NEWSPAPER FRENCH

Adrian C. Ritchie, MA (*Manc.*), Doct de l'Univ. (Strasbourg), is Lecturer in French at the School of Modern Languages, University College of North Wales, Bangor.

NEWSPAPER FRENCH

A VOCABULARY OF
ADMINISTRATIVE AND
COMMERCIAL IDIOM

With English translations

Adrian C. Ritchie

CARDIFF
UNIVERSITY OF WALES PRESS
1990

© Adrian C. Ritchie, 1990

British Library Cataloguing in Publication Data

Ritchie, Adrian C. (Adrian Charles), 1942–
  Newspaper French: a vocabulary of administrative and
  commercial idiom.
  1. French language. Idioms
  I. Title
  448

ISBN 0–7083–1060–5

Typeset by Megaron, Cardiff
Printed in Great Britain by Billing and Sons Limited,
Book Plan, Worcester

INTRODUCTION

Scope and purpose

In drawing up this glossary of French idiom, my aim has been to help those who wish to read and understand contemporary French, in particular the language of the press, of journalism, and of the media. I have assembled a selection of useful terms and common idioms which the reader of the 'quality' press [*Le Monde, Le Figaro, Libération* etc.] and of news periodicals like *Le Point* and *L'Express* will regularly encounter. The emphasis therefore is firmly on the language and usage of today. I have concentrated on a few semi-specialized areas, the language of **administration, economics, business** and **commerce,** of **politics, the law** and **journalism.** Also included are some more run-of-the-mill terms and expressions where these were felt to be useful, and also the occasional proper name [e.g. **Marianne, Maghreb**].

Conventional foreign-language technical or commercial dictionaries can often be unsatisfactory in that, however comprehensive their scope, they rarely offer sufficient illustration or explanation. In this handbook, however, I have tried to adopt a new approach. Because words are only truly meaningful when seen and understood in a context, each headword will be followed by one or more examples of its use, chosen from a broad range of situation and register. Some very common French words [e.g. **appel, bien, compte, droit, fonds,** among others] form the basis of a large number of idioms. I have had to be very selective, and so my choice will inevitably seem a trifle arbitrary. However, I have made a point of including recent coinages [e.g. **fuite en avant**] and newer meanings [e.g. **bavure, dérapage, dérive**] which either do not yet appear in existing bilingual dictionaries or, if they do, are inadequately explained. In the case of neologisms or unusual words like **beur,** I have tried to find an illustration which is both a definition ['jeune

Français issu de l'immigration maghrébine'] and an explanatory gloss. Though few if any of the entries exhaust the potential meanings of the headword, the examples chosen do serve to indicate the variety and range of idiom and meaning associated with that word.

The **marché unique européen** represents an opportunity and a challenge to us all, and a familiarity with specialized lexis in fields like administration, economics and politics is becoming essential for meaningful intercultural exchange. This glossary of contemporary French, with its emphasis on a wide range of idiomatic usage, embodies a fresh approach. It is intended to fill a gap in the current market, by offering what conventional dictionaries do not consistently supply, namely authentic contexts and real-life situations. I am confident that, used in conjunction with a good dictionary, it will prove a useful tool for translation from and into French, and a valuable aid, not only to the businessman needing to correspond or conduct discussion in French, but to all who wish to read, understand and use actively these essential registers of the contemporary French language.

Adrian C. Ritchie   BANGOR, February 1990

In many entries, the headword reappears in inflected form in one or more of the illustrative examples given. In the interest of clarity, headwords, inflected or otherwise, are printed in **bold** wherever they appear in the entry. Likewise, all idioms and expressions formed on the headword are in bold.

Translations — italicized — take the form either of renderings of the headword [e.g. **échelon** (*step, grade, rung*)] or, in the case of phrases and expressions incorporating the headword [e.g. **à l'échelon des villes**], translations of that particular idiom or set phrase [(*at the urban/city level*)]. Commas are used to separate equivalents in the target language; a semicolon indicates a clear shift in meaning.

Hyphenated compound words are put under the most suitable headword in each case. Hence **arrière-pensée** and **congé-conversion** are classified under **arrière** and **congé**, while **pré-retraite** comes under **retraite** and **expert-géomètre** under **géomètre**. So also with non-hyphenated compounds and other collocations: thus, **mise au point** and **prise en compte** are ranged under **point** and **compte** respectively, but **conseil général** will be found with **conseil** and **retenue à la source** with **retenue**.

Past participles with adjectival force [e.g. **accru, éclaté**] are normally treated as headwords. Where it seems necessary, some syntactical information [prepositions etc.] is included [e.g. **aller à l'encontre de** (*be contrary/opposed to*)], emboldened to facilitate correct use of the word or expression.

In the interest of clarity, much of the usual lexicographical paraphernalia [phonetic transcriptions of headwords, semantic categories, field and style labels etc.] has been omitted. Reflexive verbs are identified, as are adjectives; noun genders are marked, but indications of grammatical categories are otherwise kept to an absolute minimum.

The following are the most commonly used symbols:

(*m*)	masculine noun
(*f*)	feminine noun
(*pl*)	plural noun
(*adj*)	adjective
< >	feminine endings where indicated are shown within oblique brackets
[se] or [s']	reflexive/pronominal verb
≃	where the French word/phrase has no exact equivalent, the nearest English/American cultural equivalent is given
(*fam.*)	familiar/colloquial

A

abaissement (*m*): l'**abaissement** à 60 ans de l'âge de la retraite (*lowering*)

abaisser: le nouveau gouvernement a promis d'**abaisser** les taux d'intérêt (*lower*)

abattement (*m*): un **abattement** forfaitaire de 10% sur le revenu imposable (*reduction*); l'**abattement d'âge** des jeunes travailleurs a été supprimé (*reduction/allowance given to specific age-group*)

ABC: la prospection en profondeur des marchés, c'est l'**ABC** de l'exportation (*first requirement*)

aberrant <e> (*adj*): il tente de mettre de l'ordre dans une économie **aberrante** (*disorganized; chaotic*)

aberration (*f*): ceci aboutit à de véritables **aberrations** (*aberration*)

abonder: le parquet semble **abonder dans son sens** (*be in full agreement with*)

abonné (*m/adj*): 100 000 **abonnés** ont été privés d'eau courante (*customer*); les **abonnés** ont priorité pour la location des places (*subscriber; season-ticket holder*)

aboutir: le seul moyen d'**aboutir** à une paix durable (*reach, arrive at*); ces manœuvres pour isoler le Maroc pourraient **aboutir** (*succeed, come to fruition*)

aboutissement (*m*): la France souhaite l'**aboutissement** des négociations (*end; successful conclusion*)

abrogation (*f*): l'**abrogation** de la loi n'était pas pour plaire aux partisans de la peine capitale (*annulment*)

abroger: ils ont **abrogé** les récentes mesures de bannissement (*annul, repeal*)

absorption (*f*): rachat de trois firmes suisses, **absorption** de Le Flohic (*takeover; acquisition*)

abstenir [s']: le porte-parole du gouvernement **s'est abstenu de tout commentaire** (*decline to comment*)

abstention (*f*): le taux d'**abstention** très élevé en mars inquiète la majorité à l'approche du scrutin (*abstention*)

abus (*m*): il faut sanctionner les **abus** partout où on les trouve (*abuse; misuse*); huit employés ont été inculpés d'**abus de confiance** (*breach of* *trust*); on lui reproche des **abus de pouvoir** flagrants (*abuse of power*)

abuser: le Premier ministre a **abusé** des droits que lui accorde la Constitution (*misuse; abuse*)

abusif <-ive> (*adj*): si le licenciement est '**abusif**', le salarié reçoit des indemnités complémentaires (*wrongful*); on parle d'utilisation **abusive** de la procédure (*unauthorized; unjustified*)

abusivement: les journalistes **abusivement** assimilés à des 'fauteurs de troubles' (*wrongly*)

académie (*f*): un enseignant qui s'estime lésé peut s'adresser à l'**Académie** (*regional education authority*)

accablant <e> (*adj*): le témoignage de son ancien collaborateur était **accablant** (*damning*)

accalmie (*f*): l'**accalmie** de vendredi sur la Bourse de Paris n'aura été que de courte durée (*calmer conditions, improvement, lull*)

accédant (*m*): un effort a été fait en faveur des **accédants à la propriété** (*house-buyer*)

accéder: il faut que les femmes puissent **accéder** aux postes de responsabilité (*arrive at, attain*); l'an dernier, 50 000 ménages ont **accédé à la propriété** (*become a home-owner*)

accession (*f*): des garanties sur l'**accession** du territoire à l'indépendance dans les cinq ans (*attaining, achieving*); ces mesures permettent aux Français rapatriés l'**accession à la propriété** de leur logement (*house purchase; ownership*)

accomodement (*m*): il faut que Londres trouve un **accomodement** avec l'Afrique du Sud (*arrangement, agreement*)

accord (*m*): un **accord** a été conclu entre les deux pays (*agreement*); une réunion avec les syndicats signataires des **accords salariaux** pour 1988 (*pay/wage agreement*)

accorder [s']: les négociateurs ont pu **s'accorder** sur un calendrier de retrait des troupes (*agree, come to an agreement*)

accréditer: on voudrait ainsi **accréditer** la thèse des enquêteurs (*give credit to; believe*)

accroc (*m*): un nouvel **accroc** dans la cohabitation (*hitch*); **sans accrocs**, ni retards excessifs, les réformes envisagées voient donc le jour (*without a hitch, smoothly*)

accrochage (*m*): des **accrochages** ont de nouveau opposé manifestants et forces de l'ordre (*clash, incident*)

accroître [s']: le nombre des emplois **s'est accru** en 12 ans de plus de 20 millions (*increase, grow*)

accru <e> (*adj*): l'ouverture à l'extérieur implique une spécialisation **accrue** (*increased*)

2

accueil (*m*): la France, **terre d'accueil** des réfugiés politiques (*land of welcome; refuge*)

accueillir: il fut **accueilli** par une foule en délire (*welcome*); en France, on **accueillait** de plus en plus d'immigrés clandestins (*admit, let in*); **mal accueillis** au début, les Maghrébins ont réussi à s'intégrer (*unwelcome*)

acculer: une concurrence féroce **accula** la firme à la faillite (*force into; drive to the brink of*)

accusation (*f*): l'**accusation** a fait valoir que l'inculpé avait été pris en flagrant délit (*prosecution*); l'instruction terminée, le dossier fut transmis à la **chambre d'accusation** (*Office of Director of Public Prosecutions*)

accusé (*m*): l'**accusé** nie avoir été mêlé au trafic de devises (*defendant*)

accuser: l'industrie automobile **accuse** une des plus fortes baisses, 3 300 salariés en moins (*show, register*); [s'] le décalage entre les deux partis **s'accuse** (*grow, increase; widen*)

acharner [s']: des centaines d'hommes **s'acharnent** à détruire cette forteresse (*endeavour, strive*)

acheminement (*m*): les Postes ne s'occupent pas que de l'**acheminement** du courrier (*distribution, forwarding*)

acheminer [s']: les négociations **s'acheminent** vers leur conclusion prévisible (*head, move towards*)

achèvement (*m*): les sommes nécessaires à l'**achèvement** des travaux (*completion*)

achever [s']: l'année 1982 vit **s'achever** le programme de nationalisation (*come to completion*)

acompte (*m*): il faut verser un **acompte** de 30% du prix d'achat (*deposit, down payment*)

acquéreur (*m*): l'appareil devrait donc trouver **acquéreur**, quel que soit son prix (*buyer, purchaser*); il **s'est porté acquéreur** d'un terrain construisible pas loin de la ville (*buy; offer to buy*)

acquérir: des sociétés ont été cédées et d'autres **acquises** (*acquire; take over*); [s'] les titres peuvent **s'acquérir** aux guichets de la Poste (*obtain, purchase*)

acquêts (*m pl*): l'avantage de la **communauté réduite aux acquêts**, régime du mariage sans contrat (*agreement whereby only goods acquired since marriage are owned in common*)

acquis (*m*): il faut maintenir les **acquis** de notre politique de redressement financier (*achievement; possession*); (*adj*) le soutien de l'aile gauche du parti est **acquis** au leader du Labour (*certain, guaranteed*); il est d'ores et déjà **acquis** au projet (*in favour of*)

acquisition (*f*): une véritable fièvre d'**acquisitions** a gagné les pays membres de la CEE (*taking of control; take-over*)

3

acquit: sur la facture était marqué '**pour acquit**' (*received with thanks*)

acquitter: les entreprises doivent désormais **acquitter** la taxe professionnelle qui remplace la patente (*pay*); [s'] il **s'est acquitté** des factures impayées (*pay; pay off*)

acte (*m*): et ils **passent à l'acte**, en arrêtant toute vente de pétrole aux pays occidentaux (*carry out a threat*); ces dispositions **prennent acte** de la nouvelle configuration des frontières (*take into account*)

actif (*m*): en 1988, le nombre d'**actifs** occupés a augmenté en France de 103 000 (*person in/seeking employment*); **à l'actif** du gouvernement, on cite sa législation sociale (*to the credit of*); (*adj*) le chômage a atteint 10% de la **population active** (*population of working age*); ceux qui sont en âge d'**entrer dans la vie active** (*enter employment*)

action (*f*): une offre publique d'échange [OPE] sur la base d'une **action** X pour trois titres Y (*share*); mener une **grande action** pour la protection de l'environnement (*concerted drive; initiative*); il y a lieu d'engager une **action en justice** (*court case, proceedings*); une **action** de 24 heures paralyse les transports parisiens (*industrial action; strike*)

actionnaire (*m*): le conseil d'administration conseille aux **actionnaires** d'accepter la proposition (*shareholder*)

actionnariat (*m*): un système d'**actionnariat** où les salariés détiennent 15% du capital (*share-holding; share-ownership*); partisan de l'**actionnariat du personnel** (*employee share-ownership*)

activité (*f*): la croissance de l'**activité** féminine (*employment; work*); en cas de cessation d'**activité** (*trading*); la société du Nord a vendu ses **activités** de peignage et de tissus (*interests; operation*)

actualiser: cet accord a été **actualisé** au mois de juin 1987; pour **actualiser** ces chiffres, il faut les multiplier par deux (*renew; update, bring up to date*)

actualité (*f*): la question retrouve tout à coup toute son **actualité** (*topicality, relevance*); l'**actualité** politique est peu fournie en ces mois d'été (*current affairs*)

actuel <-elle> (*adj*): l'**actuel** chef de l'exécutif; l'**actuelle** majorité au parlement (*present*)

acuité (*f*): le problème prend maintenant une **acuité** particulière (*urgency, acuity*)

adduction (*f*): la société du Havre a emporté un important marché d'**adduction d'eau** (*water supply*)

adepte (*m/adj*): les **adeptes** de l'interventionnisme (*advocate; supporter*)

adéquat <e> (*adj*): la demande sera examinée par la commission **adéquate** (*relevant*)

adéquation (*f*): il n'y a pas **adéquation** entre l'offre d'emplois et la demande d'emplois (*correspondence; equivalence*)

adhérent (*m*): les **adhérents** du parti conservateur y sont en majorité

4

favorables (*member; supporter*)

adhérer: la Libye **adhérait** au traité de fraternité entre pays maghrébins (*adhere; belong; join*)

adhésion (*f*): l'**adhésion** de la Grande-Bretagne à la CEE risquait de faire éclater la Communauté (*membership; joining*); l'idée a recueilli une très large **adhésion** (*support; agreement*)

adjoint (*m/adj*): employé en tant qu'**adjoint** au directeur (*assistant; deputy*); les **adjoints au maire** faisaient le gros du travail (*deputy mayor*)

administrateur (*m*): les affaires en dépôt de bilan sont confiées à l'**administrateur judiciaire** (≃ *official receiver; insolvency practitioner*)

administration (*f*): mars 1982 donna à l'**administration locale** — de la commune à la région — un regain de vie (*local government*); la transaction a été acceptée par le **conseil d'administration** de la société (*board, board of management*)

administré (*m*): le maire est soutenu par la plupart de ses **administrés** (*citizen; subject*)

affaire (*f*): le pilote croyait **avoir affaire** à un bâtiment iranien (*be involved/ confronted with*); les ennuis du Labour **font l'affaire** des Conservateurs (*suit*)

affairisme (*m*): l'inquiétude de la gauche face aux accusations d'**affairisme** (*shady dealing; political racketeering*)

affaissement (*m*): on craignait un nouvel **affaissement** des cours à Wall Street (*fall, collapse*)

affectation (*f*): dispensé, il a reçu son **affectation** dans la réserve du service militaire (*posting*); l'opposition s'inquiète de l'**affectation** du produit de ces privatisations (*allocation, allotment; use*)

affecter: les objecteurs de conscience sont souvent **affectés** dans une formation militaire non-armée (*attach*); on a **affecté** les sommes économisées à l'aide au tiers monde (*apply, use*)

afférent < e > (*adj*): les dépenses **afférentes** à l'habitation principale ouvrent droit à déduction d'impôt (*pertaining to*)

affichage (*m*): une campagne d'**affichage** à l'échelon national (*bill-sticking; placarding*)

affiché < e > (*adj*): son approbation **affichée** de la politique du gouvernement (*open, declared*)

afficher: côté français, on **affiche** une complète satisfaction (*show, demonstrate*); les statistiques récentes **affichent** une diminution de 5% du chômage en Isère (*reveal*)

affilié (*m/adj*): la Sécurité sociale répartit les **affiliés** en deux groupes, Français et étrangers (*affiliated/registered member*)

affilier [s']: 20 000 membres supplémentaires **se sont affiliés** cette année (*join* *up, affiliate*)

affluer: Libanais et Ghanéens **affluent** en République fédérale (*flood into*)

afflux (*m*): un **afflux** massif de dollars risquait de provoquer une crise du système monétaire international (*influx, flood, inflow*)

affréter: un avion gros porteur, **affrété** par la Croix-Rouge (*charter*)

affrontement (*m*): les **affrontements** ont fait 16 morts et plusieurs blessés (*clash*); la volonté d'**affrontement** des Français vis-à-vis du pouvoir (*confrontation*)

affronter: le pays **affronte** une sérieuse crise politique (*face*)

agenda (*m*): cette visite, inscrite sur l'**agenda** du Premier ministre, a été annulée (*timetable, diary*)

agent (*m*): deux **agents** communaux honorés (*employee; operator*); l'arrestation de 19 courtiers et **agents de change** (*exchange broker*); sur 450 employés et **agents de maîtrise**, 35 ont été licenciés (*supervisor*)

agglomération (*f*): une commune de l'**agglomération** caennaise (*urban/built-up area*)

aggravation (*f*): Fidji: **aggravation** de la crise; face à l'**aggravation** du déficit extérieur (*worsening*)

aggravé <e> (*adj*): une peine maximale de deux ans pour les délits, même **aggravés** (*serious*)

agissement (*m*): les **agissements** des fauteurs de trouble ne sont pas passés inaperçus (*scheme, intrigue*)

agitation (*f*): l'**agitation** dans les territoires occupés par Israël (*unrest*)

agréer: une réduction dont le principe a été **agréé** lors du sommet d'octobre dernier (*accept; approve; agree*)

agrément (*m*): l'**agrément** des pouvoirs publics est nécessaire avant de procéder (*consent, approval*)

agro-alimentaire (*m/adj*): un secteur, l'**agro-alimentaire**, prospecté par le groupe Bouygues (*the farm-produce industry*)

aide (*f*): les **aides** versées par l'État à la régie Renault (*aid, assistance; support*); environ 100 milliards de francs d'**aides publiques** (*government aid; public money*); une réduction d'impôt pour **aide alimentaire** (*alimony*); il faut **venir en aide** aux plus démunis (*aid, help*)

aisé <e> (*adj*): les concessions fiscales accordées aux contribuables **aisés** (*prosperous; well-off*)

ajout (*m*): le principal **ajout** de la loi Pasqua (*addition*)

aléa (*m*): comme tous les placements, il est soumis aux **aléas** de la Bourse (*uncertainty, risk*); **sauf aléa**, il sera au rendez-vous de Paris (*if all goes well*)

aléatoire (*adj*): malgré le caractère **aléatoire** des contrats avec l'étranger

6

(*risky, uncertain*)

alerte (*f*): l'**état d'alerte** a été décrété le 4 août (*emergency*); la situation paraît avoir atteint la **cote d'alerte** (*danger/crisis point*)

aliéner [s']: le ministre **s'est aliéné** les organisations syndicales (*alienate; antagonize*)

aligner: on veut **aligner** la pratique française sur les dispositions en vigueur à l'étranger (*align; keep in step with*); [s'] tant qu'ils ne **s'alignent** pas sur les accords conclus l'an dernier (*respect, comply with*)

alimentation (*f*): les sociétés ont la responsabilité de l'**alimentation** en eau potable de la ville (*supply*)

alimenter: un compte bancaire **alimenté** par des versements d'argent (*pay money into*); les immigrés **alimentent la chronique** depuis quelques jours (*be in the news*)

alinéa (*m*): le gouvernement actuel a fait grand usage de l'article 49, **alinéa** 3 de la Constitution (*paragraph*)

alléchant <e> (*adj*): des perspectives **alléchantes** pour les entreprises investissant en Indonésie (*very attractive*)

allégation (*f*): il a formellement démenti les **allégations** portées contre lui (*allegation, accusation*)

allégement (*m*): un **allégement** des contrôles aux frontières se révèle nécessaire (*reduction; lightening; relaxing*); la répartition des 15 milliards d'**allégements fiscaux** (*reduction of tax burden*)

alléger: la volonté du gouvernement d'**alléger** les impôts (*reduce; lighten*)

allier [s']: le français Thomson **s'allie** avec British Aerospace (*join up with; go into partnership*)

allocataire (*m*): une incitation à la paresse pour les **allocataires** (*recipient of benefit*)

allocation (*f*): on vient d'annuler l'**allocation** de parent unique (*allowance*)

allocution (*f*): au cours de son **allocution** radiophonique (*speech, address*)

allongement (*m*): il préconise un **allongement** de l'année scolaire (*lengthening*)

allouer: les 500 millions de francs que l'État a **alloués** au musée de la Villette (*grant, allocate*)

allure (*f*): un catalogue **aux allures de** magazine, il coûte 39F et paraît semestriellement (*with the look/appearance of*)

alourdir: de telles dépenses ne font qu'**alourdir** le budget national (*increase*); [s'] en outre, la fiscalité **s'est alourdie**, notamment depuis 1981 (*become more onerous*)

alourdissement (*m*): en imposant aux enseignants un **alourdissement** de leurs charges de travail (*increase*)

altérer: une crise de confiance **altère** les relations entre Londres et Dublin (*impair, affect*)

alternance (*f*): la Ve République a enfin connu l'**alternance** au pouvoir avec la victoire de la gauche en 1981 (*alternation of Right and Left in power*); le système allemand de **formation en alternance** (*'sandwich' course*)

ambiant <e> (*adj*): ses propositions reflètent le discours libéral **ambiant** (*fashionable, current*)

ambitionner: ils **ambitionnent** de faire repartir l'introuvable Europe politique (*aim, hope*)

aménagement (*m*): depuis les traités de Rome, des **aménagements** ont été faits (*change, modification*); ces problèmes d'**aménagement urbain** peuvent être négociés autour d'une table (*urban development*); l'**aménagement du territoire** vise à remédier aux déséquilibres régionaux (*town and country planning*); cette région ne bénéficie pas de **prime d'aménagement du territoire** (*development zone grant*)

aménager: la ferme volonté des professeurs d'**aménager** les propositions du ministre (*alter; modify*)

amende (*f*): le ministère public a demandé une condamnation à une **amende** de 2 millions de francs (*fine*)

amenuiser [s']: l'écart **s'amenuisa** encore en 1990 (*reduce, become less*)

amiable (*adj*): Panama: accord **à l'amiable** avec Washington; des négociations qui débouchent sur un règlement **à l'amiable** (*by mutual agreement; out of court, without recourse to litigation*)

amont: l'usine sera construite à 30 kms **en amont** de Bordeaux (*upstream from*); les entreprises situées **en amont** dans la chaîne de production (*earlier; at an earlier stage*)

amorce (*f*): ses propos constituent peut-être une **amorce** de solution (*beginning, first stage*)

amorcer: le déclin **amorcé** en 1972 se poursuit (*initiate, introduce*); [s'] mais on ne voit pas encore **s'amorcer** ce mouvement (*begin*)

amortir: le prêt sera **amorti** en cinq ans (*pay off, reimburse*); l'embauche d'un personnel supplémentaire, **amortie** à moyen terme, résoudrait le problème (*recoup the cost*)

amortissement (*m*): l'**amortissement** de la dette exigera de longues années d'efforts (*paying off; repayment*); compte tenu de l'**amortissement**, elle ne vaut plus que 5 000F (*depreciation*)

ampleur (*f*): il a souligné l'**ampleur** de la réforme envisagée; on a peu d'informations sur l'**ampleur** des combats (*size, extent; scale*)

amplifier [s']: la baisse **s'est amplifiée**, jeudi, au Stock Exchange; si le terrorisme continuait à **s'amplifier** (*increase, grow*)

amputer: les salariés voient leur pouvoir d'achat **amputé** (*drastically reduce*)

ancien (*m/adj*): les **anciens** des Grandes Écoles prestigieuses, telle Polytechnique (*former student*)

ancienneté (*f*): la progression automatique, **à l'ancienneté** (*by seniority/ length of service*)

ancrage (*m*): il est important de préserver l'**ancrage** à gauche du Parti socialiste; l'**ancrage** du parti en Picardie reste fort (*solid base, entrenchment*)

animateur (*m*): mouvement dont il était l'**animateur** incontesté (*leading figure*)

animation (*f*): mal préparé aux fonctions de gestion et d'**animation** (*leading, inspiring*); il faisait de l'**animation sociale** dans les Maisons de jeunes (*social activities/entertainment*)

annexe (*f/adj*): renvoyez la déclaration de revenus et les |pièces| **annexes** (*enclosure*)

annexer: ceux qui n'ont pas été **annexés** par les gros (*take over*)

annoncer [s']: la tâche du gouvernement **s'annonce** difficile (*be likely/promise to be*)

annonceur (*m*): les **annonceurs** reçoivent un exemplaire gratuit (*advertiser*)

annuaire (*m*): tout abonné a droit à titre gratuit à l'**annuaire** du département (*telephone directory*)

annulation (*f*): la CGT exige l'**annulation** de 55 licenciements (*cancellation, quashing*)

annuler: dans ce cas, le sommet devra être **annulé** (*cancel*)

antenne (*f*): la décision d'interdire d'**antenne** les membres du Sinn Fein (*broadcasting*); le **temps d'antenne** accordé aux petits partis est dérisoire (*broadcasting time*); les locaux abritent l'**antenne** parisienne de l'ancien Premier ministre (*agency; branch*)

anticipé <e> (*adj*): on annonce des **élections anticipées** pour le 11 juillet (*early elections*); les mineurs n'ont plus qu'à prendre leur **retraite anticipée** (*early retirement*)

apaisement (*m*): le conflit scolaire semble en voie d'**apaisement** (*abatement; calming down*)

apaiser [s']: la tension en Cisjordanie **s'apaise** (*abate*)

aplomb (*m*): il compte **remettre d'aplomb** une industrie en triste état (*set back on its feet, turn round*)

appareil (*m*): il a gravi un à un les échelons de l'**appareil** local (*organization*); l'**appareil du parti** est tout absorbé à la préparation du prochain congrès (*party organization*)

apparenté (*m*): étaient présents les seuls socialistes, sans les **apparentés** radicaux de gauche (*close ally*); (*adj*) ancien député **apparenté** socialiste des Alpes-Maritimes (*closely allied*)

appartenance (*f*): on ne connaît pas leur **appartenance** précise (*affiliation; membership*)

appartenir: c'est au Président qu'il **appartient de** trancher (*be the responsibility/duty of*)

appât du gain (*m*): l'**appât du gain** représente l'unique motivation (*profit motive; greed*)

appel (*m*): elle avait été relaxée **en appel** (*on appeal*); il annonça son intention de **faire appel** contre la décision du tribunal de Rennes (*appeal, lodge an appeal*); s'il n'avait pas été algérien, le ministère public n'aurait pas **fait appel 'a minima'** (*appeal for a heavier sentence*); la direction a **lancé un appel** à la reprise du travail (*make an appeal*); la firme de Rouen a remporté l'**appel d'offres** pour la construction de l'autoroute (*invitation to tender/bid*)

appelant (*m*): l'appel étant injustifié, l'**appelant** est condamné aux dépens (*appellant against a judgement*)

appelé (*m*): 400 postes de militaires de carrière et 2 183 postes d'**appelés du contingent** (*conscript; national serviceman*)

appeler: un jeune Français est normalement **appelé** à l'âge de 19 ans (*call up for service*); les rebelles musulmans ont **appelé** au boycottage des élections (*appeal/call for*); il **en appelle** au respect des droits de la personne (*appeal for*); tant que le pétrole reste un produit indispensable, l'inégalité est **appelée** à persister (*be certain to*)

appellation (*f*): il y a des centaines de personnes répondant à cette **appellation** (*label, name, title*)

appoint (*m*): les petits partis servent souvent d'**appoint** au gouvernement minoritaire (*support*)

apport (*m*): l'**apport** du tourisme étranger ne compense pas l'évasion de capitaux vers l'étranger (*contribution; input*); faute d'**apport personnel** suffisant, les plus pauvres dépendent de l'aide publique pour l'achat d'un logement (*financial contribution; down payment*)

appréciation (*f*): à Paris et à Bonn on a des **appréciations** assez différentes sur cette affaire (*view, interpretation*); l'**appréciation** de la monnaie favorise les achats à l'étranger (*appreciation; increase in value*)

approbation (*f*): la politique des États-Unis a rencontré une large **approbation** (*approval*)

approfondi <e> (*adj*): une étude **approfondie** de la question (*in depth*)

approfondissement (*m*): un **approfondissement** du fossé entre gauche et droite (*widening*); il faudrait pour cela un **approfondissement** du dialogue (*deepening*)

approprier [s']: en s'**appropriant** un marché qu'il a lui-même qualifié de 'juteux' (*take over, monopolize*)

approvisionnement (*m*): les tensions dans le Golfe font peser de sérieuses inquiétudes sur l'**approvisionnement** pétrolier (*supply*)

approvisionner: aubaine qui lui permit d'**approvisionner** son compte en banque (*credit; pay money into*); un compte bancaire **non-approvisionné** (*overdrawn; in the red*)

appui (*m*): le président salvadorien cherche des **appuis** diplomatiques (*support*)

appuyer: pour **appuyer** leurs revendications, ils menacent de faire grève (*support, back*)

apurer: l'URSS a totalement **apuré** ses vieilles dettes financières avec l'ONU (*settle, pay off*)

arbitrage (*m*): les tout derniers **arbitrages** en la matière seront rendus fin octobre (*decision*); on a soumis le litige à l'**arbitrage** de l'ONU (*arbitration*)

arbitraire (*m*): dans aucun pays le citoyen n'est à l'abri de l'**arbitraire** de l'internement (*arbitrary/unfair treatment*)

arbitrer: le Front National est en mesure d'**arbitrer** cette confrontation (*decide the result*)

ardoise (*f*): la balance industrielle affiche une **ardoise** de deux milliards en juin (*deficit*)

argentier (*m*): à l'issue de la réunion des **grands argentiers** (*Finance Minister*)

arguer: en **arguant** que ce pacte ne constitue pas une garantie (*argue*)

argumentaire (*m*): son **argumentaire** n'a guère ébranlé les convictions des Sénateurs (*argument*)

armateur (*m*): les **armateurs** veulent briser la grève des marins (*shipowner*)

arnaque (*f*): une belle histoire d'**arnaque** et de magouilles politiciennes (*swindling; dishonesty*)

arnaquer: il s'est fait **arnaquer** par un démarcheur peu scrupuleux (*swindle*)

arraisonner: le juge fit **arraisonner** le bateau (*stop and inspect*)

arranger: la fermeture de l'aéroport **arrangerait** tout le monde (*suit, be convenient*); [s'] il n'y a guère de chances que les choses **s'arrangent** d'ici à la date de la réunion (*improve; be settled*)

arrérages (*m pl*): il s'est acquitté des **arrérages** de loyer et des factures impayées (*arrears of payment*)

arrêt (*m*): l'**arrêt** des hostilités n'est pas pour demain (*halt, cessation*); une journée nationale d'action, avec **arrêts de travail** et manifestations (*stoppage; stopping work*); le tribunal a enfin rendu son **arrêt** (*judgment, decision*)

arrêté (*m*): le SMIC sera augmenté par **arrêté** du ministre si l'indice des prix augmente de 2% (*decree, order*)

arrêter: un calendrier de réformes vient d'être **arrêté** par le gouvernement

11

(*decide; fix*)

arrhes (*f pl*): il a dû verser des **arrhes** pour l'achat du terrain (*advance, down payment for purchase/rent of property*)

arriéré (*m*): aucun nouveau contrat, tant que l'Irak n'aura pas réglé ses **arriérés** (*arrears of payment*)

arrière (*adj*): les ports maritimes doivent disposer de liaisons avec un **arrière-pays** le plus large possible (*hinterland*); cette initiative anglaise n'est certes pas sans **arrière-pensées** politiques (*ulterior motive, intention*)

arrondissement (*m*): cet **arrondissement** est, sur le plan industriel, un des plus sinistrés de France (*administrative sub-division of* département; *district*)

article (*m*): dans son **article de fond**, l'éditorialiste traite longuement de cette question (*leading article*)

articuler [s']: la position de la CFDT **s'articule** autour de deux principes (*be based on/organized around*)

artisan (*m*): les petits commerçants et les **artisans** sont les plus nombreux (*craftsman; self-employed person*); il se veut l'**artisan** de l'Europe (*builder; creator*)

artisanal <e> (*adj*): une forte explosion produite par un engin **de fabrication artisanale** (*home-made; amateurish*); des **activités artisanales** lucratives (*small-scale cottage industry*)

artisanat (*m*): le transfert de tâches des grandes entreprises vers l'**artisanat**, à travers la sous-traitance; les structures d'accueil relèvent encore de l'**artisanat** (*cottage industry; small-scale production*)

ascendance (*f*): l'association des Français d'**ascendance** polonaise (*origins; ancestry; stock*)

ascension (*f*): il a fait une **ascension** éclair en passant au privé (*rise*)

asphyxie (*f*): la crise de la production et l'**asphyxie** du marché sont préoccupantes (*suffocation; economic strangulation*)

assainir: des décisions visant à **assainir** la trésorerie du régime local de l'assurance maladie (*reform; put on a sounder footing*)

assainissement (*m*): signes d'**assainissement** de l'économie au premier semestre (*improvement*); dans le cadre de l'**assainissement** de l'appareil et des procédures judiciaires (*reform*); la pose des canalisations d'**assainissement** (*drainage; sanitation*)

assemblée (*f*): toute sa carrière politique s'est déroulée à l'**Assemblée nationale** (*National Assembly*); depuis les élections sénatoriales, il occupe un fauteuil à la **Haute Assemblée** (*Senate; Upper House*)

assentiment (*m*): les autorités ont voulu obtenir, par voie de référendum, l'**assentiment** de la population (*assent, agreement*)

asseoir: le Premier ministre eut à cœur de **mieux asseoir** son pouvoir

(*consolidate*)

assermenter: il fut **assermenté** et tenu au secret (*swear in*)

assiette (*f*): l'impôt sur la fortune est calculé sur une **assiette** beaucoup plus large en France; l'**assiette** de l'impôt sur le revenu est devenue trop étroite et injuste (*basis for taxation*)

assignation (*f*): quatre **assignations à résidence** après le coup manqué d'hier (*house arrest*)

assigner: la société a été **assignée en justice** pour rupture de contrat (*serve writ on; summons*); il était **assigné à résidence** depuis trois ans (*put under house arrest*)

assimilé (*m/adj*): sans compter les modérés et **assimilés** (*ally*)

assise (*f*): depuis les **assises** du parti à Marseille, en 1972 (*annual meeting, conference*)

assistanat (*m*): comment sortir d'une condition d'**assistanat** (*being in receipt of State aid*)

assistance (*f*): l'accroissement de l'**assistance** militaire fournie par l'Iran aux Kurdes (*aid, help*); les régimes d'indemnisation et d'**assistance** sont très différents d'un pays à l'autre (*State aid; care*); inculpé de coups et blessures et de **non-assistance à personne en danger** (*crime of failing to come to the aid of person in danger*)

assisté (*m/adj*): on ne saurait encourager chez eux une mentalité d'**assisté**; une population d'**assistés**, où tous les risques sont pris en charge par l'État (*in receipt of public assistance/aid*)

assister: nous **assistons** à une recrudescence de la violence (*witness*)

associatif <-ive> (*adj*): les autorités mettent tout en œuvre pour favoriser la **vie associative** dans les villes neuves (*leisure/ social activities; clubs*); dans un **local associatif**, rue Alésia (*meeting room*)

association (*f*): la loi de 1901 constitue le texte de base régissant toutes les **associations** (*association; society*)

associé (*m*): il a remercié son ancien **associé** (*colleague; partner*)

associer [s']: les deux groupes **s'associent** pour la reprise de la firme allemande (*join together, link up*)

assortir: l'achat d'avions américains est **assorti** d'importantes concessions aux industriels français; il a rendu hier son rapport, qu'il a **assorti** de quelques propositions (*accompany*)

assouplir: le chancelier n'envisage-t-il pas d'**assouplir** sa position? (*relax, make more flexible*)

assouplissement (*m*): l'**assouplissement** des conditions de détention intervenu depuis hier (*relaxing*)

assujetti (*m/adj*): les **assujettis** au régime ordinaire de la Sécurité sociale (*person liable/subject to*); les **assujettis à l'impôt** nouveau vont sans doute se plaindre (*taxpayer; person liable to tax*)

assujettir: tous les jeunes gens ne sont pas **assujettis** au service national; taxe à laquelle sont **assujetties** les entreprises (*render liable*)

assurances (*f pl*): compte tenu des services comme le fret et les **assurances** (*insurance*); dans la branche **assurance-dommages** (*accident insurance*)

assuré (*m/adj*): le courtier, défenseur de l'**assuré** (*insured person*)

assurer: il **assure** provisoirement la direction du pays (*provide, ensure; be responsible for*)

astreindre: en tant que Président, il est **astreint** à un stricte devoir de réserve (*oblige; obligate*)

astreinte (*f*): métier qui implique jusqu'à 120 heures d'**astreinte** par semaine (*obligation, service*); on ordonna le retrait des librairies de tous les exemplaires sous **astreinte** de 100F par livre (*penalty for failure to honour agreement/contract*)

atelier (*m*): à l'**atelier** comme à l'usine (*workshop, workplace*)

atermoiement (*m*): après dix ans d'**atermoiements**, ils ont paraphé les accords (*delay, hesitation*)

atout (*m*): sa présence est-ce un handicap ou un **atout**?; cette région a de sérieux **atouts** (*trump card; advantage*)

attacher [s']: il **s'est attaché** surtout à se distinguer de l'extrême droite (*seek, endeavour*)

atteinte (*f*): on y voyait une **atteinte** au principe de l'égalité entre les sexes (*denial; infringement*); la mauvaise gestion de la gauche a **porté atteinte** à notre crédibilité (*harm, injure*)

attentat (*m*): un **attentat** à l'explosif a été commis dans la soirée (*attack*)

attente (*f*): les **attentes** politiques des Français sont plus sobres (*expectation*); son dossier demeure **en attente** (*held over, pending*)

attentisme (*m*): du côté de la France, l'**attentisme** semble la règle; **attentisme** et prudence à Amman (*wait-and-see attitude*)

attentiste (*adj*): de nombreux investisseurs ont observé une attitude **attentiste** (*cautious; wait-and-see*)

attestation (*f*): il faut joindre au dossier l'**attestation** de prise en charge Sécurité sociale (*proof; attestation*)

attribution (*f*): l'**attribution** d'actions gratuites dans le cadre de l'actionnariat des salariés (*granting, distribution*); l'**attribution** du prix Nobel aux forces de la paix de l'ONU (*award*); ils ont jugé que leur collègue sortait de ses **attributions** (*go beyond one's remit*)

aubaine (*f*): ce faux pas commis par le ministre fut une **aubaine** pour l'opposition (*godsend; gift*)

audience (*f*): l'**audience** fut consacrée à l'audition des témoins (*session;*

hearing); les syndicats perdent une grande partie de leur **audience** auprès du personnel (*attention; popularity*)

audit (*m*): un **audit** a mis en lumière de graves irrégularités de gestion (*audit; financial analysis*); c'est un des plus importants **cabinets d'audit** (*accountancy practice*)

audition (*f*): au premier jour des **auditions** publiques; après une ultime **audition** de témoins (*hearing, examining*); il a été conduit à la gendarmerie pour **audition** (*questioning*)

auditoire (*m*): il a exposé les faits devant un **auditoire** très attentif (*audience*)

augmentation (*f*): le pourcentage d'Italiens est en forte **augmentation** (*increase*); les ouvriers réclament de fortes **augmentations salariales** (*wage rise/increase; pay award*); Saint-Gobain lance une **augmentation de capital** de 3,27 milliards de francs par émission de 5 million d'actions (*share-issue; raising of capital*)

augmenter: les ouvriers ont été **augmentés** de 50 cts de l'heure à compter du 1ᵉʳ septembre (*give a pay rise*)

austérité (*f*): le budget d'**austérité** norvégien est vivement contesté (*austerity; severity*); en 1983, en pleine **austérité** (*period of austerity measures*)

austral <e> (*adj*): manifestations sanglantes en Afrique **australe** (*southern*)

auteur (*m*): les trois **auteurs** présumés ont été arrêtés; une attaque à main armée dont il a reconnu être l'**auteur** (*perpetrator*)

autochtone (*m*): les plus déshérités, tous, ou presque, des **autochtones** (*native inhabitant*); (*adj*) les habitants **autochtones** de la région (*indigenous*)

autodétermination (*f*): il était hostile à l'idée du référendum d'**autodétermination** (*self-determination*)

autofinancement (*m*): l'**autofinancement** des entreprises a retrouvé son niveau d'avant 1984 (*self-financing; ploughing back of profits*)

autogestion (*f*): un vieux rêve du socialisme français, l'**autogestion** (*worker-management*); ouverture de la campagne pour le référendum d'**autogestion** (*self-administration/government*)

autonome (*adj*): une liste centriste **autonome** aux élections européennes (*separate; independent*)

autonomie (*f*): l'aspiration à l'**autonomie** sinon à l'indépendance; son **autonomie** par rapport aux organismes qui le soutiennent (*autonomy, freedom of manœuvre*)

autonomiste (*m*): les **autonomistes** basques revendiquèrent l'attentat (*autonomist*); (*adj*) les mouvements **autonomistes** ne sont pas les seuls à utiliser la violence (*autonomist*)

autorisation (*f*): 175 **autorisations** de permis de construire enregistrées cette année (*authorization; permit*)

autorisé <e> (*adj*): dans les milieux **autorisés** français (*official*)

autoriser: autant d'éléments qui l'**autorisent** à être confiant dans l'avenir (*justify; entitle*)

autorités (*f pl*): les **autorités** empêchent les journalistes de faire correctement leur travail (*authorities*)

autosatisfaction (*f*): il leur reste deux motifs d'**autosatisfaction** (*satisfaction, self-congratulation*)

autosuffisance (*f*): ce pays mène une politique d'**autosuffisance** (*self-sufficiency*)

autruche (*f*): on ne peut plus pratiquer la **politique de l'autruche** (*burying one's head in the sand*)

aval (*m*): les Douze ont donné leur **aval** à l'accord CEE-États-Unis (*agreement, endorsement; approval*); l'usine est située à 15 kilomètres **en aval** de Rouen (*downstream*); fournisseur, la société de Rennes peut encore récupérer des bénéfices **en aval** (*afterwards; at a later stage*)

avaliser: le Conseil constitutionnel doit **avaliser** le découpage électoral (*endorse, agree to, ratify*)

avance (*f*): la droite a pris une sérieuse **avance** dans les sondages (*lead*)

avancée (*f*): les deux parties se sont félicitées des **avancées** réalisées (*progress*); **avancée** du 20ᵉ congrès au mois d'octobre 1990 (*bringing forward*)

avancement (*m*): le conseil municipal sera informé de l'**avancement** des négociations (*progress*); l'**avancement** est à l'ancienneté (*promotion*)

avanie (*f*): cette nouvelle **avanie** infligée à la France par ses partenaires (*insult, snub*)

avant: il faut **mettre en avant** les avantages de l'ouverture; il **met en avant** les liens qui unissent les partis de la gauche (*emphasize*)

avantage (*m*): le cumul des **avantages en nature** représente le quart du salaire d'un cadre (*bonus, perk*)

avarier: il ne reste plus sur l'étal que des produits **avariés** (*spoil, damage*)

avenant (*m*): une simple lettre valant **avenant** au contrat initial suffit (*additional clause to insurance policy; codicil to treaty*)

avènement (*m*): le prix à payer pour l'**avènement** d'une société plus juste (*advent*)

avérer: même si l'authenticité du document est **avérée** (*prove, confirm; show to be true*); [s'] la rentrée sociale s'**avère** 'chaude' cette année (*prove to be*)

avertissement (*m*): un **avertissement** au gouvernement à deux ans des élections; un **avertissement** de Jérusalem à la Syrie (*warning*)

aveu (*m*): les *mafiosi* qui sont **passés aux aveux** (*confess, make a confession*)

avis (*m*): un **avis** de prélèvement vous sera envoyé par votre banque (*notice, intimation*); le Conseil d'État a émis un **avis** négatif sur le décret sur les loyers parisiens (*opinion; judgement*)

avocat (*m*): un dernier échange d'arguments entre le ministère public et les **avocats** (*defence lawyer*); l'importance du barrister le désigne comme l'équivalent anglais de l'**avocat** (≃ *barrister*); l'Algérie **se fait l'avocat** de Tunis auprès du colonel Kadhafi; il **s'est fait l'avocat** de la fabrication et du déploiement de l'arme nucléaire (*advocate, support*); l'**avocat général** a demandé une peine de dix ans (*public prosecutor*)

avoir (*m*): après le gel des **avoirs** panaméens aux États-Unis; les **avoirs** japonais s'élèvent à 90 milliards de dollars (*asset; holding*)

avoisiner: la population **avoisine** les 300 000; la charge de la Sécurité sociale **avoisine** 30% du budget de l'État (*approach*)

avorté <e> (*adj*): coup d'État **avorté** en Guinée; le référendum **avorté** de 1984 sur l'école (*failed; abortive*)

avoué (*m*): c'est l'**avoué** qui représente les plaideurs (≃ *solicitor; attorney*); (*adj*) les partisans **avoués** de l'Europe dominent (*avowed, declared*)

avouer: les auteurs des attentats ont **avoué** (*confess*)

axe (*m*): il précisera le 15 septembre les **grands axes** de sa politique de la mer (*directions, lines*)

ayant droit (*m*): l'abaissement de l'âge de la retraite a pour effet d'augmenter le nombre d'**ayants droit** (*beneficiary; person eligible for benefit*)

azimut (*m*): la force de frappe **tous azimuts** ; elle a mené une offensive médiatique **tous azimuts** (*generalized, multi-directional*)

B

B.A.-BA (*m*): il fait de l'hostilité aux États-Unis le **B.A.-BA** de sa politique (*ABC; guiding principle*)

bachelier (*m*): **bachelier**, il commence dès 1941 ses études supérieures (*holder of* Baccalauréat)

bafouer: la présence de l'armée indienne **bafoue** la souveraineté nationale sri-lankaise (*insult; expose to ridicule*)

bail (*m*): lors d'un renouvellement de **bail**, le propriétaire demande souvent une hausse de loyer (*lease*); les **baux locatifs** sont, outre-Manche, de 25 ans (*tenant's lease*); il va **prendre un bail** de dix ans sur une propriété sur la côte (*take out a lease*)

bailleur (*m*): une réforme des relations entre **bailleurs** et locataires est indispensable (*lessor; landlord*); ses **bailleurs de fonds** étrangers qui lui ont apporté leur aide (*financial backer*)

baisse (*f*): nette **baisse** de la production: mises en chômage en perspective (*downturn, fall*); les vins de Bordeaux **à la baisse**: les prix chutent de 15% (*falling*); l'INSEE **révise à la baisse** ses estimations (*revise downwards*)

baisser: ceci a permis de **faire baisser** le chômage (*lower, reduce*)

baissier <-ère> (*adj*): sur le marché des changes, le dollar était **baissier** hier (*tending to fall, falling*); les cambistes sont devenus **baissiers** sur le dollar (*inclining to sell; 'bearish'*)

balance (*f*): l'annonce d'un excédent record de la **balance commerciale** allemande pour le mois de juillet (*trade balance, balance of trade*); la **balance des paiements** courants est déficitaire pour le mois d'aôut (*balance of payments*)

balbutiant <e> (*adj*): cette innovation encore **balbutiante** (*in its infancy; hesitant*)

balbutiement (*m*): cette activité n'est en France qu'aux **balbutiements** (*very beginnings, earliest stages*)

ballon (*m*): sa lettre est perçue comme un **ballon d'essai** (*test of public opinion; 'kite-flying'*)

ballottage (*m*): le premier tour s'est soldé par un **ballottage**; le député sortant se trouve **en ballottage** avec le candidat socialiste (*without overall majority; required to stand in a run-off ballot*)

banalisation (*f*): la **banalisation** du crime et des menus larcins est inquiétante (*spread; becoming commonplace*)

banalisé <e> (*adj*): trois policiers à bord de véhicules **banalisés** (*unmarked*); un local **banalisé** en banlieue (*multi-purpose*)

banc (*m*): la présence du Premier ministre **au banc du gouvernement** (*on the government front bench*); sur le **banc des accusés** aux Assises de Rouen une infirmière de 25 ans (*dock*)

barème (*m*): un **barème des prix** doit obligatoirement être affiché devant l'établissement (*price list*)

baron (*m*): la guerre de succession est ouverte entre les grands **barons** du régime (*principal personality*)

baroud d'honneur (*m*): la population va opposer bien plus qu'un simple **baroud d'honneur** à la construction de l'autoroute (*last-ditch stand; gesture of defiance*)

basculer: le mouvement n'a que rarement **basculé** dans les affrontements violents (*degenerate into*)

base (*f*): les organisations syndicales vont consulter leur **base** (*rank and file; members*); on a **jeté les bases** d'un consensus introuvable depuis près de 16 ans (*sow seeds, prepare the ground*)

bâtiment (*m*): un **bâtiment** américain battant pavillon libérien (*ship*); la bonne activité du **bâtiment** et des travaux publics (*construction industry*)

bâtonnier (*m*): une plainte a été déposée par le **bâtonnier** du barreau de Nancy (*president of barristers in French lawcourt*)

battage (*m*): le gouvernement fait un énorme **battage** autour de cette affaire (*publicity*)

bavure (*f*): pas mal de **bavures** et de maladresses ont été commises; la triple **bavure** policière, politique et judiciaire de Marseille (*mistake, blunder*)

bénéfice (*m*): l'impôt sur les **bénéfices** des sociétés (*profit*); quelques **prises de bénéfice** font baisser le cours du titre (*profit-taking*)

bénéficiaire (*m*): ce pays est le deuxième **bénéficiaire** de l'aide publique française (*person/body in receipt of*); (*adj*) la sidérurgie française serait **bénéficiaire** en 1993 (*profitable*)

bénéficier: ce type de placements **bénéficient** d'une déduction fiscale (*enjoy*)

bénévole (*m/adj*): une équipe d'amateurs dirigés par des **bénévoles** (*unpaid worker*)

bétonner: Perrier était en train de **bétonner** sa première place mondiale en eaux minérales; il ne reste plus qu'à **bétonner** la nouvelle formation et à lui donner un programme (*consolidate, give a solid basis*)

beur (*m/adj*) (*fam.*): les '**beurs**', ou les Français issus de l'immigration maghrébine; il a appelé aux jeunes **beurs** à s'inscrire sur les listes électorales (*young Arab, born in France of immigrant parents*)

biais (*m*): la lutte contre le trafic des stupéfiants **par le biais** de la direction des douanes; la société a choisi de s'implanter en Corée **par le biais** de partenaires locaux (*via, through*)

bien (*m*): la poussée des importations de **biens de consommation courante** (*consumer goods*); ils continuent à exporter, notamment des **biens d'équipement** (*capital goods*); maisons, terrains ou autres **biens immeubles**, ou biens fonciers (*real estate, property*); il fallait inventorier tous ses **biens meubles** (*personal estate; moveables*); les importations de **biens et services** devraient encore progresser de près de 5% (*goods and services*)

bien-fondé (*m*): il ne mettait pas en cause le **bien-fondé** des assurances soviétiques; il convainc les compagnies du **bien-fondé** de sa stratégie (*cogency; reliability; justification*)

bilan (*m*): le **bilan** de quatre jours d'affrontements s'élève à 44 morts; le **bilan** est loin d'être glorieux (*final result; balance sheet*); la société vient de **déposer son bilan** (*go into liquidation; file a bankruptcy petition*)

bisbille (*f*) (*fam.*): nouvelle **bisbille** entre l'Élysée et Matignon (*squabble, tiff*)

blanchiment (*m*): le **blanchiment** de fonds d'origine criminelle ('*laundering*')

blanchir: la filiale new-yorkaise de la banque a '**blanchi**' un million de dollars en trois ans ('*launder*')

bleu <e> (*adj*): pour discuter de la réforme de l'**Europe bleue** (*EEC fisheries policy*); trois hommes, en **bleu de travail** (*overalls; dungarees*)

19

bloc (*m*): les pays du **bloc** soviétique votèrent contre (*bloc*); contre lequel tous les candidats avaient **fait bloc** (*come together, form a group*)

blocage (*m*): les deux syndicats ont constaté hier un **blocage** total des négociations (*block; stalemate*); le gouvernement opte pour un **blocage des prix** pour résoudre le problème (*price freeze/controls*); la direction décide le **blocage des salaires** (*wage restraint/freeze*)

blocus (*m*): le **blocus** imposé par l'Iran aux exportations irakiennes (*blockade*)

bloqué <e> (*adj*): la situation pour l'instant reste **bloquée** (*in stalemate; insoluble*)

bloquer: il faudrait pour cela **bloquer** les pensions pendant trois années consécutives (*freeze*)

bombardement (*m*): la reprise des **bombardements** par l'Irak (*bombing raid*)

bombarder (*fam*.): il a été récemment '**bombardé**' ministre de l'enseignement supérieur (*appoint an inexperienced/unsuitable person*)

bonification (*f*): départ à 55 ans avec **bonifications** d'ancienneté (*bonus*)

bonus-malus (*m*): le système dit '**bonus-malus**' est appliqué différemment selon la société d'assurance; deux accidents entraînent la suppression du **bonus** (*no-claims bonus*)

boom (*m*): l'économie britannique est **en plein boom** (*expanding*)

bord (*m*): même ceux du même **bord** que le maire ne partagent pas son enthousiasme (*side; party*)

bordereau (*m*): le **bordereau** annuel de renouvellement d'adhésion au club (*slip, counterfoil*)

bouc émissaire (*m*): la France ne tient pas à être un **bouc émissaire** (*fall guy; scapegoat*)

boucler le dossier doit être **bouclé** avant la fin de l'année (*finalize; settle*); le quartier fut immédiatement **bouclé** par les forces de l'ordre (*seal off, close*)

bouder beaucoup de jeunes immigrés **boudent** ces activités communautaires; les petits épargnants ont **boudé** la Bourse cette semaine (*reject; stand aloof from*)

bourse (*f*): la reprise a été confirmée à la **Bourse** de Londres (*Stock Exchange*)

bousculer: ils ont **bousculé** toutes les prévisions (*overturn, disprove*); ceci a **bousculé** bien des habitudes au sein de l'entreprise (*shock, disturb; change*)

bout (*m*): ces propositions ont peu de chance de **venir à bout de** la grogne des syndicats (*satisfy, calm*)

box (*m*): dans le **box** [des accusés], la jeune femme s'est défendue vaillamment (*dock*)

boycottage (*m*): son parti appelle au **boycottage** des élections (*boycott*)

bradage (*m*): les Socialistes crient au **bradage** du patrimoine national (*selling off*)

brader: on l'accuse de **brader** l'héritage de De Gaulle (*sell off*); [se] en pleine crise de surproduction, l'aluminium **se bradait** à 1 000 dollars la tonne (*be sold cheaply; be 'given away'*)

brancard (*m*): les infirmières **ruent dans les brancards**: manifestations et arrêts de travail (*complain; rise up, rebel*)

bras (*m*): une **partie de bras de fer** se joue entre eux; le '**bras de fer**' continue entre la direction et les grévistes (*deadlock; trial of strength*); **bras droit** du Premier ministre japonais (*right-hand man*)

bretelle (*f*): il a pris la **bretelle de raccordement** avec l'autoroute (*connecting/linking section of road*)

brevet (*m*): il a **décroché son brevet** (*gain a school-leaving certificate*); ceci est considéré comme une sorte de **brevet** de loyalisme (*proof, guarantee*); la société payera une redevance à IBM pour l'utilisation de ses **brevets** (*patent*)

breveter: il a fait **breveter** son nouveau procédé (*patent*)

briguer: Hachette **brigue** le troisième rang mondial de l'édition; il a la ferme intention de **briguer** l'Élysée aux prochaines élections (*make a bid for*)

briscard (*m*): reste les **vieux briscards** du PS, le Premier ministre en tête (*old soldier; veteran*)

brochure (*f*): il a diffusé une **brochure** à l'intention des électeurs immigrés (*booklet*)

brouille (*f*): normalisation des relations entre les deux pays après 12 ans de **brouille** (*quarrel, being on bad terms*)

brûlant <e> (*adj*): le conflit sera l'un des sujets **brûlants** évoqués; autre dossier **brûlant**: le projet d'autoroute (*difficult, controversial*)

brut (*m*): le prix du **brut** est en chute libre (*crude oil; crude*); (*adj*) le salaire **brut** recouvre les versements aux salariés et les cotisations et autres retenues (*gross*)

bulletin (*m*): près de 10% ont déposé dans l'urne un **bulletin** blanc ou nul (*vote; voting paper*); l'accroissement des **bulletins blancs** ou **nuls** (*blank/spoiled voting paper*); les délégués ont élu, **à bulletin secret**, le nouveau comité central (*by a secret vote*); pour avoir un **bulletin de naissance**, il faut s'adresser à la mairie (*birth certificate*)

bureau (*m*): la décision a été annoncée au cours du **bureau** national de la centrale syndicale (*committee*); le **bureau exécutif** du PS, réuni mercredi soir (*board*)

buter: les négociations ont toujours **buté** sur des problèmes de vérification (*come to grief; come up against*)

butoir (*m*): la nouvelle date **butoir** est reportée au 15 janvier prochain (*last; final*)

butte (*f*): il se trouve **en butte** à l'incompréhension de l'opinion (*butt, object of*); il **est en butte** à une grave crise au sein de sa majorité (*be faced with*)

C

cabale (*f*): la **cabale** récemment montée contre lui (*plot; faction*)

cadastral <e> (*adj*): le **plan cadastral** de la commune permettra de le situer avec exactitude (*plan of commune*)

cadastre (*m*): en consultant le **cadastre**, on a pu établir les limites exactes de la commune (*land register*)

cadence (*f*): les syndicats dénoncent les **cadences** trop élevées à l'usine de Selongey (*production rate*); en diminuant ses effectifs **à la cadence de** 8 000 emplois par an (*at the rate of*)

cadre (*m*): 400 **cadres** seront embauchés l'an prochain (*managerial / executive staff*); **dans le cadre** de la lutte contre le terrorisme (*in the context/framework*); Renault: échec de l'**accord-cadre** (*outline agreement*); préfet **hors cadre** en 1984 (*detached; seconded*)

caduc <-que> (*adj*): l'OPA **devient caduque** ce vendredi (*expire; lapse*)

cahier (*m*): en les soumettant à la stricte contrainte des **cahiers des charges** (*schedule of conditions; operating guidelines; specifications*)

caisse (*f*): l'expansion actuelle apporte d'abondantes recettes fiscales dans les **caisses** de l'État (*coffers, purse*); un médecin contrôleur de la **caisse** d'assurances sociales (*office*)

calendrier (*m*): aucun accord sur un **calendrier** du retrait des forces d'intervention (*timetable*)

cambiste (*m*): d'après les **cambistes**, la baisse de la devise américaine continuera (*foreign-exchange dealer*)

camelote (*f*): un vendeur de **camelote** à bon marché (*cheap/poor quality merchandise; junk*)

camouflet (*m*): on avait ainsi infligé un grave **camouflet** aux extrémistes palestiniens (*snub*)

canaliser: les élections sont une occasion de tenter de **canaliser** le mécontentement populaire (*channel, give expression to*)

candidat (*m/f*): deux fois il **fut candidat à la présidence** (*run for president*); un débat télévisé entre les six **listes candidates** (*competing electoral list*)

canton (*m*): le **canton** a perdu beaucoup de son importance (*administrative* *subdivision of* département); dans un **canton** de l'Isère particulièrement sensible (*electoral district*)

cantonal <e> (*adj*): nos chances d'emporter les **élections cantonales** sont très réelles (*elections to the council of the* département)

cantonner [se]: la France **se cantonne** dans un rôle de gendarme aux frontières tchadiennes (*restrict/limit oneself*)

capital (*m*): des joint-ventures, ou **sociétés à capitaux mixtes**, montées avec les Soviétiques (*joint venture*)

capitalisation (*f*): les entreprises françaises souffrent d'une trop faible **capitalisation** (*capital base*)

capoter: dispute qui risque de faire **capoter** les négociations (*fail*)

caractérisé <e> (*adj*): il estime qu'il s'agissait là de dumping **caractérisé** (*a classic case of*)

carcéral <e> (*adj*): les conditions **carcérales** déplorables des détenus (*of/in prison*)

carence (*f*): ces pays n'ignorent pas la **carence** alimentaire (*shortage*); la **carence** des pays socialistes dans ce domaine (*shortcoming*)

caritatif <-ive> (*adj*): la ville ne subventionne plus les associations, même **caritatives** (*charitable*)

carnet (*m*): le **carnet de commandes** s'élève à 40 satellites à lancer; l'amélioration des **carnets** ne saurait tarder (*order-book*)

cartel (*m*): l'**office des cartels**, chargé de faire respecter la libre-concurrence (*Monopolies Board*)

cas (*m*): depuis 1860, ce **cas de figure** s'est présenté huit fois (*situation; scenario*); un autre **cas de figure** étant alors envisagé (*eventuality, possibility*)

caser: il n'est pas facile de **caser** un jeune Maghrébin (*insert, place in a job*)

caserne (*f*): les gendarmes sont rentrés à leur **caserne** (*barracks*)

casier (*m*): son **casier judiciaire** est déjà fourni; il a un **casier judiciaire** vierge (*police record*)

casque (*m*): incidents entre **casques-bleus** et Chypriotes turcs (*United Nations peace-keeping troops*)

cassation (*f*): les condamnés à mort peuvent **se pourvoir en cassation** dans un délai de sept jours (*appeal*); un recours possible devant la **Cour de cassation** (*Court of Final Appeal*)

casser: le renchérissement de la consommation **casse** la consommation (*arrest; bring to a halt*); ce verdict avait été **cassé** par la Cour de cassation (*overturn, quash*); pour rester compétitifs, ils sont obligés de **casser les prix** (*reduce prices*)

casse-tête (*m*): le dossier des transports aériens est un vrai **casse-tête** pour le ministre; désarmement: le **casse-tête** de la vérification (*problem; difficulty*)

cassure (*f*): la **cassure** entre les syndicats et la base (*break, divide*)

catégoriel <-elle> (*adj*): il n'est pas toujours possible de satisfaire des revendications **catégorielles** (*group; sectional*)

cause (*f*): les variations de prix ne sont pas seules **en cause** (*to blame, responsible*); c'est l'avenir de la démocratie qui est **en cause** (*at stake*); l'enquête risque de **mettre en cause** des personnalités importantes (*implicate*); cette agitation va **remettre en cause** la croissance de l'économie (*endanger, imperil*); une défaite qui signifie sans doute la **remise en cause** des réformes envisagées (*re-examination*); les enquêteurs vont **mettre hors de cause** le système de sécurité (*exonerate*); il ne dément ni ne confirme l'éventuelle **mise en cause** du banquier suisse (*involvement; arraignment*)

caution (*f*): la France voudrait apporter sa **caution** à un éventuel compromis (*support, backing, authority*); il vous suffit de verser une **caution** de 250F (*down payment*); il avait été **laissé en liberté sous caution** pendant toute la durée du procès (*free/release on bail*); son récit reste **sujet à caution** (*unreliable; unconfirmed*)

cautionnement (*m*): chaque candidat doit payer un **cautionnement** de 10 000F (*surety; guarantee*)

cautionner: ils se refusent à **cautionner** la politique désastreuse du maire; il ne voulait pas **cautionner** un événement à ses yeux anti-républicain (*give approval; support*)

céder: elle n'a rien **cédé** sur sa vision politique (*give up, abandon*); le titre a **cédé** 0,75 à 1067F (*fall back, lose*)

cédétiste (*m/adj*) (*fam.*): la raison du mauvais score **cédétiste** aux élections à la Sécurité sociale (*of the CFDT trade union*)

cégétiste (*m/adj*) (*fam.*): dans cette municipalité communiste et ce fief **cégétiste** (*of the CGT trade union*)

centrale (*f*): les mutins ont été transférés dans des **centrales** (*county jail*); les **centrales** [syndicales] réclament toutes une hausse du pouvoir d'achat (*group of affiliated trade unions*)

cessation (*f*): les ouvriers recourent à la **cessation** de travail pour appuyer leur revendication (*ceasing; stop*); la société a été déclarée **en cessation de paiements** auprès du tribunal de commerce de Paris (*unable to pay its creditors; ≃ insolvent; bankrupt*)

cession (*f*): la **cession** de leurs activités minières (*sale, selling-off; disposal*); l'ensemble des **cessions d'actifs** (*disposal of assets*)

chaîne (*f*): la suppression du travail **à la chaîne** est l'objectif prioritaire (*on the production line*)

chance (*f*): il faut donner toutes ses **chances** au nouveau gouvernement (*chance*); l'**égalité des chances** est inscrite sur le fronton de la

République (*equal opportunity*)

chancellerie (*f*): situation explosive dans les prisons: la **Chancellerie** élabore de multiples projets (*Ministry of Justice*)

change (*m*): cette hausse est imputable aux seules variations des **taux de change** (*exchange rate*); il procédera à un démantèlement du **contrôle des changes** (*exchange control*)

chantage (*m*): le **chantage** aux innocents n'est certes pas une technique nouvelle (*blackmail*)

chantier (*m*): le gouvernement veut **mettre en chantier** un nouveau projet de loi (*start, work on*); le nombre de logements **mis en chantier** (*start, commence*); les **mises en chantier** s'élèvent à 310 000 logements cette année (*building start*); on attend toujours la **mise en chantier** des réformes annoncées l'an dernier (*carrying out; execution*)

chapeauter: il **chapeautait** l'éducation spéciale en Ile-de-France (*oversee; be at the head of*)

chapelle (*f*): ils font étalage de leurs querelles **de chapelle** (*domestic, internal, parochial; cliquish*)

charcutage (*m*): on a procédé à un véritable **charcutage** de la carte électorale (*butchery; radical redrawing of boundaries*)

charge (*f*): quant au Président, sa **charge** lui impose de se taire (*office; position*); un transfert de responsabilités et de **charges** (*responsibility*); aucune **charge** n'a été retenue contre lui (*charge, accusation*); une **charge** d'agent de change s'appelle maintenant une société de Bourse (*practice; office*); il faut réduire les **charges sociales** pesant sur les salariés (*social security contribution*); qui va **prendre en charge** les frais de déménagement? (*pay*); la **prise en charge** par l'État des frais de justice et des honoraires d'avocat (*undertaking to reimburse/pay*); la CGT réclame 200F par mois par enfant **à charge** (*dependent*); le coût du repas est **à la charge** des parents (*payable by; the responsibility of*)

chargé de mission (*m*): ancien **chargé de mission** sous X (*official representative*)

charnière (*f*): ce sera une année-**charnière** (*decisive; central, pivotal*)

chassé-croisé (*m*): il y a eu un véritable **chassé-croisé** entre Tokyo et Washington (*continual coming and going*)

chef (*m*): l'un des **chefs de file** de cette tendance (*leader*); deux **chefs d'inculpation** qui peuvent lui valoir la prison à vie (*charge; indictment*); c'est au **chef-lieu** du département que les décisions sont prises (*main town; administrative centre*)

cheminot (*m*): semaine agitée dans le secteur public: les **cheminots** en grève (*railway worker*)

cher <-ère> (*adj*): la lutte des travailleurs contre la **vie chère** (*high prices/ cost of living*)

cherté (*f*): tous se plaignent de la **cherté de la vie** (*high cost of living*); une prime que la **cherté des prix** dévorera en quelques mois (*high prices*)

chevronné <e> (*adj*): parlementaire **chevronné**, et plusieurs fois ministre (*experienced, skilled*)

chiffre (*m*): un bénéfice de 2 millions pour un **chiffre d'affaires** de 2,2 millions (*turnover*)

chiffrer: quant au coût de cet ensemble de propositions, il n'est jamais **chiffré** (*cost; put a figure on*)

choc (*m*): le **choc** de deux nationalismes (*conflict; collision*); depuis le premier **choc pétrolier** en 1973 (*oil crisis*)

chômage (*m*): à 16 ans, il est déjà **inscrit au chômage**; renvoyé, il n'a plus qu'à **pointer au chômage** (*sign on the 'dole'*); la grève risque de **mettre au chômage technique** de nombreux salariés (*lay off*); la résorption du **chômage partiel** se poursuit (*short-time working*)

chômé <e> (*adj*): la fête est **chômée** lorsqu'elle tombe un jour ouvrable (*designated a holiday/rest-day*)

chômer: la Bourse **chôme** en raison de la fête de la Toussaint (*close; shut*)

ciblage (*m*): son message doit être clair et son **ciblage** précis (*targeting*)

cibler: l'annonce est **ciblée** sur les lecteurs du *Point* (*aim at, target*)

circonscription (*f*): il regrettait que le député de la **circonscription** ne fût pas présent (*electoral constituency*)

citation (*f*): une sommation — ou **citation** — à comparaître en justice (*summons*)

cité (*f*): les populations laborieuses de la **cité** de Mons-en-Barœul (*town; housing estate*); le syndicalisme a conquis une place **dans la cité** (*in public life*)

citer: il fut **cité** à comparaître comme témoin (*subpoena; summon*)

citoyenneté (*f*): pour faciliter l'accession à la **citoyenneté** de certains jeunes étrangers (*citizenship*)

civil (*m/adj*): la mort de deux **civils** après l'attentat à la bombe hier (*civilian*)

civisme (*m*): le pouvoir appelle au **civisme** et au sang-froid de la population (*public spiritedness; respect for the law*)

clair <e> (*adj*): ce qui veut dire **en clair** la fermeture de l'usine (*put simply, in simple language*); il doit **le plus clair** de son pouvoir à son armée de 20 000 hommes (*most/largest part of*)

clandestin (*m*): la reconduite à la frontière des **clandestins** (*illegal immigrant*); (*adj*) la résorption du travail **clandestin** (*illegal; undeclared*)

clandestinité (*f*): le chef des rebelles, aujourd'hui **en clandestinité** (*underground; in hiding*)

classe (*f*): une **classe d'âge**, c'est encore 420 000 jeunes (*contingent; class of conscripts*); l'accès de 80% d'une **classe d'âge** au baccalauréat (*age-*

group); la **classe politique**, des conservateurs aux travaillistes, s'interroge (*political community*)

classer: l'affaire de l'assassinat a été **classée sans suite** (*close a file on a legal case; decide there is no case to answer*)

clé/clef (*f*): la présence de femmes à des postes-**clés**; c'est un personnage-**clé** (*key, major*); l'usine sera livrée, **clés en main**, fin mai (*ready for occupation*); ces bases sont la **clef de voûte** de la stratégie américaine en Asie-Pacifique (*keystone; key component*)

clientélisme (*m*): le maire ne faisait quasiment que du **clientélisme** (*favours to one's political supporters*)

clivage (*m*): la décentralisation dépasse les **clivages** politiques (*divide, rift*)

clochardisation (*f*): les universités sont au bord de la **clochardisation** (*beggary; impoverishment*)

clocher (*m*): une campagne marquée par des rivalités **de clocher** (*parochial, petty*); stratégies industrielles et **esprit de clocher** (*parochialism*)

clôture (*f*): dès la **clôture** de la Bourse vendredi soir (*close of trading; end*)

clôturer: à la Bourse de Paris, l'indice CAC a **clôturé** à 523,9 (*close; register at close of trading*); [se] l'exercice qui vient de **se clôturer** (*end, finish*)

clou (*m*): la Fête de la liberté, **clou** de la campagne pour le référendum (*centre-piece*)

club (*m*): fondateur de l'Union des **clubs** pour le renouveau de la gauche (*political club*)

coche (*m*): le pays a **raté le coche** de la modernisation (*miss the boat*)

coefficient (*m*): on estime à 2,5 points la baisse du **coefficient d'occupation** des avions (*occupancy rate*)

coiffer: le même ministre '**coiffe**' à la fois l'aménagement du territoire et l'urbanisme (*oversee, run*); la liste du PCF était **coiffée** par celle du PS (*beat, defeat*)

col (*m*): dans la même période, se sont accrus les **cols blancs** et les emplois féminins (*white-collar worker*)

co-listier (*m*): ses **co-listiers** l'appuyent à cent pour cent (*candidate on same electoral list*)

collaborateur (*m*): le P-DG a remercié ses **collaborateurs** au sein de la rédaction (*colleague*); la firme recrute même de nouveaux **collaborateurs** à l'étranger (*associate; partner*)

collaborer: il avait **collaboré** à plusieurs journaux, dont *Le Monde* (*contribute to; write in*)

collecte (*f*): des **collectes** seront organisées pour venir en aide aux sinistrés (*collection*)

collecter: les agences de presse **collectent** et diffusent les informations

(*collect, assemble*)

collectif (*m*): la principale résistance est venue du **collectif** Pléneuf-Val André (*joint community*); un certain nombre de projets de loi comme le **collectif budgétaire** (*supplementary Finance Bill*)

collectivité (*f*): son inlassable dévouement au service de la **collectivité** (*community*); les **collectivités territoriales** apportent à l'université un soutien régulier et non négligeable; certaines **collectivités locales** contrôlées par le Labour (*local authority*)

collège (*m*): désigné par un **collège** de notables (*college; assembly*)

collimateur (*m*): les médecins sont **dans le collimateur** (*under attack; under scrutiny*)

colombe (*f*): il est à classer parmi les **'colombes'** de l'Administration (*'dove'*)

combinaison (*f*): une lutte pour le contrôle de la municipalité sur fond de **combinaisons** et d'âpres rivalités (*conspiracy; plot*)

combler: pour **combler** le déficit prévisionnel de la seule année 1988 (*make up, make good*)

comité (*m*): ils se sont rencontrés **en petit comité** au Kremlin (*in a small group; in private*); les projets de licenciements furent révélés au cours d'un **comité d'entreprise** (*works committee, works council*)

commande (*f*): il a montré qu'il est toujours **aux commandes** (*in charge, at the controls*); les **prises de commandes** ont été très flatteuses (*order; placing of an order*)

commanditer: accusé d'avoir **commandité** la tentative d'assassinat (*organize; master-mind*)

commerce (*m*): malgré un mauvais résultat du **commerce extérieur** (*foreign trade*)

commercialiser: il emploie 1 650 personnes et ses marques sont **commercialisées** dans 70 pays (*market; sell*)

commis (*m*): plusieurs **grand commis de l'État** étaient présents (*top civil servant*)

commissaire (*m*): seuls les **commissaires** socialistes ont voté contre (*committee member*); on revient à l'appellation d'avant 1982: le **Commissaire de la République** redevient Préfet (*Commissioner of the Republic*)

commissariat (*m*): il a été conduit au **commissariat** de police (*police station*)

commission (*f*): la **commission** des affaires culturelles, familiales et sociales (*committee*); la **commission d'enquête** vient de publier son rapport (*committee of enquiry; fact-finding committee*); des **commissions permanentes** pourraient être créées, chacune traitant d'un problème particulier (*standing committee*); des investigations, sur **commission rogatoire** du juge d'instruction (*commission to take evidence*)

commun <e> (*adj*): dans les villes, les **transports en commun** recommencent à fonctionner (*public transport*)

communautaire (*adj*): la réglementation **communautaire** en la matière est stricte (*pertaining to the EEC*)

communauté (*f*): le régime matrimonial de la **communauté** réduite aux acquêts (*shared ownership*); Talence, une ville clé pour la **communauté urbaine** de Bordeaux (*grouping of urban communes*)

compagne (*f*): il avait été expulsé de France avec sa **compagne** (*common-law wife*)

compagnon (*m*): il faut un diplôme [CAP, **compagnon**, apprentissage artisanal] (*workman; member of trade-guild*)

comparaître: les sept détenus ont **comparu** devant la chambre correctionnelle (*appear in court of law*)

comparution (*f*): en attendant une **comparution** devant le conseil de discipline (*appearance before tribunal/court of law*)

compensation (*f*): les entreprises accordent toutes sortes de **compensations** pour fidéliser leurs cadres supérieurs (*perk, bonus*)

compétence (*f*): 1982 — nouvelle répartition des **compétences** entre communes, départements et régions (*power; responsibility; sphere, ambit*); les diplômes ne suffisent pas à définir les **compétences** professionnelles d'un candidat (*ability*)

compétent <e> (*adj*): selon la Constitution, les régions sont **compétentes** en matière d'urbanisme (*responsible; competent*)

complaisance (*f*): il prétend avoir été attaqué, avec la **complaisance** de la police (*connivance; full knowledge*); un navire sous **pavillon de complaisance** (*flag of convenience*)

complicité (*f*): il a touché des sommes importantes grâce à des **complicités** haut placées (*collusion; aiding and abetting*); elle fut inculpée de **complicité d'homicide volontaire** (*be accessary to murder*)

composante (*f*): les immigrés sont une **composante** essentielle de la société (*element, constituent part*)

composer: même s'il doit **composer** avec une Assemblée hostile à ses idées (*come to terms with*)

compréhensif <-ive> (*adj*): il est assez **compréhensif** pour ne pas le leur reprocher (*understanding; tolerant*)

compréhension (*f*): Bonn compte sur la **compréhension** de Paris dans l'affaire des Euromissiles (*sympathy; understanding*)

compression (*f*): il s'opposa à toute tentative de réduction de salaires et de **compressions** des effectifs (*reduction, cut*); le plan de restructuration conduira à une **compression du personnel** (*reduction of work-force; redundancies*)

compromettre: la commission a blanchi sa femme, également **compromise** (*compromise*); il a su rétablir in extremis une situation **compromise** (*perilous*); [se] un diplomate qui **s'était compromis** dans une affaire d'espionnage (*be compromised*)

compromis (*m*): le **compromis de vente** entre le conseil général et la Société d'économie mixte du Périgord; l'offre d'achat en Angleterre n'est pas la même chose que le **compromis de vente** français (*preliminary contract/agreement to sell*)

compromission (*f*): il a perdu toute crédibilité par ses **compromissions** avec l'ancien pouvoir (*shady deal; compromise of principle*)

comptabiliser: de nombreuses dépenses sont **comptabilisées** dans d'autres rubriques (*post*)

comptabilité (*f*): les enquêteurs ont épluché la **comptabilité** de la firme d'armements (*accounts, accounting*)

comptage (*m*): des erreurs ont été commises dans le **comptage** des voix (*count, calculation*)

comptant: une remise sera accordée sur tout achat **comptant** (*cash; in cash*)

compte (*m*): l'Assemblée générale a approuvé les **comptes** de l'exercice 1991 (*financial accounts*); il veut **se mettre à son compte** sans tarder (*set up in business*); trois éléments doivent être **pris en compte** (*take into account*); il faut une meilleure **prise en compte** des problèmes écologiques (*understanding; taking into account*); la manière peu objective dont les médias ont **rendu compte** de l'affaire (*report*); on n'y **tient compte** ni des grèves ni du chômage technique (*take into account*); les banques annoncent pour bientôt les **comptes à vue rémunérés** (*interest-bearing current account*); le ministre lui consacre des crédits **au compte-gouttes** (*in very small quantities; in driblets*); un **compte-rendu** de la gestion financière est porté à la connaissance du personnel (*report*); le **compte-rendu** de la réunion permettra de le savoir avec précision (*minutes; record*)

compter: la capitale **compte** 17 synagogues (*contain, hold*); l'**on ne compte plus** les articles parus sur le travail au noir (*innumerable*); la Constitution de 1970 est annulée, **à compter** du 25 septembre (*with effect/as from*)

concert (*m*): une personne ou un groupe de personnes agissant **de concert** (*together*)

concertation (*f*): la réforme annoncée sera précédée d'une large **concertation**; le début d'une **concertation** franco-britannique sur la sécurité européenne (*consultation*)

concerté <e> (*adj*): une politique économique **concertée** au niveau de la CEE (*concerted; common*)

concerter [se]: après **s'être concertés**, ils ont rejeté l'accord signé deux semaines avant (*consult, discuss*)

conciliateur (*m*): nommé **conciliateur** par le ministre dans le conflit de la RATP (*conciliator; mediator*)

conciliation (*f*): en soumettant le litige à une **commission de conciliation** on évitera la grève (*conciliation/arbitration tribunal*)

concordant <e> (*adj*): des témoignages partiels, mais tous **concordants** (*in agreement; which tally*)

concourir: cet office **concourt** à l'orientation et au contrôle de la politique foncière agricole (*contribute*)

concours (*m*): avec le **concours** de la Ville de Paris; 200 personnes prêteront leurs **concours** (*help, support*); le **concours** d'entrée peut être sur titres ou sur épreuves (*competitive examination*)

concrétisation (*f*): l'emploi dépend de la **concrétisation** éventuelle de commandes en cours de négociation (*confirmation; coming into being*)

concrétiser: sa visite permettra de **concrétiser** des projets de coopération entre les deux pays (*materialize, bring to fruition*); [se] si le plan **se concrétise**, ce sera la catastrophe (*be carried out*)

concurrence (*f*): il pratique des prix **défiant toute concurrence** (*unbeatable*); ils sont plutôt sous-payés par rapport à la **concurrence** (*competitor; competition*); la **concurrence déloyale** des grandes surfaces vis-à-vis du petit commerce (*unfair competition*); ils ont voté une majoration de 1 000F pour les deux premiers enfants et **à concurrence de** 2 000F par enfant à partir du troisième (*up to the sum/limit of*)

concurrencer: le tunnel sous la Manche va **concurrencer** le trafic trans-Manche (*compete against; challenge*)

concurrent (*m/adj*): entretemps, il a racheté un de ses principaux **concurrents** (*competitor*)

condamnation (*f*): il a trois **condamnations** à son actif (*conviction*)

condamner: il a été **condamné** pour détournement de fonds (*convict; sentence*)

conduire: il **conduira** une liste concurrente aux municipales de mars (*head an electoral list*)

conduite (*f*): la **conduite** de la politique étrangère (*running, management*); des mouvements sociaux des **agents de conduite** (*supervisory staff/personnel*)

confiance (*f*): l'Assemblée nationale a **voté la confiance** au gouvernement (*pass a vote of confidence*)

confiant <e> (*adj*): les Républicains sont plus **confiants** que jamais (*confident*)

confisquer: ni le Premier ministre ni le chef de l'État ne peut **confisquer** la politique extérieure (*monopolize*)

conflictuel <-elle> (*adj*): les grévistes ont obtenu raison sur deux sujets

conflictuels (*of disagreement*)

conflit (*m*): il faut essayer d'empêcher de futurs **conflits sociaux** (*industrial strife*)

confondre: les partis, toutes tendances **confondues**, sont d'accord là-dessus; le pouvoir d'achat du salaire net moyen [secteurs privé et public **confondus**] (*without distinction*)

conforme (*adj*): ce qu'il a fait est **conforme** à la Constitution (*in accordance with*)

conformer [se]: le juge d'instruction, **se conformant** aux réquisitions du parquet, fit arrêter le jeune homme (*conform with; obey*)

conforter: les entreprises soucieuses de **conforter** ou d'accroître leurs parts de marché (*consolidate; strengthen*)

confusion (*f*): cela pourrait **prêter à confusion** (*cause a misunderstanding; be misunderstood*)

congé (*m*): le plan social offre à tout licencié 24 mois de **congé-conversion** (*paid retraining*); tout travailleur aura droit à des **congés payés** (*holidays with pay*); on peut occuper les lieux même après avoir **reçu congé** du propriétaire (*be expelled/turned out*)

congédier: le Premier ministre a **congédié** les commissions de spécialistes mises en place par son prédécesseur (*sack, dismiss*)

conjoint (*m*): le **conjoint** de l'assuré est aussi couvert; quel que soit le **conjoint** qui est décédé (*spouse, partner*); (*adj*) d'où une offensive **conjointe** de patrons et de syndicats (*joint; combined*)

conjoncture (*f*): l'activité de la société du Mans n'a pas été épargnée par les aléas de la **conjoncture**; en 1988–9, la **conjoncture** boursière s'était dégradée (*general situation*); le ralentissement de la **conjoncture** aux États-Unis (*economic conditions*)

conjoncturel < -elle > (*adj*): l'environnement **conjoncturel** était plutôt bon (*caused by economic variations; cyclical*)

conjoncturiste (*m*): les **conjoncturistes** prédisent une reprise de l'activité économique (*economic analyst*)

conjuguer: dans le domaine des transports, la Ville et l'État **conjuguent** leurs efforts (*co-operate, combine*); la chute **conjuguée** des prix du pétrole, du café et du cacao (*combined*)

conjurer: la crise de Wall Street n'est pas **conjurée** (*avert, cure*)

conscience (*f*): la **conscience** qu'on a en France de l'importance du nucléaire (*consciousness; realization*); la **prise de conscience** progressive de ce que le renouveau de l'Europe passe par la coopération (*realization*)

conseil (*m*): un bon vendeur, mais aussi un **conseil**, et un homme de marketing (*consultant; counsellor*); le **conseil général** est élu par tous les électeurs du canton (*departmental/county council*)

conseiller (*m*): un sénateur sur deux est lui-même maire et **conseiller général** (*departmental/county councillor*); les **conseillers municipaux** ont procédé à l'élection du maire (*town councillor*)

consensuel < -elle > (*adj*): il s'agit d'un des thèmes les plus **consensuels** (*with greatest measure of agreement; uncontroversial*)

consensus (*m*): le **consensus** sur le recours à un prélèvement sur tous les revenus (*consensus of opinion; general agreement*)

consentir: les avantages **consentis** aux locataires sont de différents ordres (*allow; offer*); chez eux, un effort important est **consenti** pour la formation (*make*)

consigne (*f*): la **consigne** de grève a été largement suivie; il refuse de donner des **consignes** de vote (*instruction; recommendation*)

consommation (*f*): la **consommation** a augmenté d'environ 50% (*consumption*); le **crédit à la consommation** est le produit le plus rentable de leur gamme (*consumer credit*); les **dépenses de consommation** des ménages sont montées en flèche en 1990 (*consumer spending*); les **prix à la consommation** n'ont augmenté que de 0,9% en août (*consumer prices*)

constant < e > (*adj*): le tableau donne les budgets militaires en francs courants et non pas **en francs constants** (*in real terms*)

constat (*m*): mauvaise administration, mauvaise gestion: le **constat** est sévère (*conclusion, finding*); la police est venue **faire un constat** sur les lieux (*make a report*)

constituer [se]: il **s'est constitué** prisonnier (*give oneself up, surrender*)

constitution (*f*): États-Unis: la **constitution** de la future équipe présidentielle (*setting-up, forming*); il annonce son intention de porter plainte avec **constitution de partie civile** (*institution of a civil action*)

consultation (*f*): l'échec de la majorité lors des **consultations** cantonales de mars 1985 (*election; vote*)

contenir: le gouvernement veut **contenir** le pouvoir d'achat (*contain, control*)

contentieux (*m*): Paris veut régler le **contentieux** avec l'Iran (*difference, dispute*)

contestation (*f*): l'ensemble des mesures fait l'objet d'une vive **contestation** syndicale (*opposition; resistance*)

continent (*m*): les fonctionnaires attirent l'attention du **continent** sur le malaise corse (*mainland France*)

contingent (*m*): un petit **contingent** d'ouvriers (*group, unit*); le **contingent** cubain, estimé à 55 000 soldats (*military unit*); les soldats du **contingent** ont été envoyés pour rétablir la paix (*conscript army*); chaque formation a reçu un **contingent** strict d'invitations (*number, quota*)

contingenter: le *numerus clausus* à l'entrée des facultés **contingente** le nombre de diplômés (*fix a quota/limit*)

33

contracter: les intérêts d'emprunts **contractés** pour acheter un bien immobilier (*undertake, arrange*)

contractuel (*m*): c'est au **contractuel** de service qu'on s'adresse (*public employee; unestablished civil servant*); (*adj*) le patronat n'a rien fait pour sauver la **politique contractuelle** (*management-worker contractual relationship*)

contraignant <e> (*adj*): des règles de procédure beaucoup plus **contraignantes** et précises (*restrictive, tight*)

contrat (*m*): d'autres financements pourraient venir du **contrat de plan** État-Région (*economic development contract*)

contravention (*f*): les faits lui reprochés ne relèvent pas du délit mais de la simple **contravention** (*petty offence*); il est **en contravention** totale avec les textes à cet égard (*contravening; in breach of*)

contrebalancer: les hausses de salaire sont **contrebalancées** par les gains de production (*offset*)

contrecoup (*m*): l'industrie subit le **contrecoup** d'un quasi-doublement de la TVA (*effect, influence*)

contremaître (*m*): pour 'passer' **contremaître** il faut avoir suivi un apprentissage (*foreman, overseer*)

contrepartie (*f*): ils n'ont pas su obtenir de véritables **contreparties** des banques (*equivalent concession*)

contre-performance (*f*): une véritable **contre-performance** qui ne se reproduira plus (*bad performance*)

contre-pied (*m*): il n'a pas hésité à **prendre le contre-pied** de la politique définie par le gouvernement précédent (*take the opposite course; do the opposite*)

contrer: il faudra en dire bien plus pour **contrer** la propagande du Parti travailliste (*counter*)

contreseing (*m*): c'est le seul cas où le **contreseing** du Premier ministre n'est pas requis (*counter-signature*)

contrevenant (*m*): aucune sanction n'est prévue contre les **contrevenants** (*offender; infringer, contravener*)

contrevenir: les pays riches n'hésitent pas à **contrevenir** aux règles qu'ils se sont données (*infringe, contravene*)

contre-vérité (*f*): il ne l'accuse pas de mentir, mais de dire des **contre-vérités** (*untruth, falsehood*)

contribuable (*m*): chaque **contribuable** estime qu'il paie trop d'impôts locaux (*taxpayer*); le déficit public est supporté par le **petit contribuable** (*low taxpayer*)

contribution (*f*): il travaillait quelques années aux **Contributions** (*tax-office, Inland Revenue*)

contrôle (*m*): la **prise de contrôle** de Lesieur par Ferruzzi (*taking control/ majority interest*)

contumace (*f*): 37 furent jugés **par contumace** (in absentia; *in one's absence*)

convaincre: ayant été **convaincu** de participation à l'attentat, il fut condamné à deux ans de détention préventive (*convict*)

convenir: les deux pays ont **convenu** de mettre davantage l'accent sur ce qui les rapproche (*agree*); le traitement qu'**il conviendra** d'appliquer aux sociétés privatisées (*be appropriate*)

convention (*f*): la nouvelle **convention** d'assurance-chômage; il vient de dénoncer la **convention** qui le liait à une société privée (*agreement*); le patronat et les syndicats représentatifs signent une **convention collective** (*national agreement between both sides of industry*)

conventionné <e> (*adj*): les **médecins conventionnés** ne sont pas concernés par ce train de mesures (≃*National Health registered doctor*)

convergence (*f*): tenant compte des points de **convergence** (*agreement*)

conversion (*f*): le nord du Tarn a été déclaré **pôle de conversion** (*redevelopment area*); des **congés de conversion** avec maintien de 90% du salaire (*retraining course*)

convocation (*f*): dans l'hypothèse où on ferait obstacle à la **convocation** d'une telle réunion (*convening; convoking*)

convoquer: des élections **convoquées** par le chef de l'État (*call*)

coopérant (*m*): après avoir passé 18 mois au Gabon, en qualité de **coopérant** (*cultural/technical/medical aide*, ≃ *VSO [GB]*, ≃ *Peace Corps [USA]*)

coopération (*f*): la '**coopération**' prend la forme d'aides financières et d'assistance technique (*cultural/technical aid*); ceci accentuera la tendance à la **coopération** entre les industriels (*collaboration*)

coopérer: pour survivre, l'industrie de l'armement est condamnée à **coopérer** (*collaborate*)

coordination (*f*): une **coordination** interministérielle en Algérie et en France pour faciliter les contacts (*joint committee*); une **coordination** leur permet de revendiquer sans passer par les syndicats traditionnels (*joint action committee*); à mi-chemin entre la fédération et la **coordination** (*loose grouping*)

coordonnée (*f*): sur le petit écran s'affichent les **coordonnées** de votre correspondant (*detail/information about*)

coquille (*f*): la version dactylographiée était pleine de **coquilles** et de fautes de frappe (*mistake*); une société désirant être cotée en Bourse peut transférer ses actifs dans une **entreprise coquille** déjà sur le marché (*shell company; shell*)

corbeille (*f*): du côté de la **corbeille**, les actions grimpent en flèche (*Paris Stock Exchange, Bourse*)

corps (*m*): dans quelle mesure le **corps électoral** appréciera-t-il les mérites de chacun? (*electorate*)

correctionnel <-elle> (*adj*): le juge d'instruction a renvoyé les malfaiteurs présumés devant la cour **correctionnelle**; le **tribunal correctionnel** statue sur les délits (*magistrate's court*)

cotation (*f*): la **cotation** reprendra lundi le 8 février (*share-price quotation*); la firme demandera une **cotation** à la bourse de Tokyo (*Stock Exchange listing/quotation*)

cote (*f*): il a une **cote** énorme en province; le Premier ministre améliore sa **cote de popularité** (*popularity rating*); la **cote d'alerte** est atteinte (*danger point*)

coter: hier, le Mark valait 3F40, aujourd'hui il **cote** 3F46 (*be quoted at, be worth*); la société vient d'être **cotée en Bourse** (*go public*)

cotisant (*m*): la réduction du nombre de **cotisants** est dûe au chômage (*subscriber, contributor*)

cotisation (*f*): la **cotisation** des adhérents seule permet à Force Ouvrière de survivre (*due, contribution*)

cotiser: on **cotise** pour le montant qui vous convient (*contribute, pay*)

couleur (*f*): en Gironde, la majorité a changé de **couleur** (*political complexion*)

coulisse (*f*): des contacts **en coulisse** ont eu lieu entre les deux pays (*secret, discreet*); ce diplomate chevronné est un habitué des **coulisses du pouvoir** (*corridors of power*)

coup (*m*): on traite les revendications catégorielles **au coup par coup** (*as they occur; one by one*); **sous le coup** d'une mesure d'expulsion (*the object of*); elles **tombent**, par leur contenu, **sous le coup de la loi** (*be a statutory offence*); un **coup dur** pour les Socialistes (*blow*); la CIA n'a participé à aucun **coup monté**, affirme la Maison Blanche (*put-up job*); ce grand amateur de secrets et de **coups tordus** (*underhand trick*); inculpé pour **coups et blessures** (*grievous bodily harm; assault and battery*); il risque dix ans d'emprisonnement pour **coups et blessures volontaires ayant entraîné la mort sans intention de la donner** ($\approx$ *manslaughter*)

coupable (*m/adj*): pris en flagrant délit de vol avec effraction, il **plaida coupable** (*plead guilty*)

coupe (*f*): il va devoir pratiquer de réelles **coupes** dans les dépenses (*cut-back, reduction*); encore une **coupe claire** dans la fonction publique: 37 000 emplois supprimés (*drastic cut-back*)

couperet (*m*): le gouvernement abusa de la **procédure couperet** de l'article 49 alinéa 3 de la Constitution (*guillotine; limitation of parliamentary debate*)

coupon (*m*): il vous suffit de remplir le **coupon-réponse** ci-joint (*detachable reply coupon*)

coupure (*f*): plusieurs **coupures** de 1 000F ont disparu (*bank-note*)

cour (*f*): il fut renvoyé devant la **Cour d'assises** de Rouen; la **Cour d'assises** seule peut juger les crimes (*Assize Court; Crown Court*)

courant (*m*): le RPR semble évoluer et reconnaître l'existence de **courants** en son sein; il existe bel et bien un **courant** centriste (*tendency, trend; group*)

courbe (*f*): ils ont les yeux rivés sur la **courbe** du chômage (*curve on map/graph*)

courir: un attentat dont les auteurs **courent** encore (*be on the run; run free*)

cours (*m*): les **cours** des produits alimentaires ont dégringolé (*price*); la faiblesse actuelle des **cours** préoccupe les spécialistes de la Bourse (*share price, market rate*)

course (*f*): la **course aux armements** entre les deux super-puissances (*arms race*)

court <e> (*adj*): il prédit une **courte** victoire pour le président sortant (*close, narrow*); la grève générale **prend de court** les dirigeants du pays (*take by surprise*); les négociations ont **tourné court** très rapidement (*be cut short; come to a premature end*)

courtage (*m*): les grandes firmes de **courtage**; à la Bourse de New York, le **courtage** est informatisé (*share brokerage*)

courtier (*m*): pour les **courtiers** et agents d'assurance (*broker*)

coût (*m*): le **coût** élevé de la main-d'œuvre (*cost*)

couver: un conflit **couve** également avec la RFA (*simmer; be brewing*)

couverture (*f*): des régimes d'assurance ont permis la **couverture** de tous les risques (*cover; insurance against*); 37 millions d'Américains sont totalement dépourvus de **couverture sociale** (*health/social cover*); le **taux de couverture** des importations par les exportations reste assez faible, soit de l'ordre de 65% (*margin; cover ratio*); la livraison de matériel de guerre avec la **couverture** des autorités (*connivance; cover*)

couvre-feu (*m*): un camp de réfugiés a été placé sous **couvre-feu**; on a levé dimanche à l'aube le **couvre-feu** imposé il y a une semaine (*curfew*)

couvrir: il dément avoir **couvert** une opération frauduleuse (*cover up*)

crapuleux <-euse> (*adj*): les meurtres **crapuleux** contre les vieillards se multiplient (*foul; heinous*)

créance (*f*): les gouvernements occidentaux détiennent les deux tiers des **créances** sur la Pologne (*money owed, debt*); la banque a accumulé une série de **créances douteuses** (*bad debt*); l'ambassadeur a présenté ses **lettres de créance** au roi (*credentials*)

créancier (*m*): les **créanciers** de Varsovie commencent à serrer la vis (*creditor*); (*adj*) les principales banques **créancières** acceptent l'étalement des remboursements (*creditor*)

37

création (*f*): plus de 800 000 **créations d'emplois** aux États-Unis en deux mois (*new job*); on a trop souvent eu recours à la **création monétaire** pour s'en sortir (*printing of money*)

crédible (*adj*): aucune dissuasion purement conventionnelle n'est **crédible** en Europe (*credible*)

crédit (*m*): le Nigéria a obtenu un **crédit** du FMI de 650 millions de dollars (*loan*); on annonce des mesures pour alléger le **coût du crédit** (*cost of borrowing*)

créneau (*m*): il faut préserver l'emploi dans un **créneau** industriel qui participe de la sécurité nationale; leader sur certains **créneaux** du marché (*sector, area*); le ministre **monte au créneau** et exige des éclaircissements (*go onto the attack*)

creuser: ceci contribue à **creuser** davantage les inégalités entre Français (*increase, accentuate*); [se] tandis que le déficit britannique **se creuse** (*get worse/larger; increase*)

creux (*m*): une très bonne année, puis le **creux** de 1989 (*low point*); (*adj*) novembre, décembre, les mois **creux** de l'année (*slack; slow*)

criant <e> (*adj*): les carences dans ce domaine apparaissent **criantes** (*flagrant*)

criminalité (*f*): le succès du gouvernement dans la lutte contre la **petite criminalité** (*petty crime; small crimes*)

crin (*m*): les Anglais, porte-parole d'un libéralisme **à tout crin** (*out-and-out; unmitigated*)

crise (*f*): la **crise** qui secoue la majorité RPR-UDF (*crisis*); chacun a ressenti les effets de la **crise** dans sa vie quotidienne (*crisis, slump*); hausse des prix, **crise du logement** (*housing shortage*)

crispation (*f*): on attend du gouvernement qu'il traite ce dossier sans **crispations** inutiles (*conflict, tension*); malgré la **crispation** dogmatique de ses dirigeants (*inflexibility*)

croire: si l'on **en croit** les derniers propos officiels (*believe*); ne voulant pas **laisser croire** qu'il se dérobait (*give the impression*)

croisade (*f*): la **croisade** rageuse qu'il a menée contre le gaspillage dans le secteur public (*crusade, campaign*)

croissance (*f*): globalement la **croissance** se maintient; les entreprises à forte **croissance** semblent à l'abri de la crise (*growth*)

croître: la production **croît** à un rythme soutenu (*grow*)

croupion (*m*): un gouvernement **croupion** dirigé par le chef de l'armée s'est installé; la grande inconnue, c'est l'attitude de ce parlement **croupion** ('*rump*')

cru (*m/adj*): le député **du cru** assistait le ministre dans sa tournée (*local*)

culpabilité (*f*): une inculpation n'implique nullement la **culpabilité** de la personne inculpée (*guilt*)

culte (*m*): les Gaullistes continuent à **vouer un culte** au général (*worship*)

cumul (*m*): grâce au **cumul** de leurs salaires, ils touchent 15 000 francs par mois (*accumulated total*); seul le **cumul** avec un mandat local devrait être possible (*multiple office-holding*)

cumuler: il devient député, poste qu'il **cumule** avec la mairie de Châteauroux; ces réformes **cumuleront** deux sortes d'inconvénients (*accumulate; add together*)

cursus (*m*): l'école propose des **cursus** de deux, trois ou quatre ans (*course of study*)

D

date (*f*): la Chine et son antagonisme **de longue date** contre l'expansionnisme soviétique (*long-standing*)

dauphin (*m*): le président choisissait personnellement son **dauphin** (*heir*); il apparaît comme le **dauphin** du dirigeant démissionnaire (*heir apparent*)

déballage (*m*): le **déballage** de l'affaire jette une lumière crue sur le financement des partis politiques (*revelation, publicizing*)

débandade (*f*): depuis, c'est la franche **débandade** (*disorder, retreat; disarray*)

débaucher: il a fallu **débaucher** du personnel fixe (*lay off, sack*)

débit (*m*): la fermeture d'un grand nombre de **débits** d'alcool (*outlet; sales point*)

débiter: on crédita son compte et **débita** celui de son créancier (*debit*); cette machine peut **débiter** jusqu'à 60 stères de bois à l'heure (*deliver, yield, output*)

débiteur (*m/adj*): le compte de la société est **débiteur** de 50 000F (*in debit; overdrawn*)

déblocage (*m*): **déblocage** de crédits destinés à des équipements de santé (*release; unfreezing*)

débloquer: Américains et Soviétiques veulent **débloquer** la négociation (*break deadlock*); tant que l'État refuse de **débloquer des crédits** pour la réfection des locaux (*release/make available funds*)

déboire (*f*): il a aussi connu des **déboires** politiques; l'idéologie libérale connaît de sérieuses **déboires** (*set-back, reverse*)

déborder: le président, **débordé** par ses ministres, est parti en claquant la porte (*outflank, outmanœuvre*)

débouché (*m*): l'Inde constitue un excellent **débouché** pour les armes soviétiques (*outlet, market*); pour informer les lycéens sur les **débouchés** des baccalauréats (*opening, prospect*)

déboucher: ces négociations vont peut-être **déboucher** sur des coopérations solides (*produce, result in*)

débouter: dans 50% des cas, le plaignant est **débouté** (*non-suit a plaintiff; throw out a court case*)

débrayage (*m*): Sochaux: **débrayage** d'une heure hier à l'usine Peugeot (*stoppage*)

débrayer: hier les ouvriers de l'entreprise ont **débrayé** pour protester contre l'agression (*go on strike, stop work*)

deçà: la RDA légèrement **en deçà** de ses objectifs pour l'année; les investissements engagés restent très **en deçà** des besoins (*below; less than, inferior to*)

décalage (*m*): le **décalage** entre les hommes politiques et les Français (*gap, gulf*); il est **en décalage** avec les vrais problèmes des gens (*out of step, touch*); il y a six heures de **décalage horaire** avec la France en ce moment (*local time differential*)

décalé <e> (*adj*): la politique américaine a eu un impact **décalé** sur la conjoncture française (*delayed*)

décennie (*f*): 4 500 emplois industriels auront disparu en une **décennie** (*period of ten years, decade*); la **décennie** 90 sera déterminante (*the nineties*)

décentralisation (*f*): le débat sur la **décentralisation** déboucha sur la fameuse loi de mars 1982 (*devolution; decentralization*)

décerner: le titre d'ingénieur est **décerné** à l'issue de quatre années de formation (*award, grant*)

décharge (*f*): il était requis comme **témoin à décharge** (*witness for the defence*); le parti peut arguer **à sa décharge** l'énorme travail accompli (*in its defence*)

décharger: le département devra **se décharger** de certaines de ses fonctions sur les communes (*relieve, unload, unburden*); certaines firmes sont **déchargées** en partie de leurs impôts (*exonerate*)

déchoir: un militant nationaliste a été **déchu** de sa nationalité soviétique (*fall/ remove from high estate/honour*)

déchu <e> (*adj*): le président **déchu** a été conduit à l'aéroport militaire (*fallen; dethroned, toppled*)

décideur (*m*): les rubriques économiques, lues par tous les '**décideurs**' (*decision-maker*)

déclarer [se]: un important incendie **s'est déclaré** hier en fin d'après-midi (*break out*)

déclencher: l'offensive a été **déclenchée** dès 8 heures du matin; on imagine le tollé que cette mesure **déclenchera** (*start, set off, trigger*)

déclin (*m*): la production industrielle est **en déclin** depuis le premier choc pétrolier de 1973 (*decline*)

décliner: il refusa de **décliner** son identité (*give, reveal*)

décloisonnement (*m*): la City a fait le pari du **décloisonnement** et de l'ouverture (*removal of barriers*)

décollage (*m*): l'État accepte de financer le **décollage** de l'économie du Sud-Ouest (*start-up; getting off the ground*)

décoller: la production agricole n'a jamais **décollé** (*get off the ground; get started*)

décommander: la visite du ministre a été **décommandée** (*call off*); [se] un empêchement l'a obligé à **se décommander** au dernier moment (*cancel; cry off*)

décompte (*m*): en attendant l'ultime **décompte** des voix; selon un **décompte** arrêté dimanche (*count; calculation*)

déconfiture (*f*): la spectaculaire **déconfiture** du gouvernement battu (*embarrassment; defeat, collapse*); la compagnie aérienne **en déconfiture** (*in difficulty*); pour rétablir une situation économique et sociale **en pleine déconfiture** (*catastrophic; in total disarray*)

déconsidérer: ses volte-face et ses erreurs l'ont **déconsidéré** pour l'instant (*disqualify; make to lose favour*)

déconvenue (*f*): c'est une **déconvenue** pour le président socialiste (*disappointment; disaster*)

décote (*f*): le titre a été coté à 68p — la **décote** atteint donc 28%; le DMark a subi une **décote** de 16% par rapport au dollar (*fall in value*)

découpage (*m*): que de débats pour arriver à voter ce nouveau **découpage électoral**! (*redrawing of boundaries*)

découplage (*m*): le **découplage** entre les États-Unis et l'Europe sera lourd de conséquences (*uncoupling, separation, divergence*)

découpler: il n'y aura rien qui puisse **découpler** les États-Unis de l'Europe (*detach*)

décousu <e> (*adj*): la politique africaine **décousue** pratiquée par le gouvernement américain (*incoherent*)

découvert (*m*): il se trouve avec un **découvert bancaire** de 10 000F (*overdraft; deficit*); son compte en banque est **à découvert** (*overdrawn*)

décret (*m*): le SMIC a été augmenté par **décret** sur décision du gouvernement (*decree, edict*)

décrispation (*f*): un nouveau signe de la **décrispation** Est-Ouest (*lowering of tension; improved relationship*)

décrisper: leur libération a contribué à **décrisper** la situation (*relax; defuse*); une France **décrispée** sur le plan politique et social (*less tense/conflict-ridden*)

41

décrochage (*m*): on assiste à un **décrochage** international de l'industrie française (*falling behind; failure to keep up with*)

décrocher: quand les salaires **décrochent** de l'inflation (*fail to keep up with, fall behind*); il affirme que le PCF a **décroché** de la société française (*lose touch*); elle vient de **décrocher** d'importants contrats en Chine (*win*)

décroître: la consommation en France a sensiblement **décru** (*fall, lessen, reduce*)

décrue (*f*): la **décrue** du chômage se confirme en Allemagne fédérale (*fall, reduction*)

décuplement (*m*): le **décuplement** en dollars du prix du pétrole pèse sur l'économie tout entière (*tenfold increase; great increase*)

dédommagement (*m*): à titre de **dédommagement**, il leur a fait don de la moitié de la recette; il leur versa un gros **dédommagement** en échange des pleins pouvoirs sur la stratégie du groupe (*compensation, indemnity*)

dédommager: pour **dédommager** partiellement les pieds-noirs de la perte de leurs biens (*compensate*)

dédoublement (*m*): le **dédoublement** de la RN 4 risque de couper en deux certaines communautés (*making into dual carriageway*)

déduction (*f*): la **déduction fiscale** d'une partie des cotisations syndicales (*deduction from taxable income*)

défaillance (*f*): les **défaillances** du tissu industriel de la Lorraine (*breakdown; collapse*); le nombre des **défaillances d'entreprises** a progressé de 10% (*company collapse*)

défalcation (*f*): crédité de 1 000 voix d'avance, après **défalcation** des voix frauduleuses (*deduction; subtraction*)

défalquer: il a fallu **défalquer** les 2 000 voix 'suspectes' (*deduct*)

défaut (*m*): le **défaut** majeur de ces propositions, c'est leur coût prohibitif (*fault, drawback*); le jeune homme a été arrêté par la police pour **défaut** de port de casque (*failure; omission*); elle importe les matières premières qui lui **font défaut** (*lack*)

défavorisé <e> (*adj*): les plus **défavorisés**, pour la plupart des immigrés; une politique de solidarité, permettant la réinsertion des plus **défavorisés** (*deprived; impoverished*)

défection (*f*): la **défection** d'une partie de son électorat lui a coûté cher (*defection, abandonment*); un pilote a **fait défection** avec son avion et demande le droit d'exil (*defect*)

défendre [se]: il **se défend** d'être un néo-libéral (*deny*)

défense (*f*): 83% des Français sont pour la **défense** de fumer dans les lieux publics (*forbidding, prohibition*)

défenseur (*m*): les détenus n'ont pas pu rencontrer leurs **défenseurs** (*defence* *lawyer; counsel*)

déférer: les parlementaires de l'opposition **défèrent** la nouvelle loi au Conseil constitutionnel (*submit; refer*); l'accusé a refusé de **déférer** à une citation à comparaître devant le tribunal de grande instance de Nancy (*defer to; obey*); avec ses complices, il a été **déféré au parquet** (*refer for trial*)

défi (*m*): il nous faut relever ensemble le **défi** des nouvelles technologies (*challenge*)

défiance (*f*): la cohabitation suscite la **défiance** de 47% des personnes interrogées; résultat: une **défiance** accrue à l'égard du dollar (*hostility, distrust*); le 19 novembre, dans la **vote de défiance** à l'égard du gouvernement (*hostile vote; defiance*)

déficit (*m*): l'aggravation du **déficit extérieur** inquiète le gouvernement (*external/trade deficit*); le **déficit d'exploitation** du groupe ne cesse de s'alourdir (*operating loss*)

déficitaire (*adj*): **déficitaire** depuis 1980, la société a dégagé un bénéfice de 3 millions de francs (*unprofitable; loss-making*)

défiscalisation (*f*): la **défiscalisation** totale est un attrait certain de cet ensemble de propositions (*freeing from tax*)

défiscaliser: des rémunérations en partie **défiscalisées** et dispensées de charges sociales (*untaxed; non-taxable*)

défrayer: la déconfiture de cette société a **défrayé la chronique** (*make the headlines; be in the news*)

dégagement (*m*): les conséquences du **dégagement** jordanien de Cisjordanie (*withdrawal*)

dégager: fin août, il **dégagera** les trois priorités de son parti pour les mois à venir (*point out, define*); la police a mis deux heures pour **dégager** les rues des manifestants (*clear*); la firme a enfin **dégagé un bénéfice** (*make a profit*); [se] deux tendances **se dégagent** de l'étude de l'OCDE (*emerge; be revealed*)

dégât (*m*): les engins explosifs n'ont guère fait de **dégâts** (*damage*); le retour d'un temps sec a permis de **limiter les dégâts** (*limit the damage*); la protection est indispensable contre le **dégât des eaux** (*floods; flooding*)

dégel (*m*): leur rencontre témoigne d'une volonté de **dégel**; le **dégel** dans les relations sino-soviétiques préoccupe l'Inde (*improvement in relations*)

dégradation (*f*): emploi industriel: la **dégradation** se poursuit; Jérusalem s'inquiète de la **dégradation** de ses relations avec le Caire (*deterioration, worsening*)

dégrader [se]: la situation commerciale commence à **se dégrader** (*worsen, deteriorate*)

dégraissage (*m*): la restructuration exigera une vente massive d'actifs, un **dégraissage des effectifs** (*reduction/slimming down of staffing levels*)

43

dégraisser: avec un appareil de production **dégraissé** (*make leaner/ fitter; slim down*)

degré (*m*): un nouveau **degré** a été franchi dans l'escalade de la tension en Transcaucasie (*step*)

dégressif < -ive > (*adj*): à la différence du système actuel, le montant sera **dégressif** dans le temps (*on a reducing scale*)

dégrèvement (*m*): les sociétés sont imposables à 50%; dans certains cas il y a des exonérations et des **dégrèvements** (*tax relief*)

dégringolade (*f*): à commencer par la **dégringolade** du marché (*rapid fall; slump*)

dégringoler: sa cote de popularité a brutalement **dégringolé** (*fall sharply*)

déjouer: un attentat anti-américain **déjoué** à Rome (*foil*)

délabrement (*m*): compte tenu du **délabrement** de l'économie (*poor/ dilapidated state*)

délai (*m*): à deux heures de l'expiration des **délais** institués par les ravisseurs; il a respecté les **délais** de livraison (*time-limit*); il faudra que la France se dote, **dans les meilleurs délais**, d'un missile performant (*as soon as possible*); on a décidé de suspendre **sans délai** l'importation d'ivoire (*immediately*)

délégation (*f*): adjoint aux finances, il a décidé de renoncer à sa **délégation** (*authority, mandate*)

délégué (*m*): elle est représentante syndicale CGT et **déléguée du personnel** (*workers' representative on works committee/council*); le **délégué syndical** a communiqué la décision patronale aux travailleurs (*shop steward*)

délibéré (*m*): lors du **délibéré**, il avait surtout été question du premier des deux chefs d'inculpation (*private hearing by a judge*); le tribunal a mis son **jugement en délibéré** au 26 juin (*deliberation, hearing*)

délicatesse (*f*): les deux pays, **en délicatesse** depuis longtemps, et en froid depuis une année (*in a strained relationship; out of favour*)

délictueux < -euse > (*adj*): on les soupçonnait fortement d'autres activités **délictueuses** (*criminal*)

délinquance (*f*): la **délinquance** 'quotidienne' a fait plus que doubler en 20 ans (*crime*); la **grande délinquance** a beaucoup décru (*serious crime*)

délit (*m*): coupable du **délit** de recel (*offence*); en prison pour **délit d'opinion** (*expression of subversive ideas*); il fut pris **en flagrant délit** de vol avec effraction (*in the act, red-handed*)

délivrance (*f*): ces études aboutissent à la **délivrance** d'un diplôme (*awarding*); la **délivrance** de plein droit d'une carte de séjour (*issue*)

délivrer: le collège ne **délivre** aucun diplôme (*award*)

délocaliser: les industriels qui **délocalisent** leur production hors Hexagone

(*relocate; resite*)

demande (*f*): l'offre n'arrive pas à rattraper la **demande** (*demand*)

demandeur (*m*): le **demandeur** a obtenu gain de cause (*plaintiff*); les **demandeurs d'emploi** représentent 15% de la population active; le chômage fait son apparition: 22 000 **demandeurs d'emploi non-satisfaits** (*unemployed person; job-seeker*)

démanteler: il est question de **démanteler** le monopole public de l'électricité (*dismantle; take to pieces*)

démarchage (*m*): il faisait du **démarchage** pour vendre des contrats d'assurance-vie (*door-to-door selling*)

démarche (*f*): ils multiplient les **démarches** pour sauvegarder la paix (*move, initiative*)

démarcher: il **démarche** systématiquement les sociétés déjà implantées en Europe (*canvass; make approaches*)

démarcheur (*m*): il se méfie des **démarcheurs** peu scrupuleux (*door-to-door salesman; canvasser*)

démarquer [se]: le souci du chef de l'État de **se démarquer** de son Premier ministre (*dissociate oneself*)

démarrage (*m*): la campagne électorale a connu un **démarrage** hésitant, même difficile (*start, beginning*)

démêlé (*m*): les **démêlés** perpétuels du Caire avec Washington (*dispute, quarrel, problem*)

déménager: on parlait déjà de **déménager** les Halles à Rungis (*remove, move out*)

démenti (*m*): le **démenti** catégorique de X concernant les accusations portées contre lui (*denial*); c'était un **démenti** cinglant à l'adresse des autorités (*challenge; rejection*)

démentir: ils ont pour leur part **démenti** ces affirmations; il a **démenti** qu'il y ait eu une répression contre les intellectuels (*deny*); une domination de la droite jamais **démentie** en 150 années d'indépendance (*challenged; denied*); [se] un boom de la consommation qui **ne se dément pas** (*continue unabated*)

démettre: le roi a **démis** son ministre de ses fonctions (*sack, dismiss*); [se] les 12 élus **se sont démis** en bloc (*resign*)

demeure: il a **mis en demeure** les autorités de se prononcer sans délai (*instruct, order*)

démission (*f*): il envoya sa lettre de **démission** (*resignation*); il a **donné sa démission** au Président (*resign, tender resignation*)

démissionnaire (*adj*): le gouvernement belge, **démissionnaire** mais toujours en fonction (*having tendered one's resignation*)

démissionner: battu sur une question de confiance, le Premier ministre a

démissionné (*resign, tender one's resignation*); le général-ministre vient d'être **démissionné** par le Président (*sack, dismiss*)

démuni <e> (*adj*): les femmes **démunies** et sans emploi; les peuples les plus **démunis** (*deprived*)

dénégation (*f*): il faut trancher entre les affirmations de la victime et les **dénégations** de l'accusé (*denial*)

denier (*m*): la population la plus déshéritée, habituée à vivre des **deniers publics** (*state/public funds*)

dénombrer: on **dénombre** plus de 20 différents taux de TVA; on en **dénombre** plus de deux millions en 1990 (*count; list*)

dénomination (*f*): la nouvelle entité prend comme **dénomination sociale** Éts Schneider (*trading name*)

dénouement (*m*): le **dénouement** tragique de la prise d'otages (*result, outcome, conclusion*)

dénoyautage (*m*): le projet de loi sur le '**dénoyautage**' des entreprises privatisées par l'ancien gouvernement (*breaking-up of hard-core group of shareholders*)

dénoyauter: le ministre de l'Économie est désireux de '**dénoyauter**' les entreprises privatisées par le gouvernement de droite (*buy out a hard core of shareholders*)

denrée (*f*): c'est une **denrée** très recherchée en Hongrie (*commodity*)

dénuement (*m*): ils vivent dans le **dénuement** le plus complet (*destitution, penury*)

déontologie (*f*): il existe un code de **déontologie** fixé par la profession (*ethics*)

déontologique (*adj*): cette solution poserait de graves problèmes **déontologiques** (*ethical, of ethics*)

départ (*m*): il faudrait hâter les **départs à la retraite**, surtout en cas d'invalidité (*retirement*); une prime de 50 000F en cas de **départ volontaire** (*voluntary redundancy*); il a rassemblé un **capital de départ** de 2 millions de francs (*start-up capital*)

dépassement (*m*): les pénalités pour **dépassement** de quotas laitiers (*exceeding*); les **dépassements** systématiques des devis qui grèvent les coûts du programme (*exceeding; overshooting*)

dépasser: encore que les médecins puissent **dépasser** ces tarifs pour certains soins (*exceed*)

dépens (*m pl*): acquitté, il a été **condamné aux dépens** (*order to pay costs*)

dépêcher: la décision française de **dépêcher** dans la région des dragueurs et chasseurs de mines (*dispatch, send*)

dépensier <-ère> (*adj*): les Français sont parmi les plus **dépensiers** pour leur santé (*spendthrift*)

déplacement (*m*): il y a en fin de campagne des **déplacements de voix** considérables (*voting/electoral swing*)

déplafonnement (*m*): le projet de **déplafonnement** des allocations familiales (*removal of ceiling/upper limit*)

déplafonner: en **déplafonnant** et en abaissant le taux des cotisations familiales (*remove ceiling/upper limit*)

déployer [se]: l'immense activité qui **se déploie** actuellement en océan Indienne (*be deployed*)

déposant (*m*): un krach ne toucherait pas les **petits déposants** (*small depositor/saver*)

déposer: il a refusé de **déposer** devant la commission du Bundestag enquêtant sur cette affaire (*testify, give evidence*); une trentaine d'amendements ont été **déposés** (*table, put down*); la firme a **déposé son bilan** hier (*file bankruptcy proceedings*)

déposition (*f*): tout au long du procès, il a maintenu sa **déposition** (*testimony*)

dépôt (*m*): la date de **dépôt** des dossiers de candidature (*submission*); lors du **dépôt** de la motion de censure (*tabling; registering*); les principales **banques de dépôt** (*clearing bank*); l'annonce du **dépôt de bilan** a surpris les milieux d'affaires (*bankruptcy petition*)

dépouillement (*m*): dès la fin du scrutin on procède au **dépouillement** des votes (*count, counting*); le **dépouillement** des dossiers prendra du temps (*perusal; inspection*)

dépourvu: la révolte, par son ampleur, risque de **prendre au dépourvu** les dirigeants (*take by surprise*)

dépoussiérage (*m*): cette entreprise de **dépoussiérage** du vieux parti travailliste (*renovation, dusting-down*)

déprime (*f*): la Bourse a eu un nouvel accès de **déprime** mercredi (*depressed trading conditions*)

déprimer: le nouveau reflux du dollar a **déprimé** le franc (*depress, force down*)

députation (*f*): candidat à la **députation** pour la première fois (*seat in French National Assembly*)

député (*m*): élu **député**, il représenta sa circonscription pendant 25 ans (*member of French National Assembly; deputy*); membre de la SFIO, et **député-maire** de Marseille (*deputy and mayor*)

dérapage (*m*): il est vital qu'il n'y ait pas **dérapage** de l'inflation (*uncontrolled rise; going out of control*); elle s'est inquiétée des **dérapages** que pourrait entraîner l'application de ce décret (*abuse, excess*)

déraper: les prix ne **déraperont** pas l'an prochain (*take off, rise sharply*); la Nouvelle-Calédonie **dérape**! (*get out of control*)

déréglementation (*f*): c'est l'ère de la **déréglementation** mondiale de la communication; nouveau pas dans la **déréglementation** du téléphone

(*decontrolling, deregulation*)

dérégulation (*f*): il voulait prendre position sur le marché britannique en vue de sa prochaine **dérégulation** (*deregulation*)

dérive (*f*): à gauche, on craint une possible **dérive** centriste du Parti socialiste; pour empêcher une **dérive** terroriste de l'islamisme (*drift*)

dérobade (*f*): la **dérobade** du gouvernement éclaire les relations du pouvoir et des milieux financiers (*concealment, secrecy; avoiding the issue*)

dérober: coupable d'avoir **dérobé** des objets de valeur (*steal, remove*); [se] beaucoup de jeunes tentent de **se dérober** à la conscription (*avoid*)

dérogation (*f*): on l'a autorisé, par **dérogation** spéciale, à consulter les archives privées (*exemption; dispensation*)

dérogatoire (*adj*): certaines monnaies ont aujourd'hui des régimes **dérogatoires** (*exceptional; dispensatory*)

déroulement (*m*): pour surveiller le bon **déroulement** des opérations (*progress, development*); ils demandent 1 000F pour tous, et de meilleurs **déroulements de carrière** (*career structure*)

dérouler [se]: les négociations de paix qui **se déroulent** à Genève; des affrontements **se sont déroulés** à Beyrouth (*take place*)

déroute (*f*): humiliante **déroute** pour le parti au pouvoir (*defeat, reverse*)

désaccord (*m*): **désaccord** entre les Dix sur l'avenir politique de la communauté (*disagreement, division*); les deux pays sont **en plein désaccord** à ce sujet (*divided; in total disagreement*)

désaffecté <e> (*adj*): il dispose d'un ancien atelier **désaffecté** (*disused, abandoned*)

désaffection (*f*): une **désaffection** des électeurs à l'égard du Parti; la **désaffection** qui menace la Maison Blanche (*loss of favour; unpopularity*)

désamorcer: la bombe fut vite **désamorcée**; il faut tout faire pour **désamorcer** la tension (*defuse*); il pensait avoir **désamorcé** d'éventuelles critiques (*pre-empt*)

désarmer: l'opposition des syndicats ne **désarme** pas (*weaken; give up the fight*)

désarroi (*m*): après le sommet raté, c'est le **désarroi** dans le camp occidental (*disarray, confusion*)

désaveu (*m*): pour le Président, le **désaveu** est cinglant (*rebuff; repudiation*)

désavouer: le ministre, **désavoué** par son parti, a été acculé à la démission (*reject, repudiate*)

désenclavement (*m*): le **désenclavement** de la façade maritime, avec le projet autoroutier (*ending of the isolation of*)

désenclaver: on se bat pour **désenclaver** la capitale de la Picardie (*put an end* *to the isolation of*)

désendetter: soucieux de **désendetter** l'État, le ministre maintient le cap choisi par son prédécesseur (*get out of debt*)

désengager [se]: le gouvernement a décidé de **se désengager** de l'opération (*withdraw*)

déséquilibre (*m*): mais on agit peu en profondeur sur les grands **déséquilibres** structurels (*imbalance*)

désertification (*f*): pour lutter contre la **désertification des campagnes** (*flight from the land; rural exodus*)

désescalade (*f*): la poursuite de la **désescalade** des taux d'intérêt (*fall, reduction*)

désétatiser: partout on cherche à **désétatiser** un secteur public tentaculaire (*privatize; remove from public ownership*)

déshérité <e> (*adj*): les plus **déshérités** sont toujours les plus durement touchés par la crise (*deprived, impoverished*)

désignation (*f*): la **désignation** d'un successeur ne saurait tarder (*naming, nomination*)

désigner: son successeur ne tardera pas à être **désigné** (*choose, designate, appoint*)

désistement (*m*): peu de **désistements**, beaucoup de candidats se maintiennent (*withdrawal in favour of another candidate*)

désister [se]: le candidat socialiste **s'était désisté** en faveur du communiste, mieux placé que lui (*withdraw, stand down*)

désolidariser [se]: il **s'est désolidarisé** de ses collègues du conseil municipal (*dissociate oneself; withdraw one's support*)

dessaisir: la décentralisation n'a pas **dessaisi** l'État de son rôle directeur (*deprive, remove from*); [se] il **s'est dessaisi** de ses fonctions d'adjoint au maire (*resign*)

dessaisissement (*m*): son avocat demanda et obtint le **dessaisissement** du juge (*taking off/ removal from a legal case*)

desserrement (*m*): la faiblesse du Mark permet à Paris un **desserrement** du coût de l'argent (*easing; reduction*)

desserte (*f*): qui assure la **desserte** de la région Pays de la Loire; Air France partage la **desserte** de Nice et de la Corse avec Air Inter (*service*)

desservir: le port de Dunkerque **dessert** tout le nord-ouest du continent européen (*serve*)

dessous (*m*): ce qui révèle de nouveaux **dessous** de cette guerre entre service secret et gouvernement (*hidden aspect, shady side*)

destituer: le Conseil d'État l'ayant **destitué**, il fit appel au Conseil constitutionnel (*dismiss, depose*)

destitution (*f*): une menace d'assassinat serait à l'origine de la **destitution** du chef d'État (*removal from power/office*)

détacher: il a été **détaché** à Athènes après la guerre (*second*); le personnel français **détaché** à l'étranger (*on secondment*)

détail (*m*): les **prix de détail** n'ont progressé que de 0,1% (*retail price*); dans le **commerce de détail** l'emploi reste un gros point noir (*retail sector; retailing*)

détaxer: l'État peut **détaxer** la partie du revenu consacrée à l'épargne (*exonerate from tax*)

détenir: il est assuré de **détenir** une position de force; l'État **détient** 45% du capital de la firme (*hold*); la police pourra **détenir** tout suspect pendant une durée de sept jours (*hold, detain*)

détente (*f*): la **détente** en cours entre les deux super-puissances ('*detente', improvement in relations*); une **détente** a été observée sur les cours des matières premières (*reduction/fall in price*)

détenteur (*m*): les **détenteurs** d'actions dans la société X; principal exportateur et **détenteur** des plus vastes réserves de pétrole (*holder, possessor*)

détention (*f*): une tentative de vol de voiture et la **détention** de faux papiers (*possession of*); sa **détention** n'a duré que six mois (*detention; imprisonment*); une mise en liberté accordée après deux mois de **détention préventive** (*remand in custody*); il a été **placé en détention provisoire** d'avril 1986 à mars 1987 (*detain; remand in custody*)

détenu (*m*): le nombre de **détenus** le 1er juillet s'élevait à 50 000 personnes (*prisoner*)

déterminant <e> (*adj*): cette victoire, **déterminante** pour l'avenir du parti (*crucial, decisive*)

détournement (*m*): la nouvelle du **détournement** de l'avion a été diffusée à 16 heures (*hijacking*); inculpé de **détournement de mineur** (*abduction of a minor; corruption of a minor*); les **détournements de fonds** s'élèveraient à une dizaine de millions de francs (*embezzlement*)

détourner: 90 millions ont été **détournés** par cet arnaqueur (*embezzle*)

dévalorisation (*f*): la progression du nombre des enseignants a facilité la **dévalorisation** de leur traitement (*lowering; falling behind*)

devancer: le maire, **devancé** au premier tour, se retira en faveur du socialiste (*head, lead*)

devant (*m*): il avait été sur le **devant** de la scène politique depuis dix ans (*forefront*); il avait préféré **prendre les devants** en regagnant précipitamment son pays (*anticipate events; take initiative*)

devis (*m*): il a fait établir un **devis** pour la réfection de la maison (*estimate*)

devise (*f*): Travail, Famille, Patrie: la **devise** de Vichy (*motto, slogan*); la **devise** américaine — le billet vert — est très demandée en ce moment

(*currency*)

dialogue (*m*): cette lettre poursuit le **dialogue de sourds** entamé avec le PS (*dialogue of the deaf*)

dialoguer: l'opposition s'est déclarée prête à **dialoguer** avec le gouvernement (*open a dialogue, have discussions*)

diffamation (*f*): ils ont porté plainte pour **diffamation** (*slander, libel*); les **procès en diffamation** se multiplient en Grande-Bretagne (*libel action*)

différé [en]: le discours du ministre est passé **en différé** sur les écrans de télévision (*pre-recorded*)

différend (*m*): puis survient sa démission et son éclatant **différend** avec le Premier ministre (*difference of opinion, disagreement*); ce **différend frontalier** est vieux de 17 ans (*frontier dispute*)

différer: la Belgique **diffère** sa décision sur l'achat de l'avion français (*defer, postpone*)

diffuser: son portrait a été **diffusé** dans les ports et dans les aéroports (*distribute; circulate*); la tension très particulière d'une émission **diffusée** en direct (*broadcast*)

diffusion (*f*): on est encore au stade de la **diffusion** du catalogue (*circulating*); c'est la seconde **diffusion** qui a été la plus suivie (*broadcast*)

dilapidation (*f*): il se consacra à la lutte contre la **dilapidation** des fonds publics (*waste, squandering*)

dilapider: l'Occident **dilapide** son crédit de confiance auprès des pays arabes (*waste, squander*)

dilatoire (*adj*): estimant qu'il s'agissait d'une manœuvre **dilatoire** (*time-wasting*)

diminuer: l'activité devra **diminuer** d'autant l'an prochain (*slow down; diminish*)

diminution (*f*): ils tablent sur une **diminution** de l'impôt direct (*reduction, fall*)

diplômé (*m*/*adj*): **diplômé** d'une grande école d'ingénieurs (*holder of a diploma; graduate*)

direction (*f*): il ne souhaite pas conserver la **direction** du parti (*leadership*); **direction** et syndicats se sont rencontrés hier (*management*); avec le concours de la **direction** des affaires culturelles (*section, department*)

dirigeant (*m*): les **dirigeants** socialistes s'y sont opposés en bloc (*leadership; leader*); deux **dirigeants** de la société ont été arrêtés (*director, manager*); (*adj*) une élite fortement intégrée à la **classe dirigeante** (*ruling class*)

dirigiste (*adj*): un gouvernement, qu'il soit libéral ou **dirigiste** (*pertaining to a planned economy*)

discours (*m*): il a changé radicalement de **discours** (*tone, vocabulary*); il **tenait un discours** bien plus ferme (*speak a language; adopt a tone*)

disculper: un communiqué de Washington semble **disculper** Ryad (*exculpate, exonerate*)

discutable (*adj*): affirmation qu'il trouvait, pour le moins, **discutable** (*arguable, questionable, debatable*)

disette (*f*): la banlieue sud était la plus touchée par la **disette** (*shortage*)

disponibilité (*f*): de bonnes **disponibilités** en logement pour les employés (*availability; supply of*); la firme possède plus de 30 milliards de **disponibilités** (*available funds*); tenu pour responsable, il a été **mis en disponibilité** (*suspend from duty*)

disponible (*adj*): le **revenu disponible** par habitant, après impôts et cotisations sociales (*disposable income*)

disposer: la plupart des ménages **disposent** du téléphone à domicile (*possess, be equipped with*)

dispositif (*m*): c'est en janvier que le nouveau **dispositif** sera mis en place (*arrangement; system*); la France renforce son **dispositif** naval dans cette zone (*military force*); au milieu d'un impressionnant **dispositif de sécurité** (*security operation*)

disposition (*f*): si ces **dispositions** sont pleinement observées par tous les États concernés (*clause, condition*); la police a **pris les dispositions** nécessaires (*take measures*); les moyens que la France peut mettre **à sa disposition** (*at the disposal of*)

disputer [se]: la Maison Blanche et le Congrès **se disputent** la maîtrise de la politique extérieure; ils **se disputent** un marché très réduit (*contest, compete for*)

dissidence (*f*): l'Église américaine serait-elle au bord de la **dissidence**? (*rebellion, breakaway*); un candidat **en dissidence** avec le parti officiel (*breakaway, in rebellion*)

dissident (*m/adj*): le PS n'entérine pas la candidature du maire sortant: il sera **dissident** (*unofficial candidate*)

dissolution (*f*): il est partisan de la **dissolution** de l'Assemblée nationale (*dissolving*)

dissoudre: le nouveau Président **dissoudra** le Parlement (*dissolve*)

dissuasif < -ive > (*adj*): la peine de mort est **dissuasive** pour les terroristes (*of a deterrent value*)

dissuasion (*f*): le refus de la **dissuasion** nucléaire; l'attachement du pays à sa force de **dissuasion** (*deterrence*)

distance (*f*): les partis de l'opposition désirent **prendre leurs distances** par rapport aux indépendantistes (*dissociate oneself*)

distancer: les communistes ont largement **distancé** les socialistes (*lead; outstrip*)

diversifier [se]: il a fait fortune dans l'immobilier, et **s'est diversifié** dans l'agro-alimentaire (*diversify; broaden one's production*)

doléance (*f*): face aux **doléances** africaines, on a fait quelques concessions de pure forme (*complaint*)

domicilier: il s'était fait **domicilier** à Paris (*have one's address; reside*)

dominical <e> (*adj*): ce quotidien à grand tirage, dans son édition **dominicale** (*Sunday*); le débat sur l'**ouverture dominicale** rebondit (*Sunday opening*)

dommage (*m*): les installations portuaires ont subi de graves **dommages** (*damage*); il demande 10 000 francs de **dommages et intérêts** (*damages*)

DOM-TOM (*m pl*): les **DOM-TOM** dépendent d'un ministre délégué auprès du Premier ministre (*overseas* départements *and territories*)

donation (*f*): si l'un des époux reçoit un bien en héritage ou **en donation** (*as a gift*)

donne (*f*): la poussée des écologistes change la **donne** politique (*complexion; balance of power*); **nouvelle donne** pour la sécurité européenne ('*New Deal*')

donnée (*f*): cette rupture complique un peu plus les **données** du conflit israélo-arabe (*fact; circumstance*); le chômage a augmenté de 0,7% en **données corrigées des variations saisonnières** (*seasonally adjusted figures*)

doper: le gouvernement allemand accepte de **doper** sa croissance pour consommer plus et exporter moins (*make artificially high*)

dos (*m*): en refusant le dialogue, il va **se mettre à dos** l'élite afrikaner (*antagonize*); un règlement politique ne peut se faire que **sur le dos** des paysans (*with the involvement of*); il les a **renvoyés dos à dos** (*reject both equally*)

dossier (*m*): les syndicats restent divisés sur les grands **dossiers** sociaux (*question, subject*); 12 000 **dossiers** ont été déposés par des demandeurs d'emploi (*file; application*)

dotation (*f*): il a notamment regretté la faiblesse des **dotations** de l'Opéra et de la Comédie-Française (*grant, subsidy*)

doter: une Hong Kong **dotée** d'institutions démocratiques; les missiles **dotés** de charges conventionnelles (*equip, supply*); [se] l'entreprise **s'est dotée** d'un ordinateur pour le traitement des commandes (*acquire*)

double-emploi: deux armes dont on peut penser qu'elles **feront double-emploi** (*be redundant/surplus to requirements*)

doublement: les spécialistes prévoient un **doublement** du volume transporté dans les dix ans (*doubling*)

doubler: les exportations de produits finis ont **doublé** (*double*)

doyen (*m*): ce magistrat quinquagénaire, **doyen** des juges de Béthune (*most senior member*)

draconien <-enne> (*adj*): des mesures **draconiennes** de rétorsion furent prises (*very severe, draconian*)

drainer: les collectivités locales **drainent** 12% des revenus fiscaux; les charges sociales **drainent** des sommes folles (*tap; use up*)

drapeau (*m*): le Nicaragua, avec plus de 100 000 hommes **sous les drapeaux** (*armed, under arms*)

drastique (*adj*): on a constaté une diminution **drastique** des visas de sortie accordés aux juifs (*drastic, very great*)

droit (*m*): leurs produits d'exportation se sont vu frappés de **droits** anti-dumping (*duty, tax*); abolition progressive des **droits de douane** frappant les véhicules japonaises (*customs duty*); une réforme des **droits de successions** s'avère indispensable (*death duty*); il est membre **de droit** de la commission (*ex-officio*); le nombre de policiers tués au cours d'affrontements avec des malfaiteurs de **droit commun** (*common law*)

droitier <-ère> (*adj*): une petite ville tranquille et **droitière** (*politically to the right*)

dumping (*m*): vendre ainsi moins cher à l'étranger équivaut à pratiquer du **dumping** (*dumping*)

duplex (*m*): il habite dans un **duplex** avenue de Paris (*split-level apartment*); les images sont venues **en duplex** de Nancy (*by TV link-up*)

duplicata (*m*): en aucun cas il ne sera délivré de **duplicata** (*copy, replacement*)

durcir: devant leur résistance, le gouvernement **durcit le ton** (*harden its attitude*); [se] la révolte **se durcit** au fil des jours (*harden*)

durcissement (*m*): il y eut un net **durcissement** à la base (*hardening of attitude*); une majorité souhaite un **durcissement** de la répression (*hardening; increase*)

durée (*f*): les contrats **à durée déterminée** sont devenus la règle et non plus l'exception (*fixed-term*); un préavis de grève **d'une durée indéterminée** (*indefinite*); les chômeurs **de longue durée**, une catégorie exclue des allocations (*long-term*)

dysfonctionnement (*m*): une table ronde sur le **dysfonctionnement** de l'économie corse (*malfunctioning; inefficiency*)

E

ébauche (*f*): le projet d'autoroute n'est qu'**à l'état d'ébauche** (*at the preliminary/drawing-board stage*)

ébranler: les débats qui **ébranlent** le Parti communiste; le parti sort durement **ébranlé** de ce scrutin (*shake; weaken*)

écart (*m*): un accroissement de l'**écart** des revenus entre les riches et les pauvres; l'**écart** de prix peut aller du simple au double (*differential*); le moindre **écart de conduite** est lourdement sanctionné (*misdemeanour*); fautes sanctionnées par mutations ou **mises à l'écart** (*banishment; imprisonment*)

écarter: cette décision visait à **écarter** un homme jugé dangereux; la police **écarte** l'hypothèse d'un meurtre (*exclude, rule out*)

échange (*m*): la bonne tenue des **échanges** avec le Japon (*trade, commerce*); le volume des **échanges** à la Bourse de Paris a doublé (*transaction*)

échanger [s']: le Mark **s'échangeait** hier à 4,090F; plus de 10% des actions de la société **se sont échangées** hier (*change hands; be traded*)

échantillon (*m*): l'enquête portait sur un **échantillon** de 3 699 personnes (*sample*)

écharpe (*f*): élections: le député PS a l'**écharpe** à portée de la main à la mairie de Verdun (*mayoral sash; mayoral office*)

échauffourrée (*f*): à Paris hier, **échauffourrées** au cours d'une manifestation de mineurs (*scuffle, disturbance*)

échéance (*f*): cette **échéance** va obliger les deux antagonistes à s'entendre (*deadline; expiry date*); contracter un nouvel emprunt pour payer vos précédentes **échéances** (*bill/payment, commitment*); à la veille de l'**échéance électorale** de 1988 (*election date*); il n'existe pas, **à échéance prévisible**, d'alternative (*in the foreseeable future*); un grand nombre de baux **parviennent à échéance** cette année (*mature; expire*); l'arrêté devrait entrer en vigueur **à brève échéance** (*soon, shortly*)

échéancier (*m*): le programme d'investissements se poursuit selon l'**échéancier** fixé (*timetable; calendar*)

échec (*m*): les **échecs** régulièrement subis par les Travaillistes (*defeat*); à la suite de l'**échec** des négociations salariales (*breakdown*); le ministre a **fait échec** à l'amendement approuvé par le groupe socialiste (*block; defeat*); le gouvernement a été **mis en échec** par une explosion sociale inattendue (*defeat*)

échelle (*f*): grâce à des **économies d'échelle** (*economies of scale*); l'influence de la France est ressentie **à l'échelle du globe** (*world-wide; on a global scale*)

échelon (*m*): on gravit les **échelons** largement à l'ancienneté; elle est au dernier **échelon** et n'a plus de promotion à attendre (*step, grade, rung of ladder*); des émissions locales, **à l'échelon des villes** (*at the urban/city level*)

échelonner: l'accord prévoit le départ **échelonné** du ministère des finances (*in stages*); la France payera **en versements échelonnés** (*by instalments*); [s'] les versements peuvent **s'échelonner** sur plusieurs mois (*extend; be spread over*)

échiquier (*m*): l'influence de notre pays sur l'**échiquier international** est en nette régression (*international scene*); une troisième force au centre de l'**échiquier politique** britannique (*political chess-board/spectrum*)

écho (*m*): les critiques dont ce journal a **fait l'écho** (*report; repeat*)

échoir: le délai de livraison vient d'**échoir** (*expire*); la présidence de la commission **échoit** au représentant anglais (*fall to*)

échouer: une tentative de cessez-le-feu et de dialogue a **échoué** (*fail; come to nothing*); ayant **échoué** à prendre le contrôle du conglomérat allemand (*fail*)

éclabousser: il fut **éclaboussé** par l'escroquerie commise par son collègue (*besmirch, tarnish the good name of*)

éclaircissement (*m*): l'**éclaircissement** du massacre se fait toujours attendre (*explanation*)

éclaté <e> (*adj*): dans une société où l'emploi est si précaire et le salariat si **éclaté** (*fragmented, splintered*)

éclatement (*m*): le mouvement est menacé d'**éclatement** (*splitting; breaking up*)

éclater: un scandale **éclate**; la guerre **a éclaté** à la frontière entre le Tchad et la Libye (*break out*)

école (*f*): pour défendre l'**école libre** contre le gouvernement de gauche (*private-sector school*)

éconduire: il les avait gentiment, mais fermement, **éconduits** (*dismiss; usher out*)

écoper: il a **écopé** de six mois de mise à pied (*receive penalty/punishment*)

écot (*m*): ceux qui ne versent pas leur **écot** (*contribution, share*)

écouler: les Polonais ont du mal à **écouler** leur production (*sell; sell off*)

écraser [s']: l'appareil **s'est écrasé** en flammes après avoir été touché par un missile (*crash*)

écritures (*f pl*): condamné à 30 000F d'amende pour fraude fiscale et omission d'**écritures** (*book-keeping entry*)

écrouer: un policier et ses complices **écroués** pour extorsion de fonds (*imprison*)

Écu (*m*): l'**Écu** fut créé le 1er janvier 1981 (*ECU; European Currency Unit*)

édification (*f*): les chefs d'État poursuivent, à Hanovre, l'**édification** de la CEE (*building, construction*)

édulcorer: il a réussi à **édulcorer** la résolution sur l'abandon des centrales nucléaires (*dilute, tone down*)

effectif (*m*): l'augmentation des **effectifs** scolaires (*numbers; strength*); les **effectifs** ont été réduits d'un tiers en cinq ans (*staffing levels; work-force*)

effectuer: il a **effectué** une étude approfondie auprès de 150 usagers; un commando a **effectué** un raid dans les faubourgs de la ville (*carry out, perform, execute*); [s'] la rentrée, qu'on avait promise 'chaude', **s'est effectuée** dans le calme (*take place*)

effondrement (*m*): l'**effondrement** de la monnaie italienne; l'**effondrement** du marché a surpris les spécialistes (*collapse*)

effondrer [s']: des sociétés bien cotées ont vu leurs cours **s'effondrer** (*collapse*)

effraction (*f*): il est **entré par effraction** dans la nuit de jeudi à vendredi (*breaking and entering*); inculpés de **vol avec effraction** (*theft with breaking and entering*)

effritement (*m*): nouvel **effritement** des voix socialistes (*crumbling away, erosion; decline*)

effriter [s']: toutes les monnaies européennes **se sont effritées** vis-à-vis de la devise allemande (*lose value*)

égalité (*f*): la justice sociale, et l'**égalité des chances** (*equal opportunity*); les femmes demandent l'**égalité devant le salaire** (*equal pay*); la pleine **égalité d'accès au travail** entre femmes et hommes (*equal opportunity*)

égide (*f*): un cessez-le-feu sous l'**égide** syrienne; ils ont constitué une société holding sous l'**égide** de la banque Worms (*control, direction*)

élargir: on **élargit** les catégories d'étrangers bénéficiant de la carte de résident (*extend, widen*); on **élargit** le détenu avant qu'il n'eût purgé la moitié de sa peine (*free, release from prison*)

élargissement (*m*): l'**élargissement** puis l'expulsion des trois hommes (*release from prison*); l'**élargissement** du collège de 5 à 8 membres (*increase, extension*)

électeur (*m*): depuis quelques années, l'**électeur** français se rend aux urnes au moins une fois par an (*elector*); 2 708 **grands électeurs** se réunissent à Bordeaux pour les sénatoriales (*member of restricted electoral college*)

électif <-ive> (*adj*): l'avocat général est, à Dallas, une **fonction élective** (*elected office*)

élever [s']: les autorités **s'élèvent** contre les accusations de torture (*protest*); le bilan des victimes **s'élevait** samedi à 129 morts (*total*)

éligible (*adj*): le militaire est **éligible**, mais doit choisir entre sa fonction et son mandat (*eligible for election*); on lui a promis une place d'**éligible** sur la liste socialiste (*with realistic chance of election*); il figure **en place non-éligible** sur la liste socialiste (*low-placed*)

élu (*m*/*adj*): une délégation d'**élus** lorrains (*elected member, deputy, representative*)

émargement (*m*): la procédure de signature du **cahier d'émargement** par chaque électeur (*voting register*)

émarger: il avait oublié d'**émarger** la feuille de vote conformément aux nouvelles dispositions (*sign*)

emballement (*m*): l'économie donnait déjà des signes d'**emballement** (*going out of control*)

emballer [s']: pour éviter que le crédit à la consommation ne **s'emballe** (*go out of control*)

embargo (*m*): Paris assouplit l'**embargo** pétrolier vis-à-vis de Téhéran (*embargo*)

embauche (*f*): les projets initiaux ne prévoient que l'**embauche** de 50 salariés (*employment, taking on of labour*); le **monopole d'embauche** syndical est illégal en France (*closed shop*); les plus forts **salaires d'embauche** pour un premier emploi sont ceux des actuaires (*starting salary*)

embellie (*f*): l'**embellie** provoquée par la baisse du prix du pétrole; profitant d'une **embellie** dans la situation économique (*improvement*)

embrayer: une aubaine pour l'opposition, qui a pu **embrayer** derrière les rebelles sur les bancs du gouvernement (*follow the lead*)

émettre: les Postes **émettent** une nouvelle série de timbres commémoratifs (*issue*)

émeute (*f*): les **émeutes** hier ont fait 18 morts (*riot*)

émeutier (*m*): le procès des **émeutiers** passionne l'opinion publique (*rioter*)

émission (*f*): Petrofina augmente son capital par l'**émission** de deux millions de nouvelles actions (*share issue*)

émoi (*m*): c'est tout juste si les syndicats manifestent quelque **émoi**; alors que l'**émoi** suscité par sa défaite inattendue était encore vif (*emotion, excitement*)

émouvoir: l'annulation de la visite a **ému** les Autrichiens (*upset; arouse indignation of*); [s'] le Président **s'est ému** des propos de son ministre (*be stirred/aroused/angry*); il **s'est ému** auprès du ministre (*complain*)

empêchement (*m*): à la suite d'un **empêchement** de dernière minute, le Premier ministre s'est décommandé (*unforeseen circumstance; hitch*)

empiéter: on estime que le Premier ministre **empiète** sur le terrain présidentiel (*encroach*)

empirer [s']: la situation ne s'est pas améliorée: au contraire, elle **s'empire** (*get worse*)

employer [s']: Moscou **s'emploie** à resserrer ses liens avec Téhéran (*endeavour, devote oneself*)

empoignade (*f*): la perspective d'une rude **empoignade** entre les deux candidats (*row; contest*); de vigoureuses **empoignades verbales** ont eu lieu hier à l'Assemblée (*verbal set-to*)

emporte-pièce [à l']: irrités par les décisions **à l'emporte-pièce** du Président (*incisive; sudden*); il faut se méfier de toute solution simpliste **à l'emporte-pièce** (*once and for all*)

emporter: la liste emmenée par l'ancien maire a **emporté** cette élection partielle (*win*); l'intérêt du pays **l'emporte** sur toute autre considération (*prevail*); la droite **l'a emporté** le 16 mars (*win*)

empressement (*m*): il n'avait montré aucun **empressement** à rencontrer son homologue allemand (*eagerness, anxiousness*)

emprise (*f*): l'administration continue à exercer son **emprise** sur les institutions démocratiques du pays (*ascendancy, control*)

emprunt (*m*): certains ménages consacrent le tiers de leurs ressources au remboursement d'**emprunts** (*loan*); un **emprunt-logement** à un taux très avantageux (*mortgage loan*); le vif succès du dernier **emprunt gouvernemental** de 4 milliards de DMarks à 10 ans (*government loan*); la Caisse nationale de l'énergie a **émis un emprunt** d'un milliard de francs (*float new loan*)

énarque (*m*): une direction composée de 200 fonctionnaires, la plupart **énarques** (*graduate of the ENA*)

encadrement (*m*): l'**encadrement** est assuré par des officiers d'expérience (*supervision*); l'**encadrement** de la société a informé le personnel sur les circonstances de l'OPA (*management; directors*); avec la levée de l'**encadrement du crédit** (*restriction on credit/lending*)

encadrer: le conflit a été aussitôt **encadré** par la CGT; les syndicats ont du mal à **encadrer** ces mouvements spontanés (*take in hand, organize*); à l'époque, le crédit était **encadré** (*restricted; controlled*)

encaisser: il a **encaissé** de substantiels bénéfices (*receive; collect*)

encart (*m*): il a fait paraître un **encart** publicitaire dans trois journaux régionaux (*insert*)

enchérissement (*m*): par crainte d'un **enchérissement** des importations (*rise in price/cost*)

enclavement (*m*): ceci accentue l'**enclavement** actuel de l'est du pays, dépourvu de TGV (*isolation*)

enclaver: malgré son aérodrome récent, Albi est **enclavé** (*hem in, enclose; cut off*)

encontre [à l']: l'embargo commercial décrété **à son encontre** par les États-Unis (*against*); elle **irait à l'encontre de** l'évolution constatée dans les autres pays d'Europe (*be contrary/opposed to*)

encours (*m*): l'activité de crédit a progressé de 2%, les **encours** atteignant 15 milliards de francs; les prêts à taux fixe représentent 40% environ des **encours** (*credit; money lent*)

endettement (*m*): pour résoudre le problème de l'**endettement** du Tiers-Monde (*debt; getting into debt*)

endetter: la commune est fortement **endettée** (*in debt*)

endiguer: un plan destiné à **endiguer** la crise qui sévit dans ce pays; pour **endiguer** la chute du dollar (*check, arrest; contain*)

endossement (*m*): une lettre de change peut être transmise à un tiers par **endossement** (*endorsement*)

endosser: il a dû **endosser** la responsabilité des activités de ses collègues (*take on, accept*); en faisant **endosser** par les États-Unis son projet d'élections dans les territoires occupés (*endorse*)

énergétique (*adj*): la France peut conquérir son indépendance **énergétique** en dix ans (*in energy resources*)

engagement (*m*): on accuse le Nicaragua de ne pas respecter ses **engagements** (*promise*); son **engagement** personnel dans la lutte contre le terrorisme (*involvement*); quel que soit l'**engagement** politique ou philosophique de chacun (*alignment; commitment*)

engager: les super-puissances viennent d'**engager** un timide dialogue (*open, start, initiate*); les décisions à prendre **engagent** l'avenir (*commit*); [s'] la lutte contre le terrorisme **s'engage** dans une nouvelle phase (*enter*); c'est une triple bataille qui **s'engage** à Washington (*start, begin*)

engin (*m*): un bâtiment porteur d'**engins** nucléaires endommagé par un incendie (*weapon*); il a lancé une grenade: l'**engin** a explosé faisant dix morts (*device*)

englober: ces projets doivent **englober** les autres pays européens (*include*)

engloutir: à quoi ont pu servir les sommes **englouties** par le gouvernement démissionnaire? (*swallow up*)

engorgement (*m*): les investisseurs redoutent un **engorgement** du marché (*glut*)

engouement (*m*): la privatisation a confirmé l'**engouement** nouveau des petits épargnants pour la Bourse (*passion, enthusiasm*)

enjeu (*m*): le pays, l'**enjeu** des rivalités de ses puissants voisins (*object*); tel est l'**enjeu** crucial en cette fin d'année (*stake; what is at stake*)

enlever: en Jordanie, les islamistes **enlèvent** 31 sur 80 sièges (*capture, win*)

enliser [s']: cette stratégie marque le pas, et les négociations **s'enlisent** (*fail to advance; get bogged down*)

enquête (*f*): la police a ouvert une **enquête** (*investigation, enquiry*); lors d'une **enquête d'opinion** effectuée début mars (*survey; public-opinion poll*); une **enquête d'utilité publique** aura lieu; l'**enquête préalable à la**

déclaration d'utilité publique commencera jeudi (*public enquiry*)

enquêter: la commission qui **enquête** sur cette affaire (*investigate*)

enrayer: l'objectif est d'**enrayer** toute spirale inflationniste (*arrest; bring under control*)

enregistrer: le parti a **enregistré** un revers aux élections; c'est le chiffre le plus bas **enregistré** depuis vingt ans (*record; register*)

ensanglanter: un nouvel attentat a **ensanglanté** le pays (*bathe in blood*)

enseignement (*m*): une enquête sur l'**enseignement** qui y est dispensé (*teaching; education*); le parti a su tirer les **enseignements** du passé (*lesson*)

ensemble (*m*): il a réuni l'**ensemble** des membres du gouvernement (*whole, entirety*)

entamer: une défaite qui a largement **entamé** sa crédibilité (*impair*); ils **entament** la lutte contre ce fléau (*begin, initiate*)

entendre [s']: Paris et Alger **s'entendent** sur un prix pour le gaz algérien (*come to an agreement; agree*)

entente (*f*): l'amende infligée aux deux firmes pour **entente** illicite (*agreement; arrangement*); la **'liste d'entente'** de la majorité sortante l'a emporté aux élections (*joint electoral list*)

entériner: les principes d'un règlement global ont été **entérinés** le 20 juillet; une dévaluation vient **entériner** la perte du pouvoir d'achat de la monnaie (*ratify, confirm*)

enterrement (*m*): autre sujet de mécontentement: l'**enterrement** de la réforme agraire (*abandoning*)

enterrer: le nouveau texte **enterre** le projet de réforme fiscale (*abandon; bury*)

entier < -ère > (*adj*): le programme **en son entier** reviendrait à l'État à 400 millions de francs (*as a whole, in totality*)

entorse (*f*): il y voit une **entorse** aux règlements du libéralisme (*infringement*); ce qui avait amené l'Israel à **faire une entorse** à ses habitudes (*make an exception; infringe*)

entourage (*m*): pour son **entourage**, la question ne se pose pas (*circle; sources close to*)

entraîner: les congés de l'usine Peugeot **entraînent** ceux de sept sur dix des entreprises de la région; l'évolution technologique **entraîne** un besoin croissant de personnel qualifié (*cause, bring about*)

entrave (*f*): une action en justice pour **entrave** au droit syndical (*obstruction*)

entraver: la cherté du crédit **entrave** effectivement le commerce (*be a barrier to, prevent*)

entrée (*f*): il s'est déclaré favorable **d'entrée de jeu** (*from the outset, straightaway*)

61

entremise (*f*): Israel et l'OLP amorcent un dialogue **par l'entremise** des États-Unis (*with the mediation/intervention*)

entreprise (*f*): il hésitait entre l'**entreprise** et la finance (*business*); le retour des profits et de l'**esprit d'entreprise** (*enterprise culture; spirit of enterprise*)

entretenir: l'illusion **entretenue** par la classe dominante (*foster, maintain, promote*); [s'] il désirait **s'entretenir** avec eux du rôle du Conseil constitutionnel (*discuss*)

entretien (*m*): leur **entretien** est à la une de tous les quotidiens (*conversation, interview*); l'**entretien** de la voirie relève du maire (*upkeep, maintenance, repair*)

enveloppe (*f*): il a fixé à 15 milliards de francs l'**enveloppe** d'allègements fiscaux; le groupe prévoit une **enveloppe** d'investissements de 450 millions pour 1993 (*expenditure, budget; package*)

envenimer: cela ne peut manquer d'**envenimer** les rapports entre les deux États (*embitter, poison*); [s'] les relations sino-soviétiques **s'enveniment** (*worsen, deteriorate*)

envergure (*f*): l'URSS a des problèmes, et ils sont **d'envergure**! (*considerable, sizeable*); une action **d'envergure** est prévue par la RATP pour le 5 janvier (*large-scale, wide-ranging*)

envisager: il n'est pas **envisagé** de hausse, affirme le P-DG de la Régie (*contemplate, envisage*)

envol (*m*): le 17, le dollar poursuivait son **envol** (*rise*)

envolée (*f*): les gains réalisés, grâce à l'**envolée** des cours; l'**envolée** des prix inquiète le gouvernement (*steep rise*)

envoler [s']: les prix **se sont envolés** à Paris hier (*rise steeply*)

épargnant (*m*): une bonne partie des **petits épargnants** risque de vendre ses actions (*small investor*)

épargne (*f*): l'**épargne** a été largement détaxée; on s'enrichit plus facilement par l'**épargne** que par le travail (*savings*); il a pu accéder à la propriété grâce au **plan d'épargne-logement** (*housing savings scheme*)

épauler: le ministre est venu de Paris **épauler** le candidat dans sa campagne (*support, assist*)

éplucher: les experts **épluchent** les données économiques (*dissect, examine closely*)

épouvantail (*m*): brandissant l'**épouvantail** de la natalité galopante (*bogy; scare*)

épreuve (*f*): un sursis peut être simple ou avec **mise à l'épreuve** (*with conditions attached*); le conflit glissait vers l'**épreuve de force**; une **épreuve de force** entre partisans des deux solutions proposées (*trial of strength*)

équilibre (*m*): Renault prévoit l'**équilibre financier** pour l'an prochain (*a* *balanced budget*)

équilibrer: les PTT sont tenus d'**équilibrer** leurs recettes et leurs dépenses (*balance*); la SNCF s'est fixé pour objectif d'**équilibrer ses comptes** avant deux ans (*be in balance, break even*)

équipement (*m*): préserver un équilibre entre emplois, logements et **équipements collectifs** (*public amenities; facilities*); la décentralisation accélère le transfert aux collectivités locales de certaines **dépenses d'équipement** (*capital expenditure*)

équité (*f*): on juge un impôt sur son **équité** et sur son efficacité (*fairness, equitableness*)

équivoque (*f*): c'est ici que l'**équivoque** peut s'entretenir! (*ambiguity*); Tunisie: lever les **équivoques** entre Paris et le nouveau pouvoir (*misunderstanding; difference*); il a rejeté **sans équivoque** la thèse du porte-parole de la droite (*unambiguously*)

errement (*m*): il faut éviter les **errements** économiques des premières années (*mistake, error*)

escalade (*f*): nouvelle **escalade** dans la course aux armements (*rise, escalation*)

escale (*f*): il a fait une courte **escale** à Brazzaville (*stopover*)

escarmouche (*f*): les premières **escarmouches** sérieuses ont éclaté en fin de journée (*skirmish*)

escompte (*m*): la maison a fait un **escompte** de 6% pour paiement au comptant (*discount*); refusant encore de s'engager sur une baisse du **taux de l'escompte** (*discount rate; bank rate*)

escompté <e> (*adj*): la fin **escomptée** des hostilités entre gouvernement et rebelles; loin d'avoir l'effet **escompté** (*expected, anticipated*)

escompter: les personnes dont il **escomptait** la coopération (*expect, count on*)

escroquer: comment peut-on **escroquer** 14 millions de francs au détriment d'une institution religieuse et rester impuni? (*swindle*)

escroquerie (*f*): une peine de prison pour **escroquerie** aux chèques volés (*swindle*)

espèce (*f*): il est préférable de payer par chèque barré plutôt qu'**en espèces** (*in cash; cash*); un groupe de pression important, **en l'espèce** les agriculteurs (*in this case; namely*)

esquisse (*f*): en présentant les premières **esquisses** du Xᵉ Plan (*sketch, outline, draft*); aucun des grands contentieux n'a reçu ne serait-ce que l'**esquisse** d'une solution (*the beginnings; barest outline*)

esquisser: son premier geste fut d'**esquisser** un rapprochement avec l'URSS (*start, initiate*); dans son article, il a essayé d'**esquisser** le paysage social de l'automne (*outline, sketch out*)

essai (*m*): nouvel **essai** nucléaire français à Mururoa (*test*)

essentiel (*m/adj*): il a vendu l'**essentiel** de ses parts dans la société (*most/ majority of*)

essor (*m*): les ventes de magnétoscopes connaissent un **essor** fulgurant (*expansion, development*)

essoufflement (*m*): il mise sur l'**essoufflement** du mouvement de protestation (*running out of steam; tailing/falling off*)

essouffler [s']: le miracle économique allemand **s'essouffle** (*run out of steam; tail/fall off*)

essuyer: le parti au pouvoir **essuya** de lourds revers lors des élections; le fourgon **a essuyé** une rafale d'arme automatique (*suffer, be the target of*)

estimer [s']: le gouvernement ne **s'estime** pas concerné par les accusations portées contre le ministre (*consider*)

établi <e> (*adj*): il paraît **établi** que ces hommes étaient des espions (*certain, undeniable*)

établir: on a pu **établir** sa participation à l'attentat (*establish with certainty*)

établissement (*m*): il prône l'**établissement** d'une liste d'union pour les élections (*setting up*); l'**établissement** pyrénéen est un des leaders français des appareils ménagers (*firm*); d'**établissement public** régional, la Région devient collectivité territoriale (*public corporation*)

étalement (*m*): l'**étalement** des vacances est loin d'être la règle en France (*spreading, staggering*); ceci impliquerait un **étalement** de certains grands programmes militaires (*lengthening*)

étaler: la nécessité d'**étaler** dans le temps la réalisation des promesses (*space out, extend*); grâce aux révélations de son collègue, la duplicité du ministre est **étalée au grand jour** (*visible, plain to see, brought to light*); [s'] les versements peuvent **s'étaler** sur cinq ans (*be spread*)

étape (*f*): une nouvelle **étape** a été franchie; les **étapes** du processus de décentralisation (*stage*)

état (*m*): le **tout-État** fabrique un peuple d'assistés (*excessive State involvement*); on a publié un **état** assez détaillé des forces armées du pacte de Varsovie (*inventory; statement*); Amnesty International **fait état** de 722 disparitions (*report, put on record*); le roi **fait état** de ses prérogatives constitutionnelles (*cite; put forward*); un texte trop incohérent pour être voté **en l'état** (*as it stands, in its present form*)

état-civil (*m*): le maire reste agent de l'État pour l'**état-civil** (*civil status; department dealing with registration of births, marriages and deaths*)

état-d'âme (*m*): il saura profiter des divisions et des **états-d'âme** de ses ennemis; malgré les **états-d'âme** de plusieurs députés, dont dix se sont abstenus (*anguish, soul-searching*)

état-major (*m*): les **états-major** ont fini par rejeter l'accord avec le patronat; dans les **états-major**, on craint le pire (*administration; headquarters*);

on peut réunir un **état-major** de crise dans les 24 heures (*top-level meeting*)

État-Providence (*m*): les plus défavorisés tiennent à l'**État-Providence** (*Welfare State*)

états-généraux (*m pl*): il propose des **états-généraux** de l'Opposition après les élections de mars (*general assembly*)

étatique (*adj*): le citoyen dispose d'un système **étatique** de retraite; les dépenses **étatiques** n'ont progressé que de 5% (*State; of the State*)

étatisation (*f*): les dirigeants du PC exigent l'**étatisation** de toutes les filiales du groupe (*placing under State control*)

étatiser: le gouvernement a **étatisé** les grandes entreprises (*take under State control*)

étendre [s']: il ne **s'est** pas **étendu** sur ce sujet brûlant (*go into detail; expand upon*); la célèbre firme anglaise **s'étend** aux États-Unis (*expand*)

étiquette (*f*): il se présenta aux élections sous l'**étiquette** du Parti socialiste; les **étiquettes politiques** n'ont pas joué dans cette élection (*political label*)

étoffer: ils pourront **étoffer** le réseau actuel de 170 agences (*increase, expand*)

étouffer: on a **étouffé** l'affaire! personne n'a rien su (*hush up, keep quiet about*)

étrennes (*f pl*): sombres **étrennes** pour des milliers de licenciés en puissance (*New Year's present/gift*)

étroitesse (*f*): pour réaffirmer l'**étroitesse** de la coopération entre les deux pays (*closeness*)

étude (*f*): la France **met à l'étude** un missile de croisière nucléaire (*study, investigate; design*)

étudié <e> (*adj*): la politique des prix chez eux est très **étudiée** (*keen*); ils sont vendus **à des prix très étudiés** (*at rock-bottom prices*)

euphorie (*f*): le mouvement d'**euphorie** a touché les bourses de Londres et de Tokyo (*confidence; euphoria*)

euphorique (*adj*): conséquence de la conjoncture **euphorique** alors; Wall Street **euphorique** (*bullish, buoyant, confident*)

évacuer: ce sujet sera **évacué**, lui aussi; le ministre **a évacué** deux questions globales (*air; deal with*)

évasion (*f*): l'érosion de l'assiette de l'impôt et l'accroissement des possibilités d'**évasion fiscale** (*tax avoidance*)

éventail (*m*): des personnes d'un large **éventail** socio-économique (*range, spread, spectrum*)

éventualité (*f*): sans écarter toutefois l'**éventualité** de licenciements (*possibility*)

éventuel <-elle> (*adj*): on a dressé une liste d'**éventuelles** représailles économiques (*possible, future*)

éventuellement: la région parisienne et **éventuellement** la province sera touchée par la nouvelle réglementation (*possibly*)

évidence (*f*): le vote de censure **met en évidence** les divisions de l'opposition (*emphasize, bring out*)

évincer: il a été **évincé** de la direction (*oust; supplant*)

évoluer: le nouveau P-DG souhaite **faire évoluer** Péchiney; là aussi les choses **évoluent** vite (*develop, change*); il **évoluait** à l'époque dans les milieux d'extrême-droite (*move in, mix with*)

évolutif < -ive > (*adj*): un poste passionnant et **évolutif** (*with promotion prospects*)

évolution (*f*): il s'inquiète de l'**évolution** de la situation (*development*); l'**évolution** des coûts salariaux y est favorable si on la compare à celle de la France (*growth; movement*); le candidat à fort potentiel aura de réelles perspectives d'**évolution** (*progression, promotion*); cet accord vise à favoriser une meilleure **évolution de carrière** pour les ouvriers (*career prospects*)

exacerbé < e > (*adj*): ces pays font preuve d'un nationalisme **exacerbé** (*prickly; excessive*)

exacerber [s']: la situation risque de **s'exacerber** (*get worse, deteriorate*)

exactitude (*f*): le ministère conteste l'**exactitude** de certains de ces chiffres (*accuracy*)

excédent (*m*): les ministres de l'Agriculture ont à résoudre le problème des **excédents**, notamment laitiers (*surplus; excess production*); l'**excédent commercial** du prêt-à-porter français a atteint deux milliards de francs (*trade surplus*); à son départ, il laisse la Sécurité sociale **en excédent** ('*in the black'; in surplus*)

excédentaire (*adj*): alors que la balance des invisibles était **excédentaire** (*in surplus*)

exception (*f*): il est hostile au rétablissement de la **législation d'exception** (*emergency laws/rule*)

exclure: les dirigeants **excluent** que des emplois soient supprimés (*rule out, exclude*)

exclusive (*f*): nous devons rassembler, sans **exclusives**; ils veulent éviter toute **exclusive**, tout esprit de chapelle (*exclusion, rejection*)

exclusivité (*f*): on lui a confié l'**exclusivité** des exportations de diamants (*exclusive rights*)

exécuter: dès qu'ils auront **exécuté** leurs engagements; ils ont trois mois pour **exécuter** la décision du Conseil de la concurrence et des prix (*carry out*)

exécutif (*m/adj*): le Premier ministre et le Président partagent le **[pouvoir] exécutif** (*executive power*)

exécution (*f*): une conférence internationale chargée de l'**exécution** des accords (*carrying out/through*)

exemplaire (*m*): Delhi a commandé mille **exemplaires** pour équiper l'armée de l'air indienne (*unit*); ce livre s'est vendu à plus de 30 000 **exemplaires** (*copy*)

exercer: le Labour perd ainsi un pouvoir qu'il **exerçait** depuis 16 ans (*wield, exercise*)

exercice (*m*): les actionnaires ont approuvé les comptes de l'**exercice [fiscal]** (*financial year; accounting/trading period*); il est le président **en exercice** (*current; incumbent*); la Région est désormais une collectivité territoriale **de plein exercice** (*full; fully fledged*)

exonération (*f*): l'**exonération** des charges sociales est accordée aux entreprises embauchant des jeunes (*exoneration*)

exonérer: la RFA **exonère** de droits de douane les produits importés de la RDA (*exempt*); sont **exonérés d'impôts** les intérêts du livret A de Caisse d'épargne (*tax-free*)

exorbitant <e> (*adj*): le pouvoir **exorbitant** de quelques responsables (*excessive*)

expédient (*m*): le cabinet se voit obligé, à l'approche des élections, d'utiliser tous les **expédients** (*short-term measures*); ils en sont réduits à **vivre d'expédients** (*live on one's wits; resort to short-term means*)

expédier: le gouvernement en fin de mandat se contente d'**expédier les affaires courantes** (*deal with day-to-day business*)

expéditif <-ive> (*adj*): pour venir à bout de la guérilla, il faut des solutions **expéditives** (*quick, expeditious*)

expérimenté <e> (*adj*): un homme politique **expérimenté** qui avait servi dans plusieurs cabinets (*experienced*)

expérimenter: la formule sera **expérimentée** dans plusieurs régions de France (*try out; experiment*)

expert (*m/adj*): le terrain a été évalué par un **expert foncier** (*valuer; surveyor*); un rapport fait par un **expert immobilier** (*surveyor*)

expertise (*f*): il aurait fallu procéder à des **expertises** (*evaluation*); le **rapport d'expertise** est formel (*finding by an expert*)

expiration (*f*): son mandat ne vient à **expiration** qu'au mois d'août prochain (*expiry*)

expirer: son OPA sur la maison d'édition américaine **expire** lundi 12 septembre (*expire, lapse*)

exploitant (*m*): 2 000 **petits exploitants** font le siège du ministère de l'Agriculture (*small farmer*)

exploitation (*f*): une autorisation d'**exploitation** de salles de jeux (*operating, running*); les grandes **exploitations** dominent dans la Beauce (*farm; farming concern*); 40% des **chefs d'exploitation** ont plus de 55 ans (*farm-owner*); une entreprise, c'est d'abord un **compte d'exploitation** bénéficiaire (*balance sheet*); beaucoup d'entreprises ont connu cette année un **déficit d'exploitation** (*operating loss*)

exploiter: il **exploite** un petit fonds de commerce dans le centre ville (*run; operate*)

exposé (*m*): après l'**exposé** du ministre sur ce sujet (*presentation; talk*)

expropriation (*f*): la construction de l'autoroute a entraîné l'**expropriation** de centaines de familles (*expropriation, compulsory eviction*)

exsangue (*adj*): le pays est **exsangue**, ruiné par 12 années de guerre (*bloodless; drained, exhausted*)

extorsion de fonds (*f*): ils accusent le commissaire d'**extorsion de fonds** (*extortion*)

extrader: un ressortissant turc **extradé** des Pays-Bas (*extradite*)

extrait (*m*): un **extrait de compte** est envoyé à la fin du mois (*bank statement*); le bulletin de naissance n'est plus délivré: il est remplacé par l'**extrait d'acte de naissance** (*copy of birth certificate*)

F

fabricant (*m*): les **fabricants** de micro-ordinateurs sont mécontents (*manufacturer*)

fâcheux < -euse > (*adj*): une perte de confiance **fâcheuse**; les crises politiques ont une **fâcheuse** tendance à s'aggraver (*unfortunate*)

facilité (*f*): nous pouvons consentir des **facilités de paiement** (*easy repayment terms*)

faction (*f*): les diverses **factions** qui composent l'opposition au régime en place (*faction, group*); les policiers **en faction** devant la porte de 10 Downing Street (*on duty*)

facture (*f*): gaz: Paris et Alger d'accord sur la **facture**; la **facture** pétrolière est payée en dollars (*bill; cost*); inculpé dans une affaire de **fausses factures** (*fictitious business transaction*)

facturer: les compagnies pétrolières sont **facturées** en fin de mois (*bill, charge*)

facultatif < -ive > (*adj*): l'heure de religion **facultative** dans les écoles serait supprimée (*optional*)

faculté (*f*): les députés ont la **faculté** d'introduire une motion de censure (*right*)

faible (*adj*): on s'inquiète du **faible** niveau de la production (*low*); toutes les études montrent le **faible coût** du transport fluvial (*cheapness, low cost*); on ne fait rien pour les **économiquement faibles** (*lower-income group*)

faiblement: le commerce extérieur a **faiblement** augmenté en volume (*very slightly*)

faiblesse (*f*): la **faiblesse** du Franc représente une occasion à saisir pour les exportateurs français (*weakness*); la **faiblesse** des moyens consacrés à l'Université (*small quantity; poverty*)

faillite (*f*): le fabricant belge est au bord de la **faillite** (*bankruptcy*); le système d'assurances sociales sera **en faillite** avant la fin du siècle (*bankrupt*); contre la Mafia, toutes les solutions ont **fait faillite** (*fail*)

faisabilité (*f*): la Banque mondiale va financer une **étude de faisabilité** (*feasibility study*)

fait (*m*): la mesure **entrait dans les faits**, malgré la contestation des syndicats (*be put into practice, come into effect*); les Américains ont désormais **pris fait et cause** pour les rebelles (*give total support/backing*)

fantôme (*adj*): le ministre de l'Énergie du **cabinet fantôme** (*shadow cabinet*)

farouche (*adj*): le scrutin majoritaire conserve ses **farouches** partisans (*fierce*)

farouchement: il était **farouchement** opposé à l'entrée de son pays dans le Marché commun (*bitterly*)

faste (*adj*): l'année dernière fut une année **faste** pour les Postes et Télécommunications (*remarkable, excellent*)

faucon (*m*): les '**faucons**' sont majoritaires dans le cabinet ('*hawk*', *hard-liner*)

fausser: tout le débat a été **faussé** dès le départ (*distort*)

faute (*f*): les chantiers navals licencient, **faute de** commandes (*for lack of*); **faute de quoi**, ils menacent d'exercer des représailles (*in the absence of which; if not forthcoming*)

fauteuil (*m*): les socialistes ont donné leur accord pour qu'il conserve son **fauteuil** (*local-government seat*); les sénateurs dans leurs **fauteuils** de velours rouge (*senatorial seat*)

fauteur (*m*): les socialistes **fauteurs** d'insécurité (*responsible for*); ils ont arrêté des '**fauteurs de troubles**' (*trouble-maker; agitator*)

faux (*m*): sous le coup d'une inculpation pour **faux et usage de faux** (*forgery and use of forged documents*); il tenait à **s'inscrire en faux** contre ces allégations (*strongly deny*)

fédération (*f*): les syndicats des métaux, qui forment la **fédération** départementale de la métallurgie (*grouping of trade unions representing a single trade*)

féliciter [se]: le gouvernement **s'est félicité** du retour à la paix au Proche-Orient (*be gratified; express satisfaction*)

féodalité (*f*): il faut lutter contre les grandes **féodalités** au moyen de législations anti-trust; il faut restaurer la primauté du Parti sur les

féodalités régionales (*interest group; pressure group*)

férié <e> (*adj*): les **jours fériés**, y compris le dimanche (*public holiday*)

fermage (*m*): dans le **fermage**, un exploitant loue le fonds au propriétaire (*tenant farming*)

ferme (*adj*): ils ont été condamnés à neuf mois de prison **ferme** pour vol (*with no remission*)

fermeté (*f*): encouragé par la **fermeté** de la place new-yorkaise hier (*firmness*)

feuille (*f*): l'assuré doit fournir à la caisse primaire les trois dernières **feuilles de paie** (*pay-slip*)

feutré <e> (*adj*): le débat, jusqu'alors **feutré**, va virer à la polémique (*subdued; polite*)

fiabilité (*f*): c'est la sélection qui fait la **fiabilité** du système scolaire; la publicité met en avant la **fiabilité** du produit (*reliability*)

fiable (*adj*): ces statistiques sont jugées peu **fiables** par les experts occidentaux (*reliable*)

fichage (*m*): la réglementation relative au **fichage** informatique (*putting on file/record*)

ficher: il est **fiché** à la Préfecture, donc connu déjà par la police; ces huit personnes, **fichées** en France au grand banditisme (*on police record/file*)

fidèle (*m/adj*): **fidèle** et ami de toujours du Président (*follower; supporter*)

fidéliser: il faut essayer de **fidéliser** l'acheteur; nous conservons des services peu rentables pour **fidéliser** notre clientèle (*keep the custom of*)

fief (*m*): la troisième circonscription, **fief** traditionnel de la gauche (*stronghold*)

figure (*f*): il **faisait figure** alors de modéré; les Français **font figure** de parents pauvres dans ce domaine (*seem; appear*)

filature (*f*): les **filatures** du Nord ne connaîtront plus leur prospérité d'antan (*cotton mill*); **pris en filature** par la police, il les a menés à la cache (*tail, follow*)

filiale (*f*): le groupe, qui a des **filiales** à Genève et à Bruxelles (*subsidiary company*); **filiale à 100%** de la compagnie suisse (*wholly owned subsidiary*)

filière (*f*): de nouvelles **filières** ont été mises en place dans les lycées (*stream*); la **filière** brésilienne assure le transit des stupéfiants (*'connection'*)

fin (*f*): l'utilisation des pistes militaires **à des fins** civiles (*purposes; ends*); les plus déshérités: chômeurs **en fin de droits** ou familles en difficultés; l'**allocation de fin de droits** est portée à 70,18F (*payment made to unemployed person no longer qualifying for basic benefit*); son discours constitue une **fin de non-recevoir** à l'adresse du Conseil de sécurité (*rejection, refusal; demurral*); il a **opposé une fin de non-recevoir** à tout projet d'augmentation d'impôts (*refuse, reject outright*)

finalité (*f*): il faut développer des formations à **finalité** professionnelle (*purpose, end*)

fisc (*m*): le **fisc** estime le bénéfice qu'il a pu faire sur son chiffre d'affaires (*tax authorities*)

fiscal <e> (*adj*): un conseiller **fiscal** vous aidera à établir votre déclaration de revenus (*tax, fiscal*)

fiscalité (*f*): la **fiscalité** y est plus lourde qu'en France (*taxation*)

fixation (*f*): la **fixation** à 60 ans de l'âge de la retraite; avec la **fixation** de sommets à un rythme désormais régulier (*fixing*)

fixe (*m*): outre les commissions, on touche un **fixe** mensuel (*basic salary*); les relations franco-algériennes sont **au beau fixe** (*on an excellent footing*)

flambée (*f*): la **flambée** terroriste du mois de juin; un été humide et froid n'empêche pas la **flambée** des loyers (*sharp rise; increase*)

flamber: les prix des produits agricoles **flambent** cette année; ce qui faisait **flamber** la livre sterling (*rise sharply*)

flanc (*m*): il ne veut pas **prêter le flanc** aux critiques de ses ennemis (*invite; lay oneself open to*)

flèche (*f*): les cours du pétrole avaient **monté en flèche** (*rise sharply*)

fléchir: le nombre des sans-travail a **fléchi** pour la deuxième année consécutive (*show a slight falling-off; fall*)

fléchissement (*m*): le net **fléchissement** de la criminalité enregistré en 1990 (*fall, decrease*)

flottant <e> (*adj*): ce sont les **électorats flottants** qui décident des élections (*floating vote/voters*)

flottement (*m*): après deux semaines de **flottement,** les choses commencent à se préciser (*uncertainty*)

focaliser: en **focalisant** l'attention sur les plus superficielles apparences; [se] notre action **s'est focalisée** sur l'équilibre régional (*focus, concentrate*)

foi (*f*): selon certaines sources **dignes de foi** (*reliable*)

foire (*f*): un marché mondial aux allures de **foire d'empoigne** (*free-for-all*)

foisonnement (*m*): devant le **foisonnement** de décrets et de circulaires (*proliferation, abundance*)

foncier (*m*): jusqu'en 1993 le **foncier** est pratiquement gelé (*building, construction*); la taxe sur le **foncier bâti** est payée par les propriétaires (*building*); la taxe sur le **foncier non-bâti** est un impôt qui frappe les terres (*land*); (*adj*) une nouvelle politique **foncière** est nécessaire (*land, pertaining to land*); dans le nouveau Congrès, les **propriétaires fonciers** dominent (*landowners*)

fonction (*f*): il quittera ses **fonctions** fin août (*position, post*); les dirigeants ont été écartés 18 mois après leur **entrée en fonctions** (*taking-up a post*);

il serait prêt à **quitter ses fonctions** (*resign*); si cela continue, plus personne n'osera postuler une **haute fonction** (*high office*); un salaire mensuel généreux et une **voiture de fonction** (*company car*); les situations varient **en fonction** du type d'habitat et du niveau de revenu (*according to*)

fonction publique (*f*): faire carrière dans la **fonction publique** (*civil service; public service*)

fonctionnaire (*m*): seuls les enseignants dans le secteur public sont des **fonctionnaires** (*civil servant, functionary*)

fonctionnement (*m*): absence de contrôle financier, développement exagéré des **frais de fonctionnement** (*operating costs*)

fond (*m*): cela ne touche pas aux questions **de fond** que se posent les Français; des divergences **de fond** divisent les deux partis (*fundamental*)

fondation (*f*): lors de la **fondation** de l'État d'Israel en 1948 (*founding, setting-up*)

fondé <e> (*adj*): on serait **fondé** à considérer avec optimisme l'avenir de l'industrie; les bruits qui courent, sont-ils **fondés**? (*justified; well-founded*)

fondé de pouvoirs (*m*): il a envoyé un **fondé de pouvoirs** pour traiter avec la délégation soviétique (*authorized representative with delegated powers*)

fondement (*m*): les accusations sont absolument **sans fondement** (*groundless, without basis*)

fonds (*m*): on a prétendu que des **fonds** publics serviront à financer la campagne électorale (*money; funds*); les besoins en **fonds propres** des entreprises (*capital, funding*); ils ont gagné 1,2 milliards pour une **mise de fonds** de 600 millions de francs (*outlay; investment*); il va conserver le **fonds de commerce**, mais il cède les locaux; en achetant le **fonds de commerce**, elle estime avoir acheté aussi le stock (*business*); un dealer en **fonds d'État** britanniques (*gilt-edged stock*); la cotisation de chaque employé au **fonds de garantie** aurait dû être augmentée (*reserve fund; guarantee fund*)

forfait (*m*): le **forfait** comprend le prix de l'achat et d'éventuelles réparations (*all-in price*); on a créé le **forfait** hospitalier à la charge du malade (*fixed price/charge*)

forfaitaire (*adj*): ou une somme **forfaitaire** fixée par avance, ou une prime variable (*fixed, 'all-in'*); ceux-ci percevront des **indemnités forfaitaires** (*lump-sum compensation*)

forfaiture (*f*): accusé de **forfaiture** dans l'affaire des ventes d'armes (*maladministration; abuse of authority*)

formation (*f*): Rhône-Poulenc consacre 5% de sa masse salariale à la **formation** (*training*); des cours de **formation permanente** proposés au personnel enseignant (*in-service training*); les autres **formations** de l'opposition préféraient s'abstenir (*party; group*)

72

former: on embauche d'abord, on **forme** après (*train*)

formulaire (*m*): le **formulaire** d'inscription dûment rempli doit impérativement arriver avant le 15 septembre (*form*)

fortune (*f*): ici l'**impôt sur les grandes fortunes** frappe un nombre croissant de gens (*wealth tax*)

foudroyant <e> (*adj*): son ascension a été **foudroyante** (*extremely rapid*)

fouille (*f*): la police pratique des **fouilles** impromptues sur des individus qu'elle suspecte (*search*)

fourchette (*f*): le taux de syndicalisation se situe dans une **fourchette** comprise entre 12 et 16% (*range, margin*); les articles proposés sont dans une **fourchette de prix** assez restreinte (*price range*); la **fourchette des rémunérations** a été jusqu'ici très étroite (*wage differential*)

fournisseur (*m*): un contrat conclu avec un **fournisseur** étranger; principal pays **fournisseur**: la Chine (*supplier*)

fourniture (*f*): la France a signé un contrat pour la **fourniture** d'une usine de retraitement nucléaire (*supply*)

foyer (*m*): les principaux **foyers** traditionnels de l'industrie manufacturière (*centre, home*)

fracassant <e> (*adj*): les déclarations **fracassantes** d'un porte-parole (*sensational; excessive*)

fraîchement: les États-Unis ont accueilli très **fraîchement** cette initiative (*coolly*)

frais (*m*): il est d'ores et déjà **rentré dans ses frais** (*get a return on an investment*); c'est le Préfet qui risque de **faire les frais** de la régionalisation (*bear the brunt; pay the price*); les marges ont baissé et les **frais généraux** sont très lourds (*overheads*); (*adj*) il faut limiter les sorties d'**argent frais** (*new money; cash funds*); **frais émoulu** de l'École supérieure d'administration (*newly graduated, fresh from*)

franc <-che> (*adj*): le délai d'un jour **franc** avant l'envoi de la lettre de licenciement (*whole, complete*); quelques **francs-tireurs** centristes tenaient à montrer leur indépendance (*independent; maverick*)

franchise (*f*): les correspondances avec les services publics bénéficient souvent de la **franchise postale** (*exemption from postal charges*); une telle opération permet de réaliser un rachat **en franchise d'impôt** (*tax-free*)

franco-français <e> (*adj*): le problème est moins une affaire Est-Ouest qu'une affaire '**franco-française**' (*domestic, internal*)

frapper: l'ensemble de la fiscalité qui **frappe** le patrimoine des Français (*tax; penalize*)

fraude (*f*): la **fraude fiscale** est aussi répandue que jamais (*tax evasion*)

freiner: le souci aussi de **freiner** la hausse des prix (*slow, put a brake on*)

fréquentation (*f*): la chute de la **fréquentation** du reste du réseau de chemins de fer (*custom, use of; popularity*)

friche (*f*): la **mise en friche** d'une partie des terres agricoles en France (*leaving fallow*)

froid (*m/adj*): sa visite met fin à une période de **froid** diplomatique entre la France et la Syrie (*coolness*)

fronde (*f*): nouvelle **fronde** du Parlement européen: le projet de budget est rejeté (*revolt; rebellion*)

fronder: une partie des députés de la majorité **frondent** (*revolt; rebel*)

frondeur < -euse > (*adj*): ces initiatives **frondeuses** sont toutefois réprouvées par les inconditionnels du parti (*recalcitrant; anti-authority*)

front (*m*): il se garde bien de l'attaquer **de front**; sans aborder le problème **de front** (*head on, directly*)

frontalier < -ère > (*adj*): un incident **frontalier** fait dix morts (*frontier*)

fructifier: 200F qui auront beaucoup **fructifié** depuis; pour faire **fructifier** vos économies (*yield a profit*)

fuite (*f*): 11 000 **fuites de cerveaux** par an vers les États-Unis (*'brain-drain'*); aussi impopulaire qu'elle soit dans sa **fuite en avant**; une telle **fuite en avant** ouvre la porte à toutes les aventures militaires (*ill-considered initiative*)

fuseau horaire (*m*): Londres, dont le **fuseau horaire** permet de traiter dans la journée avec New York et Tokyo (*time zone*)

fusion (*f*): cette **fusion** entraînera des suppressions d'emplois (*amalgamation, merger*); cette année ont été conclues 163 **opérations de fusion** ou de prises de participation (*merger, amalgamation*)

fusionner: les deux entreprises ont enfin **fusionné**, au terme de négociations interminables; ils ont **fusionné** leur activités de telecom dans une société conjointe (*amalgamate; merge*)

fustiger: le porte-parole de l'opposition a **fustigé** les dépenses excessives en matière de défense (*castigate*)

G

gabegie (*f*): il a mis de l'ordre dans une société où régnait une **gabegie** financière (*muddle, disorganization*)

gage (*m*): une monnaie forte, **gage** d'une France forte; l'autocritique, **gage** d'un lendemain meilleur (*guarantee*)

gageure (*f*): c'est une véritable **gageure** que de vouloir en six mois redresser la situation (*rash promise; wager*)

gain (*m*): négocier avec les syndicats des **gains** de productivité (*gain, increase*); le **gain** horaire moyen des ouvriers s'établissait alors à 6 184F par mois (*earnings; pay*); l'imposition des **gains en capital** est un impôt sur le revenu et non pas sur le patrimoine (*capital gain*); il a fini par **obtenir gain de cause** dans son action contre son frère (*win a lawsuit*)

gamme (*f*): c'est le produit le plus populaire de la **gamme** (*range*); une firme spécialisée dans les matériels **haut de gamme** (*top of the range*)

garantie de ressources (*f*): pour un chômeur de plus de 60 ans, on applique la **garantie de ressources** (*top-up social security benefit for the out-of-work aged between 60 and 65*)

garde (*f*): il veut les **mettre en garde** contre tout optimisme déplacé (*warn*); à ce propos, il a lancé une **mise en garde** aux syndicats enseignants (*warning*); 148 personnes ont été interpellées, dont 97 sont toujours **placées en garde à vue** (*in police custody*); les 8 000 **gardes champêtres** exercent dans les communes de moins de 2 000 habitants (*country policeman*); le **garde des Sceaux** a fait le bilan de ses deux années à la tête du ministère de la Justice (*Minister of Justice; Keeper of the Seals*)

gel (*m*): un long **gel** des relations avec Paris s'en est suivi (*freezing*); le **gel des salaires** trop prolongé a conduit directement à la chute du gouvernement (*wage freeze*); la Grande-Bretagne annonce un plan de **gel des terres** (*taking land out of cultivation*)

geler: tous les cabinets ont dû **geler** les salaires et les revenus (*freeze*); la France **gèle** ses relations avec Pékin (*suspend*); l'État veut **geler les terres** (*take land out of cultivation*)

gendarmerie (*f*): la caserne de la **gendarmerie** se trouve au chef-lieu du canton (*gendarmerie, police force*)

généraliser [se]: le mouvement de mécontentement des surveillants **se généralise** (*spread; widen*)

généraliste (*m*/*adj*): les [médecins] **généralistes** sont les parents pauvres de la profession (*doctor in general practice*); en France, on a une chaîne de télévision **généraliste** de trop (*general; of general interest*)

géomètre (*m*): l'**expert-géomètre** cumule souvent le rôle d'agent immobilier (*surveyor*)

gérance (*f*): le comité exécutif, ou conseil de **gérance** (*management*)

gérant (*m*): exploitants privés ou **gérants** de fermes d'État (*manager*); la Sarl est administrée par un **gérant** (*administrator*)

gérer: 93% des citoyens estiment que leur ville est bien **gérée** (*govern*); par deux fois, il a **géré** un portefeuille ministériel (*hold; administer, run*)

gestion (*f*): on en a confié la **gestion** à un entrepreneur du privé (*running; management*); la **gestion des stocks** est cruciale dans le commerce (*stock control; inventory management*); les erreurs de la **gestion** socialiste (*government*)

gestionnaire (*m/adj*): un maire, **gestionnaire** des intérêts locaux, est aussi un homme politique (*administrator; manager*)

girondin <e> (*m/adj*): les thèses **girondines** commencent à s'imposer (*favourable to federalism/devolution*)

glissade (*f*): la **glissade** du dollar devient inquiétante (*slide*)

glissement (*m*): à la fin mai, le **glissement** des prix était déjà de 0,4% (*fall, slide*)

globalement: le bilan est **globalement** positif, affirme le ministre (*on the whole*)

gonflement (*m*): le **gonflement** de la demande suivra obligatoirement (*increase, boost*)

goulot (*m*): on a perdu quelques ventes en raison de **goulots d'étranglement** dans la production (*bottle-neck*)

gouvernant (*m*): l'incapacité des **gouvernants** à réduire des inégalités criantes (*government*)

grâce (*f*): il avait bénéficié d'une **grâce** présidentielle (*pardon; reprieve*)

gracier: condamnée à mort, elle a été **graciée** (*pardon*)

gracieusement: notre bulletin de liaison vous sera envoyé **gracieusement** (*free, without cost*)

grade (*m*): sans l'obtention d'un **grade** universitaire, il y a peu de chances de trouver un poste bien rémunéré (*degree; qualification*)

gradué <e> (*adj*): un processus **gradué** et négocié (*progressive, step-by-step*)

grand <e> (*adj*): la firme va restructurer sa division de produits électroniques **grand public** (*mass-market*); malaise au sein de **la 'grande muette'** (*French army*); les **grandes surfaces** alimentaires dominent le marché (*large store, hypermarket*)

graphique (*m*): un **graphique** permet de visualiser facilement ce genre de données (*graph*)

gratuité (*f*): la **gratuité** pour les chômeurs et les personnes âgées (*exemption from charge*); il n'est pas question de toucher à la **gratuité des soins médicaux** (*free medical care*)

gratuitement: il sera envoyé **gratuitement** à tout abonné (*without charge*)

gré (*m*): **bon gré mal gré**, l'Égypte doit faire appel aux États du Golfe; il faut amener l'employeur, **de gré ou de force**, à payer des salaires plus élevés (*willingly or otherwise*); il a montré qu'il **savait gré** au Premier ministre de l'avoir choisi (*be grateful*)

greffe (*m*): extrait des minutes du **greffe** de la Cour d'appel de Paris (*Office of Clerk to the Court*)

greffier (*m*): les notes d'audience prises par le **greffier** (*Clerk to the Court*)

grève (*f*): les **mouvements de grève** se sont limités aux houillères du

Nottinghamshire (*strike*); les syndicats ont **appelé à la grève** (*call for a strike*); le centre de tri est paralysé par une **grève illimitée** depuis lundi (*indefinite strike*); des **grèves perlées** paralysent la production (*go-slow*); la production est sérieusement perturbée par des **grèves tournantes** (*strike by rota*); la **grève du zèle** a fini par contraindre le patron à fermer l'usine (*work-to-rule*); les ouvriers ont riposté par des **grèves sur le tas** qui ont arrêté la production (*sit-down strike*); au moyen de **grèves sauvages**, ils espèrent faire pression sur l'employeur (*wild-cat strike*)

grever: les très fortes taxes qui **grèvent** les primes d'assurances en France (*burden*)

grille (*f*): l'émission a été supprimée de la **grille** des programmes (*schedule*); les salariés de base s'alignent sur la **grille de salaires** de la Banque de France (*salary structure*)

gripper [se]: l'économie **se grippe**, la productivité est en baisse; le fonctionnement des institutions est **grippé** (*seize up, jam*)

grogne (*f*): nouvelle **grogne** au Pays basque: la baisse des réservations dans l'hôtellerie s'accentue (*dissatisfaction, discontent*); ce projet risque de provoquer quelques **grognes** (*complaint*)

gros (*m*): le **gros** des manifestants s'est regroupé un peu plus loin (*most of, the majority*); **les gros** semblent à l'abri de la crise (*the wealthy, big business*); (*adj*) un avenir **gros** de périls (*full of*); les **gros contribuables** bénéficieront autant que les cadres moyens de cet allègement fiscal (*high taxpayer*)

grossir: ils ne veulent pas **grossir** les deux millions de chômeurs (*increase, swell*)

groupe (*m*): dans les diverses commissions et **groupes de travail** du mouvement (*working party*)

groupuscule (*m*): le gouvernement a interdit toutes activités politiques à ce **groupuscule** d'extrême droite (*small group; faction*)

guéguerre (*f*) (*fam.*): une **guéguerre** dérisoire face aux vrais problèmes du pays (*minor skirmish; warfare*)

guérilla (*f*): les massacres de civils perpétrés par la **guérilla** (*guerrilla force*)

guichet (*m*): au Crédit Lyonnais, 150 **guichets** vont fermer (*counter*)

guigner: deux groupes financiers puissants **guignent** la célèbre chaîne d'hôtels (*have designs upon; covet*)

H

h: à **l'heure H** du jour J (*zero hour*)

habiliter: les lois **habilitent** le gouvernement à recourir aux ordonnances

(*empower, entitle*)

habitat (*m*): la plupart d'entre eux vivent en **habitat** dispersé (*habitat*)

habitation (*f*): la **taxe d'habitation** est payée par les occupants d'un logement (*tax on house occupancy*)

hausse (*f*): ceci va entraîner des **hausses** de tarif de 10 à 15% (*increase, upturn, rise*); la tendance est **à la hausse** sur les marchés des changes (*rising; 'bullish'*)

haussier <-ère> (*adj*): le marché devrait pour le moment rester **haussier**; aucun **mouvement haussier** n'est prévisible à la bourse de Paris (*rising/ bullish trend*)

hauteur (*f*): les sidérurgistes vont procéder à des réductions de capacités **à hauteur de** 20 millions de tonnes (*up to; of the order of*); les résultats ne sont pas **à la hauteur** des espoirs (*on a level/par with*)

hebdomadaire (*m*): Unité, **hebdomadaire** du Parti socialiste (*weekly newspaper*); (*adj*) on a fixé la durée **hebdomadaire** de travail à 36 heures (*weekly; per week*)

hégémonie (*f*): la double **hégémonie** de la France et de la Grande-Bretagne au Proche-Orient (*hegemony, domination*)

hémicycle (*m*): dans l'**hémicycle** du Palais-Bourbon, les parlementaires sont répartis en groupes (*benches of the French National Assembly*)

hémorragie (*f*): taxe qui lui fait craindre une **hémorragie** des capitaux hors d'Europe (*flood; outflow*)

heure (*f*): les **heures supplémentaires** sont rémunérées au même taux (*overtime; hour of overtime*)

heurt (*m*): les **heurts** ont éclaté pendant un meeting électoral (*clash, conflict*); la transition s'est faite **sans heurts** (*smoothly*)

heurter [se]: la foule **se heurte** à l'armée; la volonté de paix chez les uns **se heurte** contre le désir chez les autres de poursuivre la confrontation (*clash; conflict*)

hexagonal <e> (*adj*): enfin sorti d'un gaullisme trop **hexagonal**; ils restent trop **hexagonaux** par rapport à leurs concurrents (*inward-looking; Gallocentric*)

hexagone (*m*): le terme '**hexagone**' reflète assez bien la configuration générale du pays (*hexagon; France*)

histoire (*f*): après trois ans de gestion **sans histoire** (*uneventful*)

homicide (*m*): condamné à deux ans de prison pour **homicide involontaire** (*manslaughter*); inculpé d'**homicide volontaire** et écroué à la maison d'arrêt de Limoges (*murder*)

homme (*m*): soupçonné d'être son principal **homme de main** en Europe (*collaborator, representative*)

homologue (*m*): le Premier ministre, comme son **homologue** anglais (*opposite *number; counterpart*)

homologuer: les nouveaux tarifs ont été **homologués** et seront appliqués dès janvier (*ratify, approve*)

hôte (*m*): l'**hôte** actuel de la Maison-Blanche (*incumbent, occupant*)

hôtel (*m*): ses chances de reconquérir l'**hôtel de ville** sont minces (*town hall; mayoral office*)

houille (*f*): le charbon britannique revient plus cher que la **houille** importée (*coal*)

houiller <-ère> (*adj*): compressions de personnel dans l'industrie **houillère** (*coal-mining*)

houillère (*f*): la tension croît dans les **houillères** (*coal-mine*)

houleux <-euse> (*adj*): débat **houleux** à l'Assemblée (*noisy, rowdy*)

huis-clos (*m*): l'audience a eu lieu à **huis-clos** (*in camera, behind closed doors*)

huissier (*m*): un **huissier** posté à l'entrée de l'hémicycle (*usher*); un **huissier de justice** inculpé d'abus de confiance; l'**huissier** est venu saisir les biens et expulser les locataires (*bailiff*)

hussarde (*f*): voté à **la hussarde**, le nouveau texte veut limiter les abus (*vigorously; energetically; unceremoniously*)

hypertrophié <e> (*adj*): la Chine souffre d'une administration **hypertrophiée** (*excessively large*)

hypothécaire (*adj*): mesures en faveur des **sociétés de crédit immobilier hypothécaire** (*building society offering mortgages*); l'octroi d'un **prêt hypothécaire** (*mortgage loan*)

hypothèque (*f*): le contrat d'**hypothèque** est obligatoirement un acte notarié (*mortgage*); l'**hypothèque** n'est pas encore levée (*doubt*); un mouvement social-démocrate débarrassé de l'**hypothèque** socialiste (*danger, threat*)

hypothéquer: il avait **hypothéqué** les deux fermes et la maison (*mortgage*); ceci avait un temps **hypothéqué** la stratégie d'Israël (*endanger; put at risk*)

hypothèse (*f*): l'**hypothèse** de sa candidature aux élections semble assez fantaisiste (*hypothesis*); dans l'**hypothèse contraire**, il n'est pas exclu qu'il se représente (*if the contrary is true*)

hypothétique (*adj*): on attend un **hypothétique** redressement (*theoretical, hypothetical*)

I

idée (*f*): retenons-en quelques **idées-forces** (*key idea*); la sécurité est une **idée fixe** de la pensée de la droite (*obsession*)

ignoble (*adj*): tentative de chantage **ignoble** (*vile, base*)

ignorer: l'industrie de l'agro-alimentaire **ignore** la crise actuelle (*be untouched by; be unaffected by*)

illusion (*f*): cette reprise ne doit pas **faire illusion** (*delude, fool*)

image (*f*): le tourisme français se doit d'améliorer son **image de marque** (*corporate identity*); à l'approche des élections, les hommes politiques soignent leur **image de marque** (*public image*)

immatriculation (*f*): les **immatriculations** devraient peu diminuer l'an prochain (*registration, especially of new cars*)

immatriculer: une Peugeot 405 verte, **immatriculée** dans le Vaucluse; la nouvelle société sera **immatriculée** au RCS de Saint-Brieuc (*register*)

immeuble (*m*): la construction de huit **immeubles de bureaux** en banlieue parisienne (*office-block*)

immiscer [s']: la France ne tolérera pas qu'un pays étranger **s'immisce** dans ses affaires (*intervene; interfere*)

immobilier (*m/adj*): en plein boom **immobilier** des années 70 (*real estate, property*); des **cabinets immobilier** anglais s'installent dans le Pas-de-Calais (*estate agency*)

immobiliser: cela éviterait d'**immobiliser** un argent rare (*tie up*)

immobilisme (*m*): les orateurs du RPR fustigent l'**immobilisme** de la politique européenne du gouvernement (*lack of initiative; opposition to change*)

impartir: dans l'enveloppe de 2% d'augmentations salariales **impartie** par le gouvernement (*allow; grant*)

impasse (*f*): les problèmes économiques compliquent l'**impasse** politique (*impasse*); les experts prévoient une **impasse** de 40 milliards de Marks pour la fin de l'année (*deficit*); un organisme caritatif qui travaille sur certains pays et **fait l'impasse** sur d'autres (*ignore, pass over*)

impayé <e> (*adj*): pour récupérer les pensions **impayées** par le divorcé (*unpaid*)

impératif (*m/adj*): l'**impératif** d'économies budgétaires est reconnu par tous les partis (*urgency; necessity*)

implantation (*f*): la société poursuit sa stratégie d'**implantations** en Asie (*setting up of operation/factory*)

implanter: les entreprises françaises **implantent** des filiales dans les pays de la CEE (*set up*); [s'] pour pouvoir **s'implanter** durablement à l'étranger (*set up business*); beaucoup d'immigrants polonais **s'implantèrent** dans le Nord (*settle*)

importance (*f*): l'**importance** des effectifs envoyés indique la gravité de la situation (*size, number*); deux entreprises publiques **de moyenne importance** (*middle-sized*)

important <e> (*adj*): la ville a subi des dégâts **importants**; la récolte de blé a été moins **importante** que prévue (*large, considerable; important*)

imposable (*adj*): à condition que le revenu **imposable** ne dépasse pas 20 000F (*taxable; before tax*)

imposer: dans tous les pays on **impose** le patrimoine sous une forme ou sous une autre (*tax*); [s'] les produits français **s'imposent** sur les marchés étrangers (*gain ground/acceptance*); les efforts d'économies **s'imposent** autant aujourd'hui qu'hier (*be necessary*)

imposition (*f*): les plus-values réalisées ne font l'objet d'aucune **imposition** (*taxation*); comment rédiger la **feuille d'imposition**, cadre par cadre (*income-tax return*)

impôt (*m*): tous sont égaux devant l'**impôt** (*tax*); l'**impôt sur les grandes fortunes** est une constante de la pensée de la gauche (*wealth tax*); l'**impôt sur les sociétés** doit descendre à 40% (*corporation tax*); on va créer un **impôt local** prélevé sur chaque citoyen et égal pour tous (*rates; local tax*)

imprévoyance (*f*): il dénonça l'incohérence et l'**imprévoyance** des politiques du gouvernement (*carelessness; lack of foresight*)

imprévu (*m/adj*): **sauf imprévu**, il assistera à la réunion (*barring unforeseen circumstances*)

imprimé (*m*): il faut remplir un nombre incroyable d'**imprimés** (*printed form*); les **imprimés** sont expédiés à un tarif réduit (*printed paper*)

impuissance (*f*): l'**impuissance** des gouvernements à réduire le chômage (*powerlessness, inability*)

impulsion (*f*): il faut donner une **impulsion** nouvelle à la décentralisation (*impetus*)

impunité (*f*): les auteurs de l'attentat ont **obtenu l'impunité** (*go free/ unpunished*)

inactivité (*f*): plus de 30% étaient retournés à l'**inactivité** ou au chômage (*unemployment*)

inadaptation (*f*): autre problème: l'**inadaptation** des institutions (*inadequacy; unsuitability*)

inadapté <e> (*adj*): son rapport est imprécis, **inadapté** et surtout maladroit (*irrelevant*)

inadéquation (*f*): il y a une telle **inadéquation** entre l'offre et la demande (*gulf; gap*)

inamical <e> (*adj*): une **OPA tout à fait inamicale** lancée par X sur la société Y; une **tentative de prise de contrôle inamicale** du groupe textile (*unwelcome/hostile bid for overall control*)

inamovible (*adj*): il faudrait que ces magistrats soient **inamovibles** (*holding appointment for life*)

incapacité (*f*): son **incapacité** apparente à enrayer cette évolution (*inability*); pour répondre à d'éventuelles **incapacités de remboursement** d'un prêt immobilier (*inability to repay*)

incarcérer: le sous-brigadier a été inculpé de coups et blessures et **incarcéré** à la maison d'arrêt de Sarreguemines (*imprison, lock up*)

incidence (*f*): cela peut avoir de lourdes **incidences** sur la rentabilité de l'opération (*effect, repercussion*)

incitatif <-ive> (*adj*): le gouvernement a pris des mesures **incitatives** en faveur de l'épargne (*encouraging; stimulating*)

incitation (*f*): **incitation** à la haine et à la violence (*incitement*); ces **incitations fiscales** comprennent des abattements de 100% pour dépenses d'équipement (*tax incentive*)

incivisme (*m*): le refus de vote est un acte d'**incivisme**, dit le ministre; la vague d'**incivisme** abstentionniste de 1988 est retombée en 1989 (*lawlessness; lack of public-spiritedness*)

incliner: ces résultats n'**inclinent** pas à l'optimisme (*induce; lead to*)

incohérence (*f*): un risque croissant d'**incohérence** dans le domaine de la défense; les **incohérences** de la gestion socialiste de la ville (*inconsistency; illogicality*)

incomber: ces responsabilités **incombent** plutôt au Premier ministre et au gouvernement (*devolve, fall to*)

incompressible (*adj*): le parquet a demandé une **peine incompressible** de 30 ans (*minimum sentence*)

incontournable (*adj*): la guérilla des Khmers rouges en fait un élément **incontournable** de tout règlement (*inescapable, inevitable; undeniable*)

inconvénient (*m*): ces réformes cumulent trois sortes d'**inconvénient** (*drawback*)

incorporation (*f*): les étudiants peuvent repousser leur **incorporation** à 24 ans (*military draft, call-up*)

incorporer: il fut **incorporé** le 5 août au régiment d'infanterie de Sarrebourg (*draft, call up*)

inculpation (*f*): la détention, sans **inculpation** ni jugement, de 200 prisonniers politiques (*formal charge*); trois **chefs d'inculpation** furent retenus contre lui (*charge*)

inculpé (*m*): il est le seul **inculpé** toujours détenu dans cette affaire (*person charged with offence; prisoner*)

inculper: mort d'un manifestant: un deuxième policier **inculpé** (*charge, bring formal charge against*)

indécis <e> (*adj*): beaucoup d'**indécis**, à dix jours du vote historique (*undecided voter, 'don't know'*)

indéfectible (*adj*): il jure une **indéfectible** fidélité gaulliste (*indestructible,* *undying*)

indélicat <e> (*adj*): des fonds détournés par des intermédiaires **indélicats** (*dishonest*)

indélicatesse (*f*): accusé d'**indélicatesse**, il fut démis de ses fonctions (*dishonesty*)

indemne (*adj*): elles ne sortent pas **indemnes** des élections du 4 novembre (*unscathed*)

indemnisation (*f*): le gouvernement instaura l'**indemnisation** à 90% pour les chômeurs (*compensation, indemnity*)

indemniser: le nombre de chômeurs **indemnisés** a légèrement baissé (*indemnify; compensate*)

indemnité (*f*): une hausse des **indemnités** de chauffage et de logement (*allowance; benefit*); il a été licencié sans **indemnité** (*compensation*); il a dépensé son **indemnité de départ** en faisant le tour du monde (*severance pay*)

indépendant (*m/adj*): le grand parti des **indépendants** et des paysans (*self-employed person*)

indice (*m*): la police ne dispose d'aucun **indice** sérieux (*clue; piece of evidence*); l'**indice des prix** permet de constater l'évolution des prix pendant une période donnée (*price index*)

indigent <e> (*adj*): même les **indigents** seront tenus de s'acquitter du nouvel impôt (*poor; impoverished*)

industrialiser: cette société a été créée pour **industrialiser** les hélicoptères au Brésil (*manufacture; produce*)

inemploi (*m*): un statut qui garantit un revenu minimum en cas d'**inemploi** (*unemployment*)

inexistence (*f*): des problèmes réels, comme l'**inexistence** d'une politique de la jeunesse (*lack; absence*)

inféoder [s']: ils accusent le PCF d'être **inféodé** à Moscou (*give allegiance to*)

infléchir: les constructeurs ont promis d'**infléchir** leur publicité dans le sens de la sécurité routière (*slant, direct; modify*); un comportement que les politiques démographiques ont peu de chances d'**infléchir** (*influence, affect*)

infléchissement (*m*): il a refusé l'**infléchissement** de la politique extérieure demandé par certains (*shift, reorientation, new direction*)

inflexion (*f*): toute **inflexion** de la politique de rigueur aurait une incidence sensible sur la santé économique du pays (*change; modification*)

information (*f*): cette **information** n'a pas encore été confirmée par la police (*report; news*); après la fin de l'enquête de la police, le parquet **ouvrit une information** (*open a judicial enquiry*)

infraction (*f*): condamné pour **infraction** à la législation sur les stupéfiants;

toute **infraction** aux dispositions du présent article sera punie d'une amende de 50 000F (*infringement, breach*)

infrastructure (*f*): un fichier central a informatisé toutes les **infrastructures** routières et aériennes (*infrastructure*); le groupe brésilien renforce ainsi son **infrastructure** européenne (*base; organization*)

ingérence (*f*): ils les considèrent comme une **ingérence** dans les affaires intérieures de l'URSS (*interference*)

initié (*m*): lors du rachat de la firme américaine, des **initiés** ont gagné des millions de dollars (*insider*); la COB enquête pour voir s'il y a eu **délit d'initié** (*insider dealing*)

innocenter: accusé de vol, mais **innocenté** par la Cour d'appel de Paris (*clear, pronounce innocent*)

innovant <e> (*adj*): une entreprise dynamique, performante, **innovante** (*innovative*)

inopérant <e> (*adj*): ce système est jugé **inopérant** par tous (*ineffective*)

inopiné <e> (*adj*): des contrôles sont faits, à grande échelle et de façon **inopinée** (*random; on-the-spot*); à moins d'un retournement de situation **inopiné** (*unexpected, surprise*)

inopinément: il a dû démissionner **inopinément** la semaine dernière (*unexpectedly*)

inquiéter [s']: il **s'est inquiété** des conséquences (*express disquiet about*)

inquiétude (*f*): l'OCDE manifeste sur ce point de réelles **inquiétudes** (*anxiety, concern*)

insatisfaction (*f*): leur **insatisfaction** vis à vis du président sortant (*dissatisfaction*)

inscription (*f*): le maire refusa l'**inscription** de sept enfants marocains (*registration*)

inscrire: 14% des Français déclarent être **inscrits** dans une bibliothèque (*take out membership*); [s'] les relations soviéto-indiennes **s'inscrivent** dans un cadre géostratégique assez clair (*be a part/element of*)

insécurité (*f*): les risques de faillite ou d'**insécurité d'emploi** (*lack of job security*); la lutte contre l'**insécurité** a permis de réduire criminalité et délinquance (*lawlessness; breakdown of law and order*)

insérer [s']: des milliers de jeunes ne sont pas parvenus à **s'insérer** socialement ou professionnellement (*find a place; integrate*)

insertion (*f*): après un stage d'**insertion** à la vie professionnelle; le ministre va mettre l'accent sur une meilleure **insertion** sociale et professionnelle des jeunes (*insertion; integration*)

inspection (*f*): s'adresser à l'**inspection académique** du département (*schools inspectorate*)

instance (*f*): une réunion des plus hautes **instances** irakiennes (*authority,* *power*); des reproches sont adressés par des militants à leurs **instances dirigeantes** (*governing body, authority*); les 471 **tribunaux d'instance** qui, en 1958, ont remplacé les 2 900 justices de paix (*magistrate's court*); le **tribunal de grande instance** siège au chef-lieu du département (≃ High Court); des dossiers **en instance** s'empilent dans les bureaux (*awaiting decision, pending*)

instauration (*f*): malgré l'**instauration** de l'état d'urgence (*instituting, setting up*); juste avant l'**instauration** de ces quotas (*fixing; setting*)

instaurer: il a l'intention d'**instaurer** en Tunisie une démocratie réelle (*install, set up*); [s'] dans le calme précaire qui **s'était instauré** depuis quelques mois (*come about*)

instruction (*f*): une **instruction** a été ouverte contre X; l'**instruction** du dossier a été confiée au juge Dupont (*examination; judicial investigation; preliminary enquiry*)

instruire: un juge d'instruction de Rennes a **instruit le dossier** (*conduct an investigation*); il en profite pour **instruire le procès** de la 'cohabitation' (*criticize; condemn*)

insuccès (*m*): en dépit de l'**insuccès** de sa démonstration (*failure; poor performance*)

insurger [s']: l'association **s'est insurgée** contre cette attitude (*deplore; condemn*)

intégral <e> (*adj*): le *Pravda* a publié le texte **intégral** de son discours (*whole, complete*)

intégralité (*f*): Téhéran exporte l'**intégralité** de son brut via le Golfe (*totality*)

intégrant <e> (*adj*): notre armement nucléaire est une **partie intégrante** de la sécurité européenne (*integral part*)

intégration (*f*): l'**intégration** des primes dans le salaire fit l'unanimité (*inclusion*)

intégrer: il compte **intégrer** la fonction publique (*join, enter*); le Premier ministre voulait l'**intégrer** dans son cabinet (*include, admit*); [s'] les nouveaux **s'y sont intégrés** parfaitement dès leur arrivée (*integrate; mix*)

intégrisme (*m*): l'**intégrisme** chiite est venu bouleverser les données de la situation (*fundamentalism*); il faut résister à la tentation de l'**intégrisme** libéral (*extremism*)

intempestif <-ive> (*adj*): les remarques **intempestives** du ministre n'ont pas été appréciées à Bruxelles (*rash, outspoken*)

intendance (*f*): au Premier ministre l'**intendance**, au Président la diplomatie (*day-to-day matters; routine administration*)

intenter: il **intenta un procès** contre les autorités françaises (*institute proceedings*)

intention (*f*): un récent sondage lui donne 52% des **intentions de vote**

(*promised/intended vote*)

interdiction (*f*): 83% des personnes interrogées sont favorables à cette **interdiction** (*ban, prohibition*)

interdir [s']: Paris **s'interdit** d'apporter une aide logistique aux Tchadiens (*refuse*)

intéressant <e> (*adj*): la banque lui propose des conditions très **intéressantes** (*attractive*)

intéressé (*m*): cette perspective fut très bien accueillie par les **intéressés** eux-mêmes (*interested party*)

intéressement (*m*): un contrat d'**intéressement au résultat** a été signé (*worker participation; profit-sharing*); il touche une **prime d'intéressement** égale à 20% de son salaire annuel (*profit-sharing bonus*)

intéresser: il faut les **intéresser** directement aux résultats de l'entreprise (*involve; make to share*); au total, 89 départements seront **intéressés** par ces mesures (*concern*)

intérêt (*m*): Péchiney cède ses **intérêts** aux Japonais (*stake; operation*)

interférer: nous n'avons pas à **interférer** dans leur politique d'investissement (*interfere; involve oneself*)

intérieur <e> (*adj*): un quart du taux de croissance était expliqué par la **demande intérieure** (*domestic demand*); la **politique intérieure** préoccupe le gouvernement (*domestic/internal politics*)

intérim (*m*): il assura par deux fois l'**intérim** de la présidence (*interim office*); il **assure l'intérim** de la direction financière (*deputize*)

intérimaire (*adj*): les partis s'accordent sur la composition d'un gouvernement **intérimaire** (*interim; stopgap*); il leur a fallu embaucher des **[travailleurs] intérimaires** (*temporary employee; 'temp'*); le **dividende intérimaire** a été fixé à 7 pence (*interim dividend*)

interlocuteur (*m*): il espère apparaître comme un **interlocuteur** privilégié pour les dirigeants soviétiques (*representative; spokesman*)

intermédiaire (*m/adj*): les ventes d'armes dégagent des commissions énormes pour les **intermédiaires** (*go-between, intermediary, middleman*)

interne (*adj*): une coalition en proie à des dissensions **internes** (*internal*); comme la demande **interne** sera comprimée (*domestic; internal*)

interpellation (*f*): il y a eu 15 **interpellations** jeudi lors des manifestations (*stopping for questioning*); les ministres n'ont plus à redouter les **interpellations** (*oral question in parliament*)

interpeller: 148 personnes ont été **interpellées** (*question; check identity*); il a l'intention d'**interpeller** directement le ministre sur ce dossier (*question; challenge*)

interprète (*m*): dans cette démarche, il **se fait l'interprète** de l'ensemble des travailleurs (*represent, speak for*)

interrogatoire (*f*): elle a subi 12 heures d'**interrogatoires** (*questioning*)

interroger: après avoir été **interrogé**, il a été écroué (*question*); [s'] l'Angola **s'interroge** sur les véritables intentions de Pretoria (*doubt, query; speculate*)

intersyndicale (*f*): l'**intersyndicale** de la réunion des Musées nationaux [CFDT, CGT, FO] (*inter-trade-union grouping*)

intervenir: l'accord **intervenu** entre les deux gouvernements (*come about*); le gouvernement **interviendra** pour éviter tout dérapage des salaires (*intervene*)

intervention (*f*): il a consacré son **intervention** aux questions européennes (*speech; contribution*); la Banque de France a baissé d'un point son **taux d'intervention** sur le marché interbancaire (*intervention rate*)

intestin <e> (*adj*): des querelles **intestines** déchirent le parti (*internal*)

intoxication (*f*): scandalisé par ce qu'il appelait la campagne d'**intoxication** (*indoctrination*)

investir: il l'avait emporté sur le candidat **investi** par l'UDF et le RPR (*invest; promote, adopt*); les sidérurgistes japonais **investissent** le marché américain (*lay siege to; attack*); une volonté farouche d'**investir** les postes clés du service public (*take over; monopolize*)

investissement (*m*): un gros effort d'**investissement** doit être fait (*investment*)

investiture (*f*): il va briguer l'**investiture** de son parti en vue des prochaines élections (*nomination as candidate; investiture*)

irrecevabilité (*f*): l'objet de l'exercice de l'**irrecevabilité**, c'est de faire admettre que le texte proposé est contraire à la constitution (*inadmissibility*)

irrecevable (*adj*): le tribunal de grande instance a **déclaré irrecevable** la requête (*reject as inadmissible*)

irréductible (*m/adj*): les **irréductibles** refusent tout compromis (*extremist; hardliner*); l'opposition **irréductible** de plusieurs députés libéraux (*out-and-out, implacable*)

irrégulier <-ère> (*adj*): on s'inquiète de la prolifération d'étrangers **en situation irrégulière** (*irregular/illegal situation*)

irresponsable (*adj*): le Président était **irresponsable**, mais le gouvernement était responsable devant le Parlement (*not accountable for one's actions before a higher authority*)

isoloir (*m*): les déserteurs de l'**isoloir** expliquent leur comportement par la faiblesse des enjeux (*voting booth*)

issu <e> (*adj*): la révolte, **issue** du mécontentement populaire (*caused by, stemming from*); un gouvernement **issu d'élections libres** (*democratically elected*)

issue (*f*): on cherche toujours une **issue** au conflit saharien (*solution, way out of*); l'**issue** la plus probable du scrutin, c'est une victoire pour la gauche (*result, consequence*)

J

jachère (*f*): il a été instauré un programme limité de **mise en jachère** des terres cultivables (*taking out of cultivation; leaving land fallow*)

jacobin <e> (*adj*): on a trop longtemps supporté la loi de l'État **jacobin** (*centralizing; Jacobin*)

jacobinisme (*m*): une certaine Gauche que son **jacobinisme** centralisateur a aveuglée (*centralizing tendency; Jacobinism*)

jaune (*m/adj*): ils furent traités de tous les noms: **jaunes**, 'sales vendus' (*blackleg, scab*); le **métal jaune**, et la pierre: deux valeurs refuges (*gold*)

jeu (*m*): leur désunion **fait le jeu** du chef de l'État (*play into the hands of*); aucun intérêt matériel n'est **en jeu** (*at stake*); la firme a pu **tirer son épingle du jeu** grâce à sa compétitivité (*extricate oneself; survive a crisis*)

jour (*m*): pour 50 anciens ouvriers de Rhône-Poulenc, c'est le **jour J** (*D-Day; the big day*); la **mise à jour** de la programmation réclamerait 20 milliards de francs (*updating; bringing up to date*)

joute (*f*): ce fut une véritable **joute oratoire** entre les deux leaders (*verbal battle, joust*)

judiciaire (*adj*): le juge l'a laissé libre, mais **sous contrôle judiciaire** (*required to report periodically to court or police station*); le **pouvoir judiciaire**, en vertu du principe de la séparation des pouvoirs, est indépendant (*judicial branch, judiciary*); on a intérêt dans ces cas à éviter la **procédure judiciaire** (*going/taking a matter to court*)

juge (*m*): les **juges** appartiennent à la magistrature assise (*State judge*); l'affaire fut confiée à un **juge d'instruction** de Rouen (*examining magistrate*)

jugement (*m*): le **jugement** sera rendu le 4 juin (*verdict; judgement*)

juger: quatre ans de détention sans être **jugé**; les inculpés vont bientôt être **jugés** (*bring to trial; try*)

juguler: comment **juguler** l'inflation si les salaires augmentent sans cesse? (*arrest, stop*)

juré (*m*): pour être **juré d'assises**, il faut être citoyen français (*juror, jury member*); **les jurés** ont conclu à une mort naturelle (*jury*)

juridiction (*f*): cette **juridiction**, créée pour statuer sur des affaires d'espionnage (*tribunal, court of law*)

jurisprudence (*f*): relaxé, il attend le verdict d'appel, qui **fera jurisprudence** (*set a precedent*)

jusqu'au-boutisme (*m*): ils risquent de payer très cher leur **jusqu'au-boutisme** (*intransigence; extremism*)

jusqu'au-boutiste (*m/adj*): les **jusqu'au-boutistes** menacent de passer à l'insurrection (*die-hard; extremist*); connu pour ses vues **jusqu'au-boutistes** (*extreme*)

justesse (*f*): nos partenaires comprendront la **justesse** de nos thèses (*rightness*); il a devancé son rival **d'extrême justesse** (*only just, barely*)

justice (*f*): sa décision de transmettre le dossier à la **justice** (*the courts; the law*); ils ont entrepris une **action en justice** (*court/legal case*); il va les **attaquer en justice** (*take before the courts*)

justiciable (*m/adj*): une formule qui offre des garanties aux **justiciables** (*person accused of a crime/on trial*)

justificatif <-ive> (*adj*): sur présentation de **pièces justificatives** (*documentary evidence*)

justification (*f*): présenter une **justification** du nouveau domicile, par exemple une quittance de loyer; sur **justification** de leur qualité de salarié (*evidence; proof*)

justifier: les étrangers souhaitant séjourner en France doivent **justifier** leur moyen d'existence (*prove, furnish evidence*)

juteux <-euse> (*adj*): la société a ainsi réalisé de **juteuses** plus-values boursières; l'occasion de fournir aux entreprises françaises des contrats **juteux** (*lucrative; considerable*)

K

krach (*m*): depuis le **krach boursier** d'octobre dernier (*stock-market crash*)

L

Labour (*m*): le **Labour** a peu de chances de former le prochain gouvernement (*British Labour party*)

laïc <-que> (*adj*): l'éducation **laïque** est sur la défensive face aux attaques du secteur privé (*lay, secular; State*)

laïcité (*f*): la **laïcité** de l'enseignement est toujours son crédo (*lay/secular ethos*)

laissé-pour-compte (*m*): ce système engendrerait-il des **laissés-pour-compte**? (*victim; reject*)

lame de fond (*f*): une véritable **lame de fond** pourrait encore le porter au pouvoir (*groundswell*)

laminer: les salariés, dont le pouvoir d'achat est **laminé**, exigent des rattrapages (*erode*); les centristes, **laminés** entre les blocs antagonistes (*squeeze; steam-roller*)

lancinant <e> (*adj*): la **lancinante** question du désarmement nucléaire (*insistent; still unresolved*)

langue (*f*): en **langue de bois** cela s'appelle le 'contrôle de la légalité' (*jargon, officialese*)

larvé <e> (*adj*): confronté à une contestation **larvée** au sein de la rédaction; vivre dans une atmosphère de haine **larvée** (*latent; barely hidden*)

leader (*m/adj*): 50 entreprises **leader** sur leur marché cherchent des candidats vendeurs (*front-runner; leader*)

lecture (*f*): le Sénat l'a adopté en première **lecture** (*reading of a parliamentary bill*); le porte-parole du gouvernement **donna lecture** du communiqué (*read aloud*)

légiférer: comment le gouvernement peut-il **légiférer** sur une question si personnelle? (*legislate, pass legislation*)

législateur (*m*): le moment est venu pour le **législateur** de faire preuve d'imagination (*legislative body; legislator*)

législatif <-ive> (*adj*): le **corps législatif** jadis avait trop de pouvoir face à l'exécutif (*legislature; legislative body*); dans les **[élections] législatives** de mars, la droite est revenue au pouvoir (*general election*)

législature (*f*): la durée actuelle d'une **législature** est de cinq ans (*life of a parliament*)

lendemain (*m*): cette initiative **restera sans lendemain** (*go no further*)

lèse-majesté (*f*): crime de **lèse-majesté** aux yeux des FLN purs et durs (*treason*)

lettre (*f*): cet accord est **resté lettre-morte**; sachant que leurs décisions **resteront lettre-morte** (*remain a dead letter; not be put into practice*)

levée (*f*): la **levée** de l'état d'urgence a été annoncée (*lifting, suspension*); la première phase du financement prévoit la **levée** de 75 milliards en capital (*raising*); l'accord a déclenché une **levée de boucliers** du côté protestant (*resistance, opposition; outcry*)

lever: Péchiney s'apprête à **lever** plus de cinq milliards de francs (*raise capital*)

levier (*m*): le secteur public doit jouer un rôle de **levier** (*lever*); c'est lui dorénavant qui **tient les leviers de commande** de l'État (*be in control, command*)

liaison (*f*): la RFA a inauguré en 1988 la nouvelle **liaison** Sarre-Moselle (*link*); la **liaison 2** × **2 voies** entre ici et Boulogne (*dual-carriageway road link*)

libeller: le chèque devrait être **libellé** à l'ordre de la Société Bissac (*draw up, make out*); on a intérêt à acheter des avoirs **libellés** en dollars (*payable*)

libération (*f*): la **libération des prix** pourrait être la cause d'abus (*price decontrolling; removal of price controls*); la loi sur la **libération des loyers** (*rent decontrolling*)

liberté (*f*): la demande de **mise en liberté** fut rejetée (*release; discharge*); il fut **mis en liberté sous caution** (*release on bail*); l'auteur présumé du crime a été **mis en liberté conditionnelle** (*bind over*)

libre-échange (*m*): le **libre-échange** avec les États-Unis créera 200 000 emplois dans les dix ans à venir (*free trade*)

lice (*f*): deux candidats sont **en lice** (*in the lists, in contention*)

licencié (*m*): aux '**licenciés** économiques' sera versée une allocation spéciale pendant un an (*person made redundant*)

licenciement (*m*): rien ne justifie le **licenciement** de la moitié des effectifs (*sacking, dismissal*); les demandeurs d'emploi qui s'inscrivent à l'ANPE pour **licenciement économique** (*redundancy; laying off*)

licencier: on a, du jour au lendemain, **licencié** 500 employés (*dismiss, make redundant*)

lieu (*m*): le vote n'a pas **donné lieu** à un débat (*give rise to*); il est allé enquêter **sur les lieux** du crime (*at the place/site of*); le développement de la démocratie sur les **lieux de travail** (*workplace*); le hameau a été ravalé au rang de **lieu-dit** (*locality smaller than a hamlet*)

ligne (*f*): dans ses **grandes lignes**, la proposition de paix semble admirable (*broad lines, outline*); le Conseil d'État **est dans la ligne de mire** du gouvernement (*be threatened, be in the firing line*)

lignée (*f*): il est à cet égard **dans la lignée** des autres Présidents de la Vᵉ République (*in the tradition of*)

limitrophe (*adj*): Aquitaine, Poitou-Charentes, Auvergne, les pays **limitrophes** du Limousin (*bordering, neighbouring*)

limogeage (*m*): son **limogeage** fit du bruit à Washington; une vague de **limogeages** a suivi les troubles dans le Caucase (*sacking*)

limoger: le ministre a **limogé** le P-DG de la société; **limogé** en 1987 de son poste de premier secrétaire (*sack, fire*)

liquidation (*f*): le tribunal de commerce de Pontoise a prononcé la **liquidation judiciaire** de la société (*winding-up*)

liquide (*m/adj*): des versements officieux directement payés **en liquide** (*in cash*)

liquidités (*f pl*): le marché regorge encore de **liquidités** prêtes à s'investir (*liquid assets; funds*)

liste (*f*): la **liste** de la majorité présidentielle l'emporte dans l'Aveyron (*list of candidates in list voting system*); PS et PC constitueront des **listes uniques** dès le premier tour (*single/joint electoral list*)

litige (*m*): il préconisa la soumission du **litige** à l'arbitrage des Nations unies (*dispute*)

litigieux < -euse > (*adj*): un service des contentieux s'occupe des questions **litigieuses** (*contentious*)

livraison (*f*): la **livraison** d'armes aux rebelles (*delivery, supply*)

livrer [se]: ils **se sont livrés** à des exactions contre la population civile (*indulge in*)

livret (*m*): titulaire d'un **livret** d'Épargne-Logement (*pass book, savings book*)

local (*m/adj*): les **locaux** administratifs du collège sont occupés depuis mardi (*premise, office*)

locataire (*m*): le précédent **locataire** n'a pas encore vidé les lieux (*tenant; incumbent, occupier*); on peut choisir à son gré entre **être locataire** ou accéder à la propriété (*live in rented accommodation*)

locatif (*m*): ceux qui plaçaient leurs économies dans le **locatif** (*rented property*); (*adj*) le **revenu locatif** des immeubles (*proceeds from rents*); acheter de l'immobilier **à des fins locatives** (*for renting out*)

lock-out (*m*): après une grève de dix jours, la direction a décidé un '**lock-out**' (*lock-out*)

locomotive (*f*): le Japon refuse d'être la '**locomotive**' économique; le secteur privé peut et doit être la **locomotive** de la croissance (*pace-setter; driving force*)

logement (*m*): il a reçu un **logement de fonction** (*tied accommodation*)

loi (*f*): le Parlement a adopté son projet de **loi-cadre** réformant le système actuel (*outline law*); tous les partis viennent de voter une **loi-programme** militaire fastueuse (*act providing framework for government programme*)

lotir: l'Europe, à cet égard, est la plus mal **lotie**; les étudiants en Lettres sont les plus mal **lotis** (*equip, provide for*)

loucher: l'énorme marché américain vers lequel **louchent** tous les pays industrialisés (*look enviously at; have designs upon*)

loyer (*m*): la libération totale des **loyers** (*rent, rental*); les HLM sont des **habitations à loyer modéré** (*cheap municipal housing*); le relèvement du **loyer de l'argent** (*money interest rates; cost of borrowing*)

lucratif < -ive > (*adj*): les associations d'entraide **à but non-lucratif** (*non-profit-making*)

M

Maghreb (*m*): l'influence de la France dans les pays francophones du **Maghreb** se maintient (*Maghreb, North Africa*)

maghrébin <e> (*m/adj*): parmi les immigrés, les **Maghrébins** sont le groupe le plus nombreux (*Maghrebin; of North African descent*)

magistrature (*f*): il fit son droit à Aix et sa carrière par la suite dans la **magistrature** (*magistracy*); battu en 1974, il accéda à la **magistrature suprême** en 1981 (*highest/supreme office; presidency of the Republic*)

magouille (*f*): devant l'accord PS/PC, certains crieront à la **magouille** politicienne; l'Opposition parle de '**magouille**' à propos du redécoupage électoral (*chicanery*)

main (*f*): le gouvernement **met la dernière main** au projet d'ordonnances (*put final touches to*); le leader du RPR **tend la main** aux partis du centre (*make overtures*); il a recours à la **main-d'œuvre** étrangère de façon temporaire; l'abondance d'une **main-d'œuvre** bon marché (*labour; work-force*); l'Inde a envoyé ses troupes pour **prêter main-forte** au gouvernement (*assist, help*)

mainmise (*f*): pour freiner cette **mainmise** du pouvoir sur la télévision; la hantise de la **mainmise** étrangère (*seizure, control; domination*)

maintenir [se]: il **s'est maintenu** au second tour des élections (*stand again*); la droite pourra-t-elle **se maintenir au pouvoir**? (*stay in power, keep power*)

maintien (*m*): le gouvernement prévoit un simple **maintien** du pouvoir d'achat du salaire horaire (*maintenance; preserving*); le Préfet demeure chargé du **maintien de l'ordre** dans le département (*law and order*); les **forces du maintien de l'ordre** étaient partout en évidence dans les rues (*police*)

mairie (*f*): ici, les Communistes ont le tiers des **mairies** (*town hall; post of mayor; municipality*)

maison (*f*): il fut écroué à la **maison d'arrêt** de Colmar (*remand centre; holding prison*)

maître <-esse> (*adj*): cet avion devait être la **pièce maîtresse** des forces israéliennes (*key element*); la flexibilité est devenue le **maître-mot** (*keyword*); la mairie de Sens **est maître-d'œuvre** du projet (*be in overall charge*)

maîtrise (*f*): les 12 ministres sont parvenus à un compromis sur la **maîtrise** de la production des céréales (*control*); lettre ouverte des ingénieurs et de la **maîtrise** au personnel (*supervisory staff*); les trois pays se disputent la **maîtrise-d'œuvre** de cet énorme projet (*leadership; overall charge*)

93

maîtriser: on a à peu près **maîtrisé** l'inflation (*curb; bring under control*)

major (*m*): étudiant en médecine, et **major** de sa promotion (*top of the list/ class*)

majoration (*f*): il n'y aura pas de **majorations** de prix (*increase*)

majorer: tous les constructeurs **majorent** leurs prix le 1ᵉʳ janvier (*increase, raise*)

majorité (*f*): cinq députés sur six de l'ancienne **majorité** y ont été réélus (*majority; governing party*); avant, la **majorité** était de 21 ans (*coming of age, attaining one's majority*)

malaisé <e> (*adj*): une loi trop complexe, et **malaisée** à appliquer (*difficult; hazardous*)

malfaiteur (*m*): un des **malfaiteurs** a tiré à cinq reprises sur lui (*criminal; law-breaker*)

malus (*m*): les Assurances frappent d'un **malus** spécial les automobilistes auteurs de graves infractions (*penalty on insurance premium*)

mal venu <e> (*adj*): une rebuffade aurait été particulièrement **mal venue** (*inappropriate; unfortunate*)

malversation (*f*): inculpé après la découverte de **malversations** financières (*embezzlement*)

mandat (*m*): le **mandat** du Premier ministre est de cinq ans (*mandate, period of office*); conseiller général et conseiller régional, il devra renoncer à un de ses **mandats électifs** (*elected office*); le procureur avait lancé un **mandat d'amener** contre les deux hommes (*arrest warrant*); sous le coup d'un **mandat d'arrêt** international (*arrest warrant*); il a été placé sous **mandat de dépôt** (*committal order*)

mandataire (*m*): en confiant ses intérêts à un **mandataire** (*proxy, representative*)

mandater: **mandaté** pour les représenter à Paris, leur député rend compte régulièrement à ses électeurs (*give a mandate; mandate*)

mandature (*f*): l'ultime conseil général de sa deuxième **mandature** (*period of office*)

manifestant (*m*): les combats opposaient **manifestants** et forces de l'ordre (*demonstrator*)

manifestation (*f*): la présence de l'armée a directement inspiré la **manifestation** (*demonstration*)

manifester: une centaine de personnes **manifestent** devant l'ambassade (*demonstrate*)

manne (*f*): la **manne** pétrolière assurait à elle seule 40% des exportations (*windfall; unexpected gift; manna*)

manœuvre (*m*): la robotisation amena la disparition progressive des postes de **manœuvres** et d'ouvriers spécialisés (*manual/unskilled worker*); (*f*): le but de sa **manœuvre** a été atteint (*manœuvre*); toutes les **manœuvres électorales** sont bonnes (*vote-catching manœuvre*)

manque (*m*): l'État récupérait par ce moyen le **manque à gagner** dû à la baisse des taxes; ce qui entraîne un **manque à gagner** de 200F pour chaque homme (*loss of earnings/revenue*)

manquement (*m*): c'était un **manquement** au respect des règles élémentaires (*breach; infringement*)

marasme (*m*): comment s'expliquer le **marasme** actuel du marché? (*depression; slump*)

marchand (*m/adj*): l'emploi salarié des **secteurs marchands** non agricoles (*trade sector*); la drogue, dont la **valeur marchande au détail** est estimée à 300 millions de dollars (*retail/street value*); entre **marchands de canons**, la bataille sera féroce (*arms supplier*)

marchandage (*m*): ces **marchandages** parlementaires nuisent à la crédibilité du parti (*bargaining; haggling*)

marche (*f*): un droit d'information et de consultation plus large sur la **marche** des entreprises (*operation; functioning*); le gouvernement vient d'effectuer une spectaculaire **marche-arrière** (*retreat*)

marché (*m*): leader européen sur son **marché** (*market sector*); ils se disputent âprement leur **part du marché** (*share of the market*); février confirme l'amélioration du **marché du travail** (*job/employment market*); le Xe Plan vise à préparer la France au **marché unique européen** (*single European market*); en vue d'obtenir le **marché** du futur lycée hôtelier de Nice (*contract*)

marge (*f*): dans cette branche, les **marges** de bénéfice sont parfois abusives (*profit/trading margin*); on dispose d'une certaine **marge de manœuvre** (*room for manœuvre*); ceux qui vivent **en marge** de la société (*on the fringe*)

marginalité (*f*): l'évolution technologique repousse les petits paysans vers la **marginalité sociale** (*fringes of society; second-class status*)

Marianne (*f*): dimanche dernier, un citoyen sur trois a boudé **Marianne** (*French Republic; allegory of the Republic*)

maroquin (*m*): autre **maroquin** éphémère, celui du secrétaire d'État chargé des travailleurs immigrés (*ministerial post*)

masse (*f*): ce train de mesures ne manquera pas de gonfler la **masse monétaire** (*money supply*); la nouvelle charge augmentera d'autant la **masse salariale** (*wage-bill*)

matière (*f*): en **matière** criminelle, les amendes peuvent aller jusqu'à cinq millions de francs; leur retard **en matière** d'investissement (*in the area of, on the subject of*); **matières premières** en hausse à la Bourse de Tokyo (*raw materials*)

mécanisme (*m*): pour que soit mis en place un **mécanisme** de contrôle (*means, mechanism*)

mécontentement (*m*): ils essayent de canaliser le **mécontentement** populaire (*discontent, dissatisfaction*)

médaillé <e> (*adj*): **medaillé** militaire en 1918 (*with a military decoration*)

médecin (*m*): le **médecin-légiste** chargé de l'expertise (*forensic surgeon*)

média (*m*): les **médias** se sont emparés de l'affaire (*mass media*)

médiateur (*m*): le ministre du Travail a fini par nommer un **médiateur** pour régler la grève (*mediator;* ≃ *Ombudsman*); nommé par le Président pour **être le médiateur** entre le gouvernement, les élus et les acteurs socio-économiques (*mediate*)

médiatique (*adj*): l'exploitation **médiatique** de l'affaire (*by/of/on the media*)

médiatiser: ces sommets exagérément **médiatisés**; jamais une maladie n'a été tant **médiatisée** (*give media coverage*)

méfiance (*f*): la **méfiance** dans laquelle il tient les États-Unis (*distrust*)

mêler: il a **été mêlé à** un trafic de devises (*be involved in*); [se] les grandes puissances **s'en sont mêlées** (*get involved; intervene*)

menacer: il **menace** de quitter le gouvernement (*threaten*)

ménage (*m*): plus d'allègements fiscaux pour les **ménages** (*household*); la **consommation des ménages** a tendance à se tasser (*domestic expenditure/spending*); Juifs et Arabes ont souvent **fait bon ménage** (*get on well together*)

menées (*f pl*): en les accusant de **menées** illégales (*intrigue, manœuvres; machination*)

mensualisation (*f*): la **mensualisation** des salaires s'est généralisée à partir de 1969 (*monthly payment*)

mensualité (*f*): ils ont vu croître à l'excès leurs **mensualités** de remboursement; la **mensualité** pour un crédit de 1 000F sur un an passe de 912F à 926F (*monthly payment/repayment*)

mensuel <-elle> (*adj*): salaire **mensuel**: 10 200F plus une indemnité de la Ville de Paris (*monthly*)

mention (*f*): nous cherchons des jeunes brillants, qui ont récolté des **mentions** (*pass with distinction*)

menu <e> (*adj*): sans compter dans ce total les **menus frais** (*incidental expenses*); il n'avait jamais commis que des **menus larcins** (*slight misdemeanour*)

méprendre [se]: cette réforme **ressemble à s'y méprendre à** celle de 1984 (*be almost indistinguishable from*)

mère (*f*): le consortium, filiale à 50% de ses deux **maisons mères**; ils pourront faire remonter leurs pertes vers la **société mère** (*parent company*)

mérite (*m*): la promotion se fera **au mérite** (*by merit*)

métropole (*f*): ancien chef de l'OAS en **métropole**; les rapports tendus que les Corses entretiennent avec la **métropole** (*home country; mainland France*); Nancy et Metz, réunies en une seule **métropole d'équilibre** (*regional growth centre*)

métropolitain <e> (*adj*): en Afrique du Nord et en France **métropolitaine** (*metropolitan, mainland*)

meurtrier <-ère> (*adj*): les auteurs de l'embuscade **meurtrière**; les attentats les plus **meurtriers** (*murderous*)

mévente (*f*): avec la **mévente** actuelle de l'avion supersonique (*slow-down of sales; poor sales*)

microcosme (*m*): la question qui obsède le **microcosme** politique marseillais (*small world; microcosm*)

mieux (*m*): un **mieux** se distingue au deuxième semestre (*improvement*); pour la résorption du chômage, pour le **mieux-être** de tous (*greater welfare; improved standard of living*)

milieu (*m*): les **milieux d'affaires** se montrent hostiles (*business community*); les **milieux financiers** redoutent une reprise de l'inflation (*financial community*)

militantisme (*m*): cette localité de la Cisjordanie n'est pas réputée pour son **militantisme** (*militancy*)

militer: il a depuis toujours **milité** au Parti communiste (*be an active/militant member*)

millésime (*m*): l'année a été excellente: 1992 s'annonce comme un **millésime** encore meilleur; au changement de **millésime**, soit à partir du premier juillet (*year; period of twelve months*)

minéralogique (*adj*): les numéros **minéralogiques** des départements (*registration*); d'après la **plaque minéralogique**, la voiture était immatriculée dans le Loiret (*vehicle number-plate*)

ministère (*m*): sous le **ministère** Rocard (*premiership*); la Gendarmerie mobile relève du **ministère** des Armées (*ministry*); le **ministère public** a requis une peine de deux ans (*prosecution; the Crown/State*)

ministrable (*adj*): après sa victoire, il prend rang parmi les **premiers ministrables** (*potential prime minister*)

minorer: le montant des frais se trouve **minoré** d'autant (*reduce, lessen*)

mise (*f*): la **mise initiale** est assez modique (*first payment*)

miser: en **misant** résolument sur une politique de qualité de leurs produits; le Niger **misait** sur l'agriculture (*bank/count on; trust*)

misère (*f*): la réalité là-bas, c'est la **misère** matérielle (*poverty*)

mitigé <e> (*adj*): ce grand lancement laisse toutefois une impression **mitigée**; satisfaction **mitigée** dans les territoires occupés (*reserved, lukewarm, qualified*)

mixte (*adj*): pour sa percée en URSS, le groupe a choisi la formule de la **société mixte** (*joint venture*)

modalité (*f*): les **modalités** de remboursement des frais sont les suivantes; les **modalités** d'application de la nouvelle loi varient selon les situations familiales (*method, mode, procedure*)

modicité (*f*): la **modicité** des impôts indirects au Japon (*modest level*)

modique (*adj*): pour la somme **modique** de 10 000F (*small*)

modus vivendi (*m*): la recherche d'un **modus vivendi** continue (*working arrangement*)

mœurs (*m pl*): les **mœurs** politiques très particuliers de l'époque d'après-guerre (*habits, manners*)

moins-value (*f*): la Bundesbank a subi en 1987 une **moins-value** d'environ sept milliards (*loss*)

moitié (*f*): nos marges sont diminuées **de moitié** (*by half*); 800 000 barils par jour, soit **moitié moins** que le normal (*half as much*); avec un volume de transactions **moitié moindre** (*smaller by half; half as great*)

monnayer: ces accords qu'il **monnayait** contre un monopole de représentativité syndicale (*trade; exchange*)

mono-: assurer un renouveau économique fondé non sur une **mono-industrie** mais sur la qualité de la vie (*a single industry*)

monopole (*m*): l'État ne dispose pas d'un **monopole** en matière de radio et de télévision (*monopoly*); ce syndicat dispose du **monopole d'embauche** ('*closed shop*'); l'**Office des monopoles et des fusions** a été saisi (*Monopolies Commission*)

montant (*m*): une indemnité d'un **montant** mensuel de 1 339 F; 120 avions pour un **montant** total de cinq milliards de francs (*sum, total*); 1971 a vu la mise en place du système des **montants compensatoires** agricoles (*compensation payment*)

monter [se]: la perte de salaire **se montait** à 2 000F par jour (*amount, total*)

montre: le patronat n'avait pas **fait montre** d'exigences excessives (*show; display*)

moralisation (*f*): la **moralisation** du financement de la vie politique (*cleaning-up*)

moraliser: ces deux textes vont **moraliser** le financement de la vie politique (*remove corruption from; make more honest*)

morcellement (*m*): d'où un **morcellement** de la fonction publique en des centaines de statuts particuliers (*division, breaking up into small units*); le remembrement a résolu les problèmes causés par le **morcellement des terres** (*division of land into small units*)

morose (*adj*): après cinq années **moroses**, le marché a bondi cette année (*depressed; poor*)

morosité (*f*): dans ce secteur, la **morosité** persiste (*depressed condition/mood*)

mot (*m*): la vigilance, ce devrait être le **mot d'ordre** de ceux qui veulent la paix (*watchword, slogan*); il a lancé un **mot d'ordre de grève générale** pour le 28 mars (*strike call*)

moteur (*m*): dans ce domaine, la France et la RFA sont les **moteurs**; les dépenses de consommation furent en France le principal **moteur** de la croissance en 1990 (*driving force; stimulus*); (*adj*) il jouait un rôle **moteur** dans la réforme des institutions (*leading; driving*)

mou <-olle> (*adj*): il s'attaque à ce qu'il appelle le socialisme **mou**; il ne décolère pas contre le règne du 'consensus **mou**' (*soft, 'wet'*)

mouiller: la flotte **mouille** en rade de Toulon (*be at anchor*); [se] le maire radical **s'est mouillé** dans une affaire de pots-de-vin (*be implicated/ involved*)

mouvance (*f*): une organisation née dans la **mouvance** des événements de 1968 (*circumstances, context*)

mouvement (*m*): des **mouvements de grève** paralysent les transports parisiens (*strike*); le gouvernement mis à l'épreuve par l'extension des **mouvements sociaux** (*strike in the social sector*); **mouvements d'humeur** et manifestations hier à Alger (*disturbance; discontent*); ce **mouvement ministériel** était attendu (*ministerial reshuffle*); il y a un parti **du mouvement**, du progrès (*progressive*)

mouvementé <e> (*adj*): séance **mouvementée** hier à l'Assemblée nationale (*eventful*)

moyennant: et ceci, **moyennant** une cotisation annuelle de 100F (*at the cost of, in exchange for*)

moyenne (*f*): chiffre plus bas que la **moyenne** nationale (*average*); les sièges sont répartis à la proportionnelle, **à la plus forte moyenne** (*system of highest average for distribution of electoral seats*)

multiplication (*f*): la **multiplication** des tarifs réduits pour les familles nombreuses (*increase in the number of*)

multiplier: Londres **multiplie** les avertissements au régime des ayotallahs (*multiply, increase*); [se] les mesures en faveur des femmes **se multiplient** (*increase in number*)

municipal <e> (*adj*): en vue des [élections] **municipales** de 1989 (*municipal elections*)

municipalité (*f*): les deux **municipalités** vont se retrouver pour discuter de cette question (*town/city council*)

musclé <e> (*adj*): il a prononcé un réquisitoire **musclé** contre le libéralisme; le parti du progrès amorce un redressement **musclé** (*vigorous, hard-hitting*)

muscler: ils voudraient **muscler** un texte qu'ils estiment un peu flou (*strengthen*)

mutation (*f*): dans la période de **mutation** profonde que traverse actuellement l'économie (*change, transformation*); un cadre peut refuser une **mutation** pour raisons d'ordre familial (*job transfer/move*)

muter: en poste dans l'Est, il se trouve **muté** dans une autre région (*transfer, move*)

mutuelle (*f*): de nombreux Français adhèrent à des **mutuelles**, qui complètent les prestations sociales (*supplementary insurance scheme; mutual benefit insurance company*)

mutuellement: les deux pays s'accusent **mutuellement** (*mutually, one another*)

N

nanti <e> (*adj*): la commune fait partie de celles qui sont particulièrement bien **nanties** (*affluent, prosperous; well-equipped*)

nantir: la France, **nantie** d'un programme très ambitieux (*equip; supply*)

napoléon (*m*): la prime du **napoléon** a subi d'importantes variations (*gold coin worth 20 old francs*)

natalité (*f*): le **taux de natalité** est partout en baisse (*birth-rate*)

nature (*f*): il a préféré se faire payer **en nature** (*in kind*)

navette (*f*): malgré les multiples **navettes** qu'il effectue (*shuttle*); le projet de loi a **fait la navette** pendant trois mois entre l'Assemblée et le Sénat (*go backwards and forwards/to and fro*)

nécessiteux <-euse> (*adj*): les familles **nécessiteuses**, vivant dans le dénuement le plus complet (*in need*)

néfaste (*adj*): les conséquences **néfastes** d'un dollar surévalué; une montée des taux d'intérêt serait **néfaste** pour l'économie (*harmful*)

négoce (*m*): le **négoce** des céréales continue entre l'URSS et les États-Unis (*trade; business*)

négocier [se]: à 232F, le titre **se négocie** peu au-dessus de son cours le plus bas de l'année (*change hands, sell*)

nervosité (*f*): **nervosité** à la Bourse de Paris hier (*tension, edginess*)

nivellement (*m*): il y aura inévitablement un **nivellement** par le bas (*levelling; evening out*)

noir <e> (*adj*): l'**économie noire** est florissante; le **travail au noir** paie mieux (*black economy*); des achats financés en grande partie par la **caisse noire** (*'slush-fund'*)

nommément: le rapport les met **nommément** en cause (*by name*)

non-lieu (*m*): l'inculpation s'est terminée par un **non-lieu**; le **non-lieu** rendu dans l'affaire des ventes illégales d'armes à l'Iran; le juge d'instruction a **rendu une ordonnance de non-lieu** (*discharge; dismiss a case for lack of evidence*)

normalien (*m*): diplômé de l'ENA et **normalien** (*graduate of the* École normale supérieure)

normaliser: il faudra **normaliser** l'écartement des voies de chemin de fer en Europe (*standardize*); [se] depuis, l'approvisionnement **s'est normalisé** (*return to normal*)

notable (*m*): il est désigné par un collège de **notables** (*notability, worthy; important personality*)

notaire (*m*): on a intérêt à passer par un **notaire** (*notary, lawyer*); tout acquéreur devrait faire appel à un **notaire en droit** (≃ solicitor)

notarié <e> (*adj*): la loi oblige à passer par **acte notarié** les contrats portant sur des immeubles (*deed drawn up by a lawyer*)

notoriété (*f*): l'exceptionnelle **notoriété** de cette société (*reputation, fame*)

novateur <-trice> (*adj*): c'est une entreprise des plus **novatrices** (*innovative*)

noyau (*m*): le **noyau dur** des chômeurs de longue durée se renforce (*hard core*); comment briser les **'noyaux durs'**, constitués par le gouvernement dans les sociétés qu'il privatisait? (*hard-core group of shareholders*)

noyautage (*m*): le **noyautage** opéré par les gauchistes paralyse le syndicat (*infiltration*)

noyauter: discrètement **noyautée** par l'État-RPR, cette firme est la nouvelle cible des Socialistes (*infiltrate; equip with hard core of shareholders resistant to renationalization*)

nuancé <e> (*adj*): la France a répondu par un 'oui' **nuancé** aux propositions américaines (*qualified*); il avait adopté une position plus **nuancée** (*moderate*)

nuancer: à vrai dire, cette analyse mérite d'être **nuancée** (*qualify*)

nul <-ulle> (*adj*): ses chances de gagner sont pratiquement **nulles** (*nil; non-existent*); ils ont préféré s'abstenir ou **voter nul** (*spoil a voting paper*)

O

obédience (*f*): les régimes d'**obédience** pro-soviétique; les sectes d'**obédience** musulmane (*allegiance; persuasion*)

objectif (*m*): l'aviation a bombardé plusieurs **objectifs** industriels (*target*)

objet (*m*): les mutins **feront l'objet** de sanctions (*receive; be the recipient of*)

obligataire (*adj*): le financement s'effectue sur le marché **obligataire** (*debenture*)

obligation (*f*): le fonds est composé d'**obligations d'État** françaises; l'idée consisterait à convertir la dette en **obligations** négociables sur le marché international (*bond; debenture; fixed-interest stock*)

obtempérer: le policier, devant son refus d'**obtempérer**, fit usage de son arme (*obey, comply*)

obtention (*f*): il faudrait accélérer la procédure pour l'**obtention** de pièces d'identité; le conflit actuel vise l'**obtention** d'un minimum vital pour les travailleurs (*attaining, achieving*)

occulte (*adj*): le problème du financement **occulte** des campagnes électorales (*undercover; secret*)

occulter: ces difficultés, un moment **occultées**, réapparaissent; ils ont **occulté** une histoire coloniale peu glorieuse (*lose sight of; obfuscate, conceal*)

octroi (*m*): le gouvernement décida l'**octroi** d'un jour de congé; les Building Societies sont spécialisées dans l'**octroi** de prêts hypothécaires (*granting, awarding*)

octroyer: une prime spéciale de fin d'année est **octroyée** au personnel (*give, award*); [s'] la France pense pouvoir **s'octroyer** 10% de ce marché (*obtain*)

œuvre (*f*): la décentralisation fut l'**œuvre** de l'ancien ministre de l'Intérieur (*work, achievement*); la politique de 'transparence' **mise en œuvre** récemment (*put into practice, implement*); 300 observateurs de l'ONU surveillent sur place la **mise en œuvre** du cessez-le-feu (*implementation*)

œuvrer: les Superpuissances **œuvrent** pour une limitation des armes; peu de maires ont autant **œuvré** pour leur commune (*work*)

office (*m*): le nouveau Premier ministre **fera office** aussi de ministre de la Justice (*hold office; serve as*); il l'a nommé **d'office** à la commission (*by virtue of office/position*)

officialiser: il a **officialisé** son hostilité au projet dans son discours d'hier (*make official*)

officieux <-euse> (*adj*): en Algérie, l'**officieux** quotidien en langue arabe, *Al Chaab* (*unofficial*); il a fait un voyage **à titre officieux** à Bonn (*unofficially*)

offrant (*m*): le droit d'un actionnaire à vendre au **plus offrant** (*highest bidder*)

offre (*f*): l'**offre** crée sa propre demande; son **offre** reste insuffisante dans beaucoup de secteurs (*supply*); le nombre des **offres d'emploi** est en forte progression (*job vacancy*); il tente une **offre publique d'achat** sur le Parti socialiste; d'autres tentatives d'**OPA** en revanche ont échoué (*take-over bid*); en **lançant une OPA** sur le grand quotidien (*launch a take-over bid*)

ogive (*m*): un retrait limité d'**ogives** nucléaires (*warhead*)

onéreux <-euse> (*adj*): la municipalité s'est lancée dans des équipements **onéreux**; les traites à payer sembleront à long terme très **onéreuses** (*expensive; heavy*)

opéable (*m*) (*adj*): une chasse aux '**opéables**' (*candidate for take-over [OPA]*)

opérationnel <-elle> (*adj*): il faut être **opérationnel** en anglais et en allemand (*competent*)

opérer: les conditions dans lesquelles les vols ont été **opérés** (*carry out*); [s'] un transfert des compétences **s'est opéré** du préfet vers le Président du conseil général (*take place*)

opinion (*f*): une bonne partie de l'**opinion** prend position en faveur du ministre (*public opinion*); une centaine de ces détenus sont des **prisonniers d'opinion** (*political prisoner*)

opportunité (*f*): il a mis en question l'**opportunité** de cette mesure (*appropriateness; timing*); c'est indispensable à qui veut saisir les **opportunités** qu'offre le marché unique de 1993 (*opportunity; chance*)

opposant (*m*): dix **opposants** iraniens expulsés de France (*opponent; member of the opposition*)

opposition (*f*): les partis de l'**opposition** se sont soudés derrière lui (*opposition*)

optimiser: il faut essayer d'**optimiser** les bénéfices (*maximize*); pour **optimiser** votre gestion de trésorerie (*optimize; get maximum benefit from*)

optique (*f*): dans l'**optique** américaine, l'affaire est plus compliquée; toujours dans l'**optique** du Marché unique de 1993 (*perspective, point of view*)

or (*m*): l'**or noir** rapporte beaucoup moins de devises; les financiers surveillent anxieusement les caprices de l'**or noir** (*oil*)

ordonnance (*f*): on a dû souvent recourir aux **ordonnances** pour accélérer les choses (*government decree; administrative decision*); la chambre d'accusation avait infirmé l'**ordonnance** de mise en détention (*order*)

ordre (*m*): l'**ordre** et la répression sont l'apanage de la droite (*law and order; public order*); les constructeurs ont, **en ordre dispersé**, augmenté leurs tarifs ce mois-ci (*one after another*); l'**ordre du jour** comportera, notamment, la question de l'emploi (*agenda*); la privatisation des monopoles publics n'est pas encore **à l'ordre du jour** (*on the agenda; imminent*)

organisme (*m*): cette initiative est subventionnée par les **organismes** régionaux et départementaux (*body, organization*)

orientation (*f*): il a défini les grandes **orientations** de sa politique étrangère (*policy direction*); l'OCDE confirme l'**orientation à la baisse** du chômage en France (*downward trend/movement*); la préparation du **projet de loi d'orientation** sur l'école (*bill laying down future guidelines*)

orienter: depuis mars, le marché est **orienté à la hausse** (*on the upturn, on the* *rise*); le dollar reste **orienté à la baisse** (*falling*)

outil (*m*): il s'est déclaré hostile à la taxation de l'**outil de travail** (*equipment; plant*)

outrage (*m*): inculpé d'**outrages à agent** (*insulting behaviour*); coupable d'**outrage aux bonnes mœurs** (*publication of indecent material; affront to public decency*); le juge d'instruction l'a inculpé d'**outrage public et attentat à la pudeur** (≃ *indecent exposure*); condamnée pour **outrage à magistrat** pour avoir injurié un juge d'enfants (*contempt of court*)

outrance (*f*): la majorité se mobilise contre les **outrances** de son discours (*excess*); la militarisation **à outrance** du Nicaragua (*large-scale; excessive, to excess*)

outre: les sociétés **d'outre-Rhin** (*German*); ceci a été abondamment commenté **outre-Manche** (*in Britain; across the Channel*); **outre-Atlantique**, on est en période d'élections (*in America; across the Atlantic*); le Sénat **passe outre** au véto que le Président a promis d'apporter à la loi (*ignore, disregard; defy*)

ouverture (*f*): on demanda l'**ouverture** d'une enquête (*opening*); l'**ouverture** des Philippines sur le monde occidental; un gouvernement d'**ouverture** vers le centre (*openness, opening up*); les **ouvertures** faites en direction de Washington (*overtures*)

ouvrable (*adj*): le Président dispose de dix **jours ouvrables** pour signer le projet du Congrès, ou s'y opposer (*working day*)

ouvré <e> (*adj*): cette augmentation résulte d'une hausse des **jours ouvrés** (*day worked*)

ouvrier (*m*): l'écart entre l'**ouvrier** le plus mal payé et le cadre supérieur est énorme (*worker; workman*); 20 000 emplois d'**ouvrier qualifié** ne trouvent pas preneurs (*skilled worker*); un maçon qui est devenu **OS** [ouvrier spécialisé] dans l'automobile (*unskilled/semi-skilled worker*); (*adj*) la gauche est majoritaire dans les banlieues **ouvrières** (*working-class; industrial*)

P

pactole (*m*): contrat qui représente un vrai **pactole** pour la société de Courbevoie (*gold-mine; windfall*)

paiement (*m*): le **déficit des paiements courants** inquiète le gouvernement (*current account deficit*)

pallier: pour **pallier** cette honteuse carence (*offset, compensate for*)

palmarès (*m*): la société s'est hissée à la première place du **palmarès** de l'agro-alimentaire (*honours list, order of merit*)

panachage (*m*): l'électeur ne peut exprimer ni vote préférentiel ni **panachage** (*alteration by the voter of the names on the voting list by subtraction or replacement*)

panacher: cette fois-ci, ils vont sans doute '**panacher**' (*alter names on voting list; vote for candidates from different parties/voting lists*)

panoplie (*f*): toute une **panoplie** de mesures ont été proposées (*battery; range*)

pantoufle (*f*): il décide de rembourser sa '**pantoufle**' de Polytechnique (*cost of study at* Grande École)

pantoufler: chargé de mission à la DATAR, il **pantoufle** ensuite comme directeur général du Club Méditerranée; les hauts fonctionnaires, '**pantouflant**' dans le privé (*move from public to private sector*)

parachever: nous voulons **parachever** la construction de l'Europe (*complete*)

parachuter (*fam.*): la direction du parti l'a **parachuté** dans l'Orne, et il fut battu sans appel dans les élections (*impose outside candidate on a local electorate*)

paradis fiscal (*m*): les enquêteurs se heurtent au système des **paradis fiscaux** (*tax haven*)

parallèle (*adj*): URSS: l'**économie parallèle** réalise un chiffre d'affaires de 145 milliards de dollars (*unofficial/'black' economy*)

parapher: les trois ordonnances que le Premier ministre n'a pas voulu **parapher** (*sign, put a signature to*)

parc (*m*): le **parc** des hypermarchés s'est accru de 42 unités en 1989 (*stock; total number*)

pari (*m*): un **pari** économique, donc, mais aussi un défi politique (*challenge*); la France veut l'aider à **gagner le pari** du développement et de la démocratie (*achieve; meet the challenge*); la RFA **fait le pari** de l'ancrage à l'Ouest (*take a risk*)

paritaire (*adj*): les syndicats participent à la gestion **paritaire** des ASSEDIC (*joint*); une **commission mixte paritaire** a été chargée de proposer un texte (*joint committee with equal representation*)

parole (*f*): il va **prendre la parole** au nom de ses collègues (*speak*); elle bénéficia d'une **libération sur parole** (*release from prison on parole*)

parquet (*m*): le **parquet** du tribunal de Douai a ordonné l'ouverture d'une enquête (*public prosecutor's department*); **sur le parquet**, les titres s'échangeaient à un rythme soutenu (*on the Stock Exchange trading floor*)

parrainage (*m*): il a insisté sur le **parrainage** du Premier ministre, qui s'engage personnellement (*support; sponsorship*); le **parrainage publicitaire** envahit les écrans (*sponsoring for publicity purposes*)

parrainer: une liste de 500 élus **parrainant** la candidature de l'écologiste (*back, support, sponsor*)

part (*f*): la **part** des hydrocarbures dans les exportations est tombée à 50% (*share, proportion*); de nouveaux pays producteurs ont pris de grosses **parts de marché** à son détriment (*market share*); en Allemagne, ces deux firmes **se taillent la part du lion** (*take the lion's share; monopolize*); la Finlande est membre **à part entière** (*full member*); **de part et d'autre**, la volonté de paix l'emporte sur le ressentiment (*on both sides*); il a **fait part de** son intention de démissionner (*announce*); six terroristes ont **pris part à** cette action (*take part; participate*)

partage (*m*): le vote de l'ONU sur le **partage** de la Palestine (*division; partition*); à moins d'envisager un **partage du pouvoir** avec les communistes (*power-sharing*); cette réforme remporta un succès **sans partage** (*unqualified; unquestioned*)

partagé <e> (*adj*): les spécialistes restent très **partagés** (*divided; in disagreement*)

partenaire (*m*): le ministre discuta de l'affaire avec tous les **partenaires sociaux** (*management and labour; boss and unions*)

partenariat (*m*): un **partenariat** avec une banque anglaise est près d'être conclu (*partnership; association*)

parti (*m*): le **parti** conservateur a triomphé à nouveau (*party*); il hésitait à **prendre parti** dans la dispute (*take sides*)

participation (*f*): les deux complices nient leur **participation** dans l'affaire (*involvement*); on a développé un système de **participation du personnel** aux grandes orientations de l'entreprise (*worker participation*); certains actionnaires ont déjà accru leurs **participations** (*share/stock holding, stake*); l'ordonnance sur la **participation des salariés aux bénéfices des entreprises** (*profit-sharing scheme*); cette faible **participation électorale** impose un second tour (*electoral turn-out*)

participer: cette réforme **participe** aussi d'un dessein plus ambitieux (*be part/ an aspect of*)

particulier (*m*): le nombre de **particuliers** à détenir directement des actions; les mesures concernent les **particuliers** et les entreprises (*individual; private person*)

partie (*f*): il faut faire venir les **parties belligérantes** autour d'une table (*warring faction; both sides*); les avocats de la **partie adverse** (*the opposing party*); des groupes qui appartiennent au mouvement ou qui **ont partie liée** avec lui (*be linked with*); l'État, l'autre **partie prenante** dans cette affaire; les Chinois sont **partie prenante** à tout règlement cambodgien (*concerned party; participant*)

partie civile (*f*): l'avocat de la **partie civile** a demandé que soient prises en compte certaines circonstances atténuantes (*defence in civil action*); si le dossier est classé sans suite, le plaignant peut **se constituer partie civile** (*institute a civil action*)

partiel <-elle> (*adj*): des **élections partielles** auront lieu dans le Doubs (*by-election*); le remplacement d'emplois stables par des emplois **à temps**

partiel (*part-time*)

partisan (*m*): les plus chauds **partisans** de la peine de mort (*advocate; supporter*); il s'est déclaré **partisan** d'un renforcement de l'autorité du chef de l'État (*in favour, for*); (*adj*) quelle que soit leur préférence **partisane** (*party political, party*)

pas (*m*): la production industrielle semble **marquer le pas** (*remain stationary, make no progress*); un débat où l'idéologie préconçue **prend le pas** sur les faits (*override, take precedence over*)

passation (*f*): au moment de la **passation des pouvoirs** à l'Hôtel Matignon (*transfer of power*)

passer: il faut utiliser différents moyens pour **faire passer** son message (*get/ put across*)

passible (*adj*): un crime **passible** de la peine de mort (*punishable*)

passif (*m*): le **passif** atteint 33 millions de francs pour un chiffre d'affaires de 29 millions en 1988 (*liabilities; deficit*); il a un **passif** très lourd de truand et de malfaiteur (*past; criminal record*)

patente (*f*): la **patente** a été remplacée par la taxe professionnelle (*tax on business*)

pâtir: le tourisme a **pâti** de la désaffection des étrangers (*suffer*)

patrimoine (*m*): la fiscalité qui frappe le **patrimoine** (*heritage; estate*); la publication du **patrimoine** des hommes politiques (*financial situation; personal fortune*); la remise à niveau du **patrimoine** des logements sociaux (*original stock*)

patron (*m*): le **patron** d'usine accueillit les invités (*boss*)

patronal <e> (*adj*): deux propositions faites par l'organisation **patronale** (*employer, employing*); la cotisation dite '**patronale**' (*of the employer*)

paumé (*m/adj*) (*fam.*): les '**paumés de la conjoncture**' ne se contentent pas d'être des assistés (*victim of economic conditions*)

pauvreté (*f*): la lutte contre la **pauvreté** dans les grandes villes (*poverty*)

pavillon (*m*): les armateurs placent souvent leurs navires sous **pavillon de complaisance** (*flag of convenience*)

payant <e> (*adj*): la stratégie s'est révélée **payante** (*profitable*)

paysage (*m*): dans un **paysage** socio-économique profondément remanié (*environment, context*)

peaufiner: le système a été constamment **peaufiné**; son image, **peaufinée** par son entourage (*polish, perfect*)

pécé (*m/adj*) (*fam.*): une ville traditionnellement d'obédience **pécé** (*Communist; of the PCF*)

peine (*f*): il a purgé sa **peine** à la prison de Melun (*prison sentence*)

peleton (*m*): il figure dans le **peleton de tête** des pays exportateurs (*leading* *group*)

pénal <e> (*adj*): la population **pénale** est en hausse de 1% par rapport au chiffre de l'an dernier (*penal; criminal*)

pencher [se]: il **s'est penché** longtemps sur la question (*study, examine*)

pénitentiaire (*adj*): l'administration **pénitentiaire** voit ses crédits augmentés d'un tiers (*prison, penal*)

pénurie (*f*): certains biens, sujets à de fréquentes **pénuries** (*shortage; scarcity, lack*); la **pénurie alimentaire** est la plus grave de l'histoire du pays (*food shortage; famine*)

percée (*f*): la firme a ainsi réalisé une **percée** de taille sur le marché américain; il a qualifié cet accord de '**percée** historique' (*breakthrough*)

percepteur (*m*): on protestait contre la suppression du poste de **percepteur** (*collector of taxes*)

perception (*f*): le ministre veut moderniser la **perception** de la redevance (*collection*); il est allé à la **Perception** payer ses contributions (*tax collector's office*)

percevoir: une baisse des revenus **perçus** par l'État (*receive, earn*); la façon dont il est **perçu** par les différents partenaires sociaux (*perceive, see*)

perchoir (*m*): l'ancien Premier ministre a été investi pour le '**perchoir**' (*office/ seat of President of the National Assembly*)

perdition (*f*): il prenait la tête de la société **en perdition** (*in a critical condition*)

pérennité (*f*): des incidents qui prouvent la **pérennité** du sentiment raciste (*permanence*); cette prise de contrôle devra assurer la **pérennité** de la firme rouennaise (*survival*)

performant <e> (*adj*): les 200 entreprises les plus grosses ou les plus **performantes** (*efficient; competitive*)

périodicité (*f*): la **périodicité** peut être semestrielle ou trimestrielle (*periodicity; interval, frequency*)

péripétie (*f*): gare à ceux qui n'y verraient qu'une **péripétie**!; les **péripéties** de la campagne électorale (*incident, episode*)

permanence (*f*): dans les **permanences** des partis de l'opposition (*committee-room; headquarters*); le député tient des **permanences** dans sa circonscription ('*surgery', consultation*); devant la **permanence** et l'ampleur des troubles en Cisjordanie (*permanence, continual presence*)

permis (*m*): un **permis** de construire a été accordé (*permit, licence*)

perpétuité (*f*): condamné à la prison **à perpétuité** (*for a life sentence*)

perquisition (*f*): la police a opéré une **perquisition** chez l'accusé (*search of premises*); ils ont obtenu un **mandat de perquisition** (*search warrant*)

personne (*f*): l'abattement est plafonné à 30 000F pour une **personne morale** (*legal/corporate entity*); cette allocation est soumise à un plafond de

70 000F pour une **personne physique** (*individual*)

perspective (*f*): la **perspective** d'un retour au pouvoir des Travaillistes (*prospect*); **dans la perspective** des élections de 1988 (*in the light of, bearing in mind; with a view to*)

perte (*f*): les **pertes** se sont élevées à 70 millions de francs (*financial loss*); l'entreprise avait enregistré 200 millions de **pertes d'exploitation** (*operating loss*); pour compenser la **perte sèche** de 1,36 milliards de francs (*total loss*); une grande partie des créances ont été **passées par pertes et profits** (*write off*)

perturbation (*f*): il y aura de nouvelles **perturbations** dans le trafic aérien (*disruption*)

perturber: les services des Finances **perturbés** par des arrêts de travail (*disrupt; disorganize*)

pervers <e> (*adj*): les réformes ont engendré des effets **pervers** (*corrupt; dangerous*)

peser: le groupe **pèse** un demi-milliard de francs de chiffre d'affaires (*be worth/valued at*)

petit porteur (*m*): 400 000 **petits porteurs** sont devenus actionnaires de TF1 (*small shareholder*)

phare (*m*): la revendication-**phare** des gardiens de prison n'a pas été acceptée (*chief, principal*)

pic (*m*): le **pic** ayant été atteint en 1985, avec 36,6% (*peak-level; high point*); la rencontre de Bruxelles **tombe à pic** (*come at the right time*)

pièce (*f*): un nouveau ministère à cet effet a été créé **de toutes pièces** (*invent; create from nothing*)

pied (*m*): la société de Rennes a **mis à pied** plus de 400 employés (*lay off; dismiss*); le patron décida la **mise à pied** immédiate des grévistes (*laying-off; suspension; dismissal*); cette décision tranche en faveur des **pieds-noirs** et d'autres rapatriés d'Afrique (*Algerian of European stock*)

pierre (*f*): la Constitution reste la **pierre angulaire** de l'édifice politique américain (*corner-stone*)

piétiner: alors que le dialogue inter-cambodgien **piétine**; le manque de crédits a fait **piétiner** le mouvement (*make little/slow progress*)

pignon (*m*): si on est une société **ayant pignon sur rue** (*successful; prominent, well-established*)

pilote (*adj*): Reims et Angers, villes-**pilotes** en matière de transports en commun (*innovative; leading*); la ville de Rennes mène une **expérience-pilote** dans ce domaine (*experiment*); le tourisme, secteur **pilote** de l'économie (*leading*)

piquet (*m*): on a installé un **piquet de grève** devant l'entrée de l'établissement (*strike picket*)

109

placarder: ils **placardent** sur les murs des milliers d'affiches (*stick up, post*)

place (*f*): la **place** française a moins baissé que les autres (*Stock Exchange/ Market*); leurs efforts pour dénoncer les **pouvoirs en place** (*powers that be, the government in office*); la **mise en place** de telles mesures serait très coûteuse (*putting into practice/effect*); on va procéder à une inspection **sur place** (*on site*)

placement (*m*): ces actions constituent un **placement** très sûr (*investment*); cinq cents offres d'emploi par semaine arrivent au **bureau de placement** (*employment office*)

plafond (*m*): le **plafond** pour le calcul des cotisations à la Sécurité sociale (*ceiling*); à 3,41F, le DMark est à 2 centimes de son **cours-plafond** (*ceiling rate*)

plafonnement (*m*): il préconise un **plafonnement** des dépenses électorales (*setting of upper limit/ceiling*); le **plafonnement** des recettes publicitaires (*levelling-off*)

plafonner: une retraite qui serait **plafonnée** à trois fois le SMIC (*set a maximum/ceiling/upper limit*); les prix de l'immobilier en région parisienne ont **plafonné** en 1989 (*reach a ceiling; level off*)

plaider: le Président **plaide** pour une coopération étroite entre leurs deux pays (*appeal*); circonstance qui **plaide** en faveur de cette dernière hypothèse (*support, argue*); il a **plaidé coupable** dans une affaire de fraude boursière (*plead guilty*)

plaidoyer (*m*): il s'est livré à un vibrant **plaidoyer** en faveur du désarmement (*defence, plea*)

plainte (*f*): une **plainte en diffamation** de quatre policiers contre *Le Républicain lorrain* (*libel suit*); ces agressions ont suscité plus de cinquante **plaintes en justice** (*complaint; legal action*); il a **porté plainte** pour incitation à la haine raciale (*lodge a complaint*)

plan (*m*): victime d'une baisse de son **plan de charge**, liée au ralentissement du programme nucléaire (*order-book*); le conseil municipal a approuvé la modification du POS [**plan d'occupation des sols**] de la commune (*cadastral plan; land register*); le **plan social** offre à tout licencié 200 000F de dédommagement (*recovery plan*)

planche (*f*): il n'entend pas financer le progrès social par la **planche à billets** (*printing of money*)

plancher (*m*): le Franc tombe près de son cours **plancher** (*bottom, minimum; floor*); la disparition de la **peine-plancher** (*minimum sentence*)

plancher: un groupe de spécialistes vont **plancher** sur le rapport (*study in detail; work on*)

planification (*f*): la **planification** à la française est de conception assez souple (*economic planning*)

planifier: l'explosion d'hier avait dû être **planifiée** depuis longtemps (*plan*)

planning (*m*): on a établi un **planning**, visualisant les réservations des appartements sur une période de trois mois (*programme, schedule*)

plat <e> (*adj*): le ministre propose de **mettre à plat** ce problème insoluble (*study, examine*); la grève a eu le mérite de permettre une véritable **mise à plat** du problème (*study, examination*)

plate-forme (*f*): il faudra qu'il applique la **plate-forme** RPR-UDF (*electoral platform, programme*)

plébisciter: le référendum du 27 juin, au cours duquel les militants socialistes l'avaient **plébiscité** (*elect by an overwhelming majority*)

plein emploi (*m*): il a obtenu une croissance soutenue qui a mené l'économie au **plein emploi** (*full employment*)

pléthorique (*adj*): la bureaucratie, souvent surpayée, est devenue **pléthorique** (*excessively large; over-staffed*)

plus-value (*f*): l'État réalisera ainsi une **plus-value** substantielle (*profit*); la **plus-value** sera alors totalement exonérée (*capital gain*)

PME (*f*): une **PME** d'Orléans se développe en élargissant la gamme de ses produits (*small/medium-sized company*)

PMI (*f*): l'État encourage l'expansion des **petites et moyennes industries** [PMI] pour faire contrepoids aux grands groupes (*small/medium-sized industry*)

point (*m*): un an après, il **fait le point** de la situation (*take stock*); il a **fait le point** sur la politique du gouvernement (*explain*); ils ont **mis au point** un système sans faille (*perfect*); la Présidence diffusa une **mise au point** pour dissiper les malentendus (*statement to set the record straight/clarify a point*); lors de son **point de presse** hebdomadaire (*meeting with the press; press briefing*)

pointage (*m*): ils ont cru, d'après leurs **pointages**, que leur candidat serait élu; au dernier **pointage**, un train sur cinq circulait en région parisienne (*count; calculation*)

pointe (*f*): après une **pointe**, le titre a fait marche arrière (*high spot; peak*); le Japon, **à la pointe** de l'innovation (*at the forefront*)

pointer: il ne lui reste plus qu'à aller **pointer** au bureau de chômage (*check in, sign on*); son mandat de député non-renouvelé, il a dû **pointer au chômage** (*register at the unemployment office*)

pointu <e> (*adj*): des formations spécifiques, très **pointues** (*advanced, specialized*)

pôle (*m*): la création de **pôles de croissance** soigneusement situés (*growth centre*)

polémique (*f*): la décision suscita de vives **polémiques** en Grande-Bretagne (*debate, argument; controversy*)

polémiquer: il évite de **polémiquer** avec la direction du parti (*debate; indulge in polemics*)

111

police (*f*): ayant souscrit une **police d'assurance** tous risques, il s'était cru protégé en cas d'accident (*insurance policy*); les contraventions relèvent du **tribunal de police** (*police court*); la **police des mœurs** enquête sur les affaires crapuleuses (*vice squad*)

politicien <-enne> (*adj*): des manœuvres **politiciennes** à courte vue (*politicking*); il dédaigne souverainement la **politique politicienne** (*politicking*)

politique (*f*): la **politique du pire** jouée par son état-major est seule responsable de la défaite de la droite (*painting things as black as possible*)

polyvalent <e> (*adj*): il s'agissait d'une brigade d'intervention **polyvalente** (*multi-purpose*)

poncif (*m*): un discours plein de **poncifs** et de lieux-communs (*cliché*)

ponction (*f*): les salariés risquent de subir une nouvelle **ponction** sur leurs revenus (*cut; reduction*); une inflation maîtrisée, et des **ponctions fiscales** en baisse (*taxation*)

ponctionner: l'impôt sur le revenu en France **ponctionne** moins de 6% de la richesse nationale (*take out, withdraw*)

ponctuel <-elle> (*adj*): l'erreur serait de se contenter de décisions **ponctuelles** et hâtives; il procède par petites touches, en multipliant les réformes **ponctuelles** (*isolated, individual*)

ponctuellement: il peut convaincre ses adversaires de se rallier **ponctuellement** à tel ou tel projet (*in individual/specific cases*)

pondérer: pour ce calcul, on a retenu sept critères, en les **pondérant** (*weight; give weighting to*); le vote majoritaire **pondéré** est le plus fréquent au Conseil des ministres (*weighted*)

porte-parole (*m*): selon le **porte-parole** de la commission d'enquête (*spokesman*)

porte-à-faux: le Président est **en porte-à-faux** après Irangate; ceci place le PCF **en porte-à-faux** (*out of step; in a delicate position*)

portée (*f*): la **portée** de ses remarques n'a pas échappé à ses interlocuteurs (*significance*); les engins de **portée** intermédiaire braqués sur l'Asie (*range*)

portefeuille (*m*): le chef de l'État lui a confié le difficile **portefeuille** de l'Intérieur (*ministerial office*); il gérait un **portefeuille** d'un montant de 2 milliards de francs (*share portfolio*)

porter: on a remarqué l'intérêt qu'on **porte à** cette affaire (*attach to*); le montant des allocations de fins de droits est **porté à** 63F par jour (*raise*); la conversation a **porté sur** les problèmes de l'Afrique australe (*treat/deal with*); l'analyse **porte sur** près de 3 000 cas (*concern*)

porteur <-euse> (*adj*): l'industrie du parfum, dopée par une conjoncture très **porteuse** (*buoyant*); des thèmes **porteurs**, des hommes crédibles

(*convincing; persuasive*)

position (*f*): il **prend position** contre la dénucléarisation dc l'Europe (*adopt a stand; declare oneself*); sa **prise de position** en faveur des minorités opprimées (*stand; position*)

positionner [se]: ICI essaie de **se positionner** sur ce nouveau créneau; il cherche à **se positionner** en vue des prochaines élections (*find a place/ niche; establish a position*)

poste (*m*): la plupart des autres **postes** du budget communal (*heading; item*); en 1995, six millions de **postes de travail** utiliseront l'informatique (*post; position, job*)

postuler: il a **postulé** une place de représentant (*apply for, make application for*)

potiche (*f*): il n'a pas l'intention d'être un PDG-**potiche** (*figure-head*)

pots-de-vin (*m pl*): toucher des **pots-de-vin** pour l'obtention de marchés; les poursuites pour versement de **pots-de-vin** (*bribe; backhander*)

poulain (*m*): toutefois il n'est pas le **poulain** de l'appareil départemental du parti (*protégé*)

poumon (*m*): l'Asie, nouveau **poumon** de l'économie mondiale (*lung; dynamic centre*)

pourparlers (*m pl*): un échec des **pourparlers** le placerait dans une situation délicate; des **pourparlers** indirects entre Kaboul et Islamabad (*talks; negotiations*)

pourrissement (*m*): ces affrontements illustrent le **pourrissement** de la situation (*worsening, deterioration*)

poursuite (*f*): craignant sans doute la **poursuite** de l'agitation (*continuation*); on a engagé des **poursuites judiciaires** pour factures non-réglées (*legal proceedings*)

poursuivre: il a été **poursuivi en justice** pour fraude; désormais, ils seront **poursuivis** devant les tribunaux (*prosecute*); [se] la campagne de dénigration **se poursuit** (*continue, carry on*)

pourvoi (*m*): le défenseur a déposé un **pourvoi en cassation** contre le verdict de la cour (*appeal*)

pourvoir: 600 emplois sont créés pour **pourvoir** aux besoins immédiats (*satisfy*); 453 sièges parlementaires sont encore à **pourvoir** (*fill, allot*); il y a 4 000 postes d'infirmière **non pourvus** (*unfilled*)

pourvoyeur (*m*): ce pays, principal **pourvoyeur** en armes de l'armée irakienne (*supplier*)

poussée (*f*): une nouvelle **poussée**, après une période d'accalmie (*progression; growth, increase*)

pouvoir (*m*): le **pouvoir** s'est ressaisi face à l'agitation universitaire (*government*); les ménages profitent de gains de **pouvoir d'achat**

consécutifs à une progression des salaires (*purchasing power*); les **pouvoirs publics** ont décrété le couvre-feu (*authorities*)

pratiquer [se]: inférieurs aux taux **pratiqués** la semaine dernière; les prix **qui se pratiquent** à Paris sont très chers (*current, prevailing*)

préalable (*m*): sa volonté de négocier sans **préalable** (*pre-condition*); ils ont fait arrêter **au préalable** un certain nombre de gens (*first of all; as a preliminary*); (*adj*) il exige le retrait **préalable** des troupes soviétiques (*prior*); le Pakistan en fait une **condition préalable** d'une normalisation de ses relations (*pre-condition*)

préalablement: si on n'a pas donné **préalablement** son accord (*already, previously*)

préavis (*m*): le licenciement sans **préavis** de 19 ouvriers (*warning, notice*); le syndicat des cheminots a **déposé un préavis de grève** pour le 15 septembre (*give notice of strike*)

précaire (*adj*): une société où l'emploi est si **précaire**; le recours aux emplois 'précaires' [temporaires, ou à durée déterminée] (*insecure, uncertain*)

précarisation (*f*): la CGT refuse ce qu'elle appelle ce 'processus de **précarisation** de l'emploi' (*endangering; putting at risk*)

précarité (*f*): la **précarité** de l'emploi s'est accentuée (*insecurity*); qui condamne à la **précarité** des milliers de citoyens (*very poor living standards*)

préciser: les détails seront **précisés** ultérieurement par décret (*announce; make clear*); [se] si l'offre **se précise** d'ici à la fin du mois (*be confirmed*)

précision (*f*): le communiqué n'a fourni aucune **précision** (*precise detail; further explanation*)

préconiser: il **préconisa** un allègement de l'horaire hebdomadaire du travail (*advocate, advise*)

prédateur (*m*): toutes les valeurs susceptibles d'intéresser les grands 'prédateurs' (*corporate predator*)

préfectoral <e> (*adj*): il rêvait à une carrière **préfectorale** (*pertaining to the office of* Préfet); des **arrêtés préfectoraux** appellent aux économies d'eau (*edict from the* Préfet)

préfecture (*f*): la circulation a été interdite par un arrêté pris par la **préfecture** (*office of the* Préfet); au chef-lieu du département, ou **Préfecture** (*prefecture; administrative centre of* département); cela s'est passé à Marseille, devant la **préfecture** (*residence of the* Préfet); Thionville, chef-lieu d'arrondissement et **sous-préfecture** (*sub-prefecture; administrative centre of* arrondissement)

Préfet (*m*): les maires ne craignent plus la tutelle du **Préfet** (*Prefect; administrative head of* département); le **Préfet de police** dépend hiérarchiquement du ministre de l'Intérieur (*Prefect of Police*)

préjudice (*m*): pour obtenir réparation du **préjudice** qui lui a été causé (*harm,* *damage, wrong*); l'attraction de Paris **porte préjudice** au développement des autres grands centres (*harm, prejudice*)

prélèvement (*m*): les **prélèvements** obligatoires — impôts et cotisations sociales — vont augmenter (*levy; deduction, stoppage*); il propose le **prélèvement à la source** de l'impôt direct (*deduction at source*); on règle la facture par **prélèvement automatique sur compte bancaire** (*direct debit of bank account*)

prélever: les versements peuvent être **prélevés** automatiquement sur un compte-chèques ou un livret (*deduct; deduct at source*)

préméditation (*f*): inculpé de meurtre **avec préméditation** (*premeditated*)

prépondérance (*f*): ceci leur y a garanti une **prépondérance** économique (*dominance; dominant position*)

prépondérant <e> (*adj*): il a joué un rôle **prépondérant** dans la recherche d'une solution pacifique (*important, major*)

préposé (*m*): le **préposé** des postes doit absolument vérifier votre identité (*official, employee*)

pré-retraite (*f*): de nouvelles règles pour les **pré-retraites** à mi-temps ont été publiées; le rythme des **départs en pré-retraite** se réduit (*early retirement*)

prérogative (*f*): il abuse des **prérogatives** présidentielles (*privilege, prerogative*)

présager: la victoire des conservateurs **laisse présager** que les réformes ne s'arrêteront pas là (*lead one to believe*)

présenter [se]: le maire décida de ne pas **se présenter** au scrutin du 25 septembre (*stand for election*)

présidence (*f*): date à laquelle débute la **présidence** française de la CEE (*chairmanship; presidency*); lors des élections à la **présidence** de la République (*presidency*)

président (*m*): c'est le **président-directeur général** lui-même qui annonça la nomination (*chairman and managing director*); mort de Félix Gouin, ancien **président du Conseil** (*Prime Minister under Third and Fourth Republics*)

présidentiable (*m*): il est, de l'avis de tous, le meilleur **présidentiable** (*potential president/candidate for presidency*)

présidentiel <-elle> (*adj*): les [élections] **présidentielles** de 1988 furent un triomphe pour la Gauche (*presidential elections*)

présomption (*f*): les dix journées de débats ont permis d'accumuler de lourdes **présomptions** contre lui (*presumption; evidence*)

presse (*f*): ce sera une année décisive pour la **presse écrite** (*press, newspaper industry*)

pressentir: le président des centristes a été **pressenti** dans la Somme (*propose* as candidate); la liste des **pressentis** s'allonge (*person whose name is put forward for office*)

pression (*f*): les magistrats dénoncent les **pressions** politiques dont ils sont l'objet (*pressure*); une aggravation de la **pression fiscale** (*tax burden/pressure*)

prestataire (*m*): les petits commerçants et les **prestataires de services** indépendants s'estiment lésés par cette loi (*operator; supplier of a service*)

prestation (*f*): on estime que les **prestations** des Postes sont devenues plus mauvaises (*service*); les **prestations** versées par la Sécurité sociale (*payment, benefit*)

présumé <e> (*adj*): l'assassin **présumé** a été écroué (*alleged, supposed; presumed*)

prêt (*m*): les **prêts au logement** comptent pour la moitié du bilan du Crédit Agricole; l'attribution de logements HLM et de **prêts immobiliers** (*housing loan*)

prétendu <e> (*adj*): une campagne de presse contre les **prétendus** excès de la politique commerciale de la CEE (*alleged, claimed*)

prétoire (*m*): les vrais fautifs seront — enfin — dans le **prétoire** (*court*)

prévaloir: il n'a pas **fait prévaloir** ses idées sur la question (*impose*); [se] il a pu **se prévaloir** du soutien de ses collègues (*profit, take advantage*); Tokyo a pu **se prévaloir** d'une très forte croissance (*claim; point to*)

prévenir: afin de **prévenir** toute augmentation du prix du brut (*anticipate*); afin de **prévenir** les dangers d'un nationalisme anti-russe (*guard against; prevent*)

préventif <-ive> (*adj*): en attendant, il a été gardé en **détention préventive**; cinq ans de prison, dont un ferme — couvert par **la préventive** (*custody while awaiting trial*)

prévention (*f*): le projet de loi relatif à la **prévention** du licenciement économique (*prevention*)

prévenu (*m*): la lenteur de l'appareil judiciaire pénalise les simples **prévenus** en attente de jugement (*person awaiting trial on criminal charge*); le **prévenu**, confronté aux témoins, reconnut les faits (*accused person; defendant*)

prévisible (*adj*): l'évolution de la situation est difficilement **prévisible** (*foreseeable; predictable*)

prévision (*f*): la **prévision** d'une croissance de 6% en 1993 paraît optimiste (*forecast*)

prévisionnel <-elle> (*adj*): un chiffre d'affaires **prévisionnel** pour 1992 de 200 millions de dollars (*anticipated, forecast*)

prévisionniste (*m*): les **prévisionnistes** parient sur une nouvelle explosion du chômage (*economic forecaster*)

prévoir: les accords **prévoient** deux réunions par an; la loi de 1987 **prévoit** deux possibilités, sans en avantager aucune (*provide for, envisage*)

prévoyance (*f*): l'assurance suppose chez l'intéressé un esprit de **prévoyance** (*forethought; provision for the future*)

primaire (*f/adj*): on désignera, dans des [élections] **primaires**, le candidat unique; l'éventualité de **primaires** à gauche n'est pas exclue (*primary; preliminary election; eliminating contest*)

prime (*f*): le syndicat réclame le versement d'une **prime** d'ancienneté (*bonus*); les élections municipales **donnent une prime** à l'opposition (*encourage; favour*); on peut résilier un contrat d'assurance quand il y a majoration de **prime** (*insurance premium*)

prise (*f*): le prolétariat n'a plus de **prise** sur les secteurs-clés de la production (*control*); la France est **aux prises** avec l'âpre concurrence de ses voisins européens (*faced by; confronted with*)

privé (*m*): le retour au [secteur] **privé** de Rhône-Poulenc lui permettra de se redéployer (*private ownership*)

priver: la récente loi les **prive** de certains droits essentiels (*deprive*); [se] l'Opposition **ne s'est pas privée** de dénoncer la lâcheté du gouvernement (*have no hesitation*)

privilégié <e> (*adj*): l'octroi de prêts sans garantie et à des taux **privilégiés** (*generous, very favourable*)

privilégier: faut-il **privilégier** la solidarité sociale aux dépens d'une relance de l'économie? (*give preference; favour*)

prix (*m*): ils diffusent auprès des pharmaciens des **prix conseillés** pour leurs produits (*manufacturer's recommended price; MRP*); la hausse des **prix de gros** s'est accélérée (*wholesale price*); le **prix de revient** est donc de 35F pièce (*cost price; manufacturing cost*)

probant <e> (*adj*): d'ores et déjà la démonstration paraît peu **probante** (*convincing*)

probatoire (*adj*): pendant une période **probatoire** (*experimental; probationary*); il s'était soustrait aux obligations du **contrôle probatoire** (*probation*)

procédé (*m*): nous nous sommes refusés à de tels **procédés** (*behaviour, conduct; methods*); le **procédé** est protégé par un brevet exclusif (*process*)

procéder: les Américains pourraient **procéder à** un essai nucléaire; il vient d'être **procédé à** une expulsion de diplomates syriens (*carry out*)

procédure (*f*): entamée depuis plus d'un an, la **procédure** pourrait bientôt aboutir (*process*); les écologistes entament une **procédure** contre les sociétés pollueuses (*legal proceedings*); réformer le Code pénal mais aussi amender la **procédure** (*legal procedure*)

procès (*m*): le **procès** s'est déroulé à huis-clos (*trial*); dans un véritable réquisitoire, il a **fait le procès** du gouvernement (*put in the dock, criticize*)

procès-verbal (*m*): extrait du **procès-verbal** des délibérations du conseil municipal (*minutes; written record*); la contractuelle de service lui a dressé un **proces-verbal pour stationnement interdit** (*parking-ticket*)

processus (*m*): il faut relancer le **processus** d'union; le **processus** de paix au Proche-Orient (*process*)

prochain <e> (*adj*): **prochain** rétablissement du trafic ferroviaire avec l'Algérie (*impending; in the near future*)

proche (*m/adj*): les **proches** du Premier ministre le nient formellement (*person/source close to*)

procuration (*f*): il a une **procuration** sur le compte en banque de sa femme (*authorization; power of attorney*); il est possible aux Français d'outre-mer de voter **par procuration** (*by proxy*)

procureur (*m*): le **procureur** a requis trois ans de prison ferme pour l'accusé (*public prosecutor*); le **procureur de la République** décidera des suites à donner (*State Prosecutor*); ancien **procureur-général** près la cour d'appel de Dijon (*public prosecutor*)

productivité (*f*): la tâche du nouveau directeur financier: renouer avec la **productivité** (*efficiency; productiveness*)

produit (*m*): que fera-t-on du **produit** de cette privatisation? (*proceeds*); la Belgique exporte 70% de son **produit intérieur brut** (*gross domestic product; GDP*); la progression du PNB [**produit national brut**] a été de 1,7% en RFA (*gross national product; GNP*)

professionnel <-elle> (*adj*): tous les loueurs en meublé sont soumis à la **taxe professionnelle** (*business licence tax*)

profit (*m*): pour améliorer le **profit** des entreprises (*profitability*); le Président ne peut que s'effacer **au profit** du Premier ministre (*in favour of; behind*)

programmation (*f*): le PS préconise une **loi de programmation** scolaire sur dix ans (*planning law*)

progression (*f*): la forte **progression** dans les ventes de magnétoscopes (*increase*)

projet (*m*): la mise en chantier d'un **projet** libéral susceptible d'attirer des électeurs (*programme*); avec l'annonce officielle du **projet de rachat** de la société française (*projected acquisition*); ils menacent de ne pas voter le **projet de loi** gouvernemental (*proposed legislation, bill*)

prolongation (*f*): il souhaite obtenir une **prolongation** de la trêve (*extension, continuation*)

prolonger: l'état d'urgence a été **prolongé** de six mois (*extend*)

promotion (*f*): il est sorti major de sa **promotion** à HEC (*year, intake*); le poste sera pourvu par **promotion** interne (*promotion*)

promouvoir: il a été **promu** au grade d'adjudant-chef (*promote, raise*)

prôner: la politique **prônée** par le gouvernement en matière d'immigration (*extol; put forward*)

prononcé (*m*): au moment du **prononcé** du verdict (*announcement, pronouncing*)

prononcer [se]: la Cour suprême **se prononcera** sur leur sort (*decide, give a verdict*); les Polonais **se prononcent** les 4 et 18 juin (*vote, go to the polls*); 38% des sondés **ne se prononcent pas** (*be undecided in opinion poll; express no opinion*)

pronostic (*m*): son **pronostic** de croissance a été révisé à la baisse (*forecast*); le **pronostic de vie** d'un malade frappé du Sida (*life expectancy*)

pronostiquer: tous deux **pronostiquent** une aggravation de la tension dans le pays (*forecast; foresee*)

proportionnel <-elle> (*adj*): le scrutin majoritaire avec une dose de [représentation] **proportionnelle** (*proportional representation*); les sièges de conseiller général sont désignés **à la proportionnelle** (*by proportional representation*); il y a peu de partisans de la '**proportionnelle intégrale**' (*strict PR*)

proposition (*f*): un certain nombre de **propositions** ont déjà été faites (*proposal, suggestion*); la **proposition de loi** émane d'un groupe de socialistes (*private member's bill*)

propriétaire (*m*): nouvelle loi sur le logement: les **propriétaires** mécontents (*landlord; owner*); plus de la moitié des Français sont **propriétaires** de leur résidence principale (*owner*); 70% d'entre eux sont **propriétaires** (*home-owner*)

prorogation (*f*): Nicaragua: **prorogation** de la grève (*continuation; extension*)

proroger: le gouvernement a annoncé qu'il **proroge** de 30 jours supplémentaires la trêve (*extend*)

protection (*f*): il a gagné le poste grâce à des **protections** (*influence; string-pulling*); la **protection sociale** [sécurité sociale, retraite, chômage] (*State-provided social protection*)

protocole (*m*): un **protocole d'accord** a été signé entre les employés grévistes et la direction (*outline agreement*)

provenance (*f*): nous avons pu nous assurer de sa **provenance** (*place of origin*); d'importantes liquidités **en provenance** de l'étranger (*originating from*)

provenir: 45% de ses recettes **proviennent** de l'assurance-maladie (*come/originate from*)

province (*f*): série d'attentats dans la capitale et en **province** (*the provinces*)

provision (*f*): le non-paiement d'un chèque en raison d'une insuffisance de **provision** (*funds*); elle paya ses achats au moyen de chèques **sans provision** (*without provision; on an overdrawn account*)

119

provoquer: accident qui a **provoqué** la mort de 37 personnes (*cause*)

prud'homal <e> (*adj*): aux **élections prud'homales**, 54% des ouvriers se sont abstenus (*election to an industrial disputes tribunal*)

prud'homme (*m*): la CGT respecte la décision des **prud'hommes**, alors que la direction fait appel (*member of industrial disputes tribunal*); il fut condamné par le **tribunal des prud'hommes** pour le licenciement d'un employé (*industrial disputes tribunal*)

pudeur (*f*): auteur de plusieurs viols et d'**attentats à la pudeur** (*indecent assault*)

puissance (*f*): la **puissance publique** dispose de la faculté de s'y opposer (*public authority; State*); pour les exportateurs **en puissance**, il existe des types d'assurances faits sur mesure (*potential*)

pur <e> (*adj*): quelques militants **purs et durs** du PC et de la CGT; coordination des infirmières: la grève **pure et dure** (*rigid, uncompromising*)

purger: cette mesure vise les détenus **purgeant** une première condamnation (*serve a sentence for*)

Q

quadrangulaire (*f*): peut-être la **quadrangulaire** la plus attendue de ce deuxième tour (*four-way electoral contest*)

quadrillage (*m*): les forces de sécurité ont accentué leurs opérations de **quadrillage** (*close supervision*)

quadriller: tout le secteur est bouclé, et **quadrillé** par la police (*under tight police control*)

quadrimestre (*m*): au premier **quadrimestre**, la baisse de l'indice INSEE était de 1,2% par rapport aux quatre mois précédents (*four-month period*)

qualifier: des idées que d'aucuns ont **qualifiées** de subversives; Londres a **qualifié** de prématurée la décision palestinienne (*describe, term*)

qualité (*f*): en sa **qualité** de secrétaire de l'Ambassadeur (*capacity, position*); le ministre **a qualité** pour signer les traités (*be competent*)

quart-monde (*m*): toutes les catégories sociales, des oubliés du **quart-monde** aux nantis (*the Fourth World*)

quasi-: il a joui longtemps d'un **quasi**-monopole (*virtual*)

quasiment: l'adoption — **quasiment** sans débats — du projet de résolution du congrès (*virtually, almost*)

quémander: ils **quémandent** des subventions (*beg*)

quête (*f*): une presse de gauche, **en quête** de financement (*in need/search of*)

quêter: ils **quêtaient** dans la rue pour soutenir les grévistes (*collect money; collect*)

queue (*f*): la France est **en queue** des nations industrielles (*in last position, at the tail-end*)

quinquennal <e> (*adj*): l'élection européenne est **quinquennale** (*five-yearly*)

quinquennat (*m*): beaucoup souhaitent abandonner le septennat et établir le **quinquennat** (*five-year period of office*)

quittance (*f*): pour pouvoir être inscrit, on demande une **quittance** de loyer (*receipt; bill*)

qui-vive: les forces en présence restent **sur le qui-vive** (*at the ready*)

quolibet (*m*): il a quitté l'hémicycle sous les **quolibets** de ses adversaires (*jeer, insult*)

quote-part (*f*): au moment de régler, chacun a tenu à payer sa **quote-part** (*share, portion*)

quotidien (*m/adj*): des **quotidiens** diversement touchés par la grève (*daily newspaper*)

R

rabais (*m*): il a bénéficié d'un **rabais** de 80F par rapport au tarif (*discount*); cette initiative est perçue comme un système de formation **au rabais** (*cut-price; on the cheap*)

rachat (*m*): le **rachat** en bourse de 5% des actions de la firme (*purchase, take-over*); la société lyonnaise, autre candidat potentiel au **rachat** (*buy-out*)

racheter: une société du Mans **rachetée** par une firme allemande (*take over*)

radiation (*f*): d'où l'idée de pratiquer des **radiations** des listes de l'ANPE (*striking off*)

radicaliser [se]: les positions **se radicalisent** dans ce conflit (*become tougher; intensify, harden*)

radier: on parle de **radier** les jeunes chômeurs qui refuseraient un emploi; il vient d'être **radié** de la fonction publique (*remove; strike off*)

raffermir [se]: la monnaie américaine **s'est raffermie** hier (*strengthen*)

raffermissement (*m*): une bonne nouvelle qui a contribué au **raffermissement** de Wall Street (*strengthening; steadying*)

rafle (*f*): le juge ordonna une **rafle** de tous les établissements du quartier

(*raid; round-up*)

rage (*f*): la guerre **faisait rage** à ce moment-là (*rage*)

raid (*m*): le groupe a fait l'objet d'un **raid boursier** (*surprise bid on the Stock Exchange*); on assiste à une fièvre d'acquisitions et de **raids** dans le monde des assurances (*take-over bid*)

raider (*m*): la firme est constamment à l'affût des **raiders**; le groupe agro-alimentaire américain semble intéresser les **raiders** (*commercial predator; corporate raider*)

raidissement (*m*): comment s'expliquer le brusque **raidissement** de l'Iran?; face à chaque crise, le premier réflexe des dirigeants est le **raidissement** (*hardening of attitude; rigidity*)

raison (*f*): 47 semaines, **à raison** de 39 heures de travail par semaine (*at a rate of*); le tribunal a **donné raison** au plaignant (*find for/in favour of*); les **raisons sociales** successives du groupe (*corporate name*)

ralenti (*m*): les chantiers navals **tournent au ralenti** (*idle, tick over*)

ralentir: les dépenses des hôpitaux ont **ralenti** (*slow down*)

ralentissement (*m*): ceci s'est traduit par un **ralentissement** de la croissance (*slowing down*)

rallier: une bonne partie des autres a **rallié** les rangs de l'UDF (*join*); [se] la Grèce **s'est ralliée** au compromis adopté la semaine dernière (*side with; come round to*)

rallonge (*f*): le ministre a obtenu une **rallonge** de 100 millions de francs (*additional payment/grant*); il revendique une **rallonge** à l'accord salarial (*extension*)

ramener: le déficit de la Sécurité sociale est **ramené** à 4 milliards de francs (*reduce, bring down*)

rang (*m*): un diplomate **de haut rang** (*high-ranking*); il a mis **au rang** de ses objectifs prioritaires la réduction du chômage (*among*)

ranger [se]: finalement il **s'est rangé** à l'argument de ses collègues (*come round to; fall in with*)

rapatrié (*m/adj*): les mesures prises en faveur des **rapatriés** (*repatriated person*)

rapatrier: les bénéfices seront **rapatriés** en France (*bring home/back capital investment*)

rappel (*m*): Bonn annonce le **rappel** de son chargé d'affaires (*recall*); à la suite d'une augmentation, il a touché un **rappel** de 2 000F (*back-pay*)

rappeler: les Douze **rappellent** leurs ambassadeurs (*recall*)

rapport (*m*): le **rapport** établira la vérité sur l'affaire (*report*); il a quelques **maisons de rapport** (*investment property*); le **rapport cours-bénéfice** de ce titre est de 12,6 en avril (*price-earnings ratio*)

rapporter: l'impôt sur le capital **rapporte** 100 milliards par an (*bring in*)

rapporteur (*m*): nommé **rapporteur** de la Commission des finances (*chairman of a committee*); le **rapporteur** d'un projet de loi (*sponsor of a bill*)

rapprochement (*m*): le **rapprochement** franco-turc intervenu récemment (*reconciliation; bringing together*); l'accord vise à favoriser des **rapprochements d'entreprise** (*collaboration; association*)

rapprocher: d'abord il faudrait **rapprocher** les taux de TVA (*bring closer together*); [se] deux géants de l'édition vont **se rapprocher**, en échangeant des participations (*collaborate; come together*)

raréfier [se]: les acheteurs solvables **se raréfient** (*become rare/scarce*)

rassemblement (*m*): créant un large **rassemblement** de tous ceux qui sont sincèrement européens (*union; grouping; party*)

raté (*m*): les **ratés** de la croissance (*stop and start; misfiring*)

ratissage (*m*): lors d'une opération de **ratissage** de l'armée israélienne (*thorough search*)

ratisser: la police **ratisse large** après l'attentat revendiqué par les séparatistes (*search widely; comb an area*)

rattachement (*m*): le **rattachement** définitif de la Sarre à l'Allemagne en 1957 (*uniting, joining to*)

ravitailler [se]: la France **se ravitaille** difficilement en sources énergétiques (*supply/equip oneself*)

raz-de-marée (*m*): le **raz-de-marée** socialiste n'épargne pas le Midi (*big electoral swing; massive vote*)

réactualisation (*f*): on a effectué une **réactualisation** des données de l'INSEE (*updating*)

réactualiser: nous **réactualisons** tous nos chiffres au 31 décembre (*bring up to date; update*)

réalisation (*f*): c'est la **réalisation** d'un rêve vieux de 20 ans (*realization*); le ministre souligna les **réalisations** de son gouvernement (*achievement*)

réaliser: les bénéfices **réalisés** sur les ventes d'armes (*achieve; obtain*); les sondages **réalisés** ces derniers mois; la Grande-Bretagne **réalise** les deux tiers de son commerce avec l'Europe (*carry out*)

réaménagement (*m*): le ministre réclame un **réaménagement** de la fiscalité des carburants (*revision; restructuring*)

rebond (*m*): baisse du chômage, **rebond** de la production industrielle (*improvement; increase*)

rebondissement (*m*): il y a eu un **rebondissement** hier dans l'affaire Greenpeace; sauf **rebondissement** de dernière minute (*fresh development*)

recaser: le tiers seulement des ouvriers licenciés ont pu être **recasés** (*re-*

employ)

recel (*m*): impliqué dans de nombreuses affaires de **recel** (*handling and receiving stolen goods*)

receler: le désert **recèle** d'importants potentiels encore inexploités (*conceal; contain*)

receleur (*m*): le butin fut retrouvé dans la cave d'un **receleur** notoire (*receiver of stolen goods*)

recensement (*m*): on a procédé à un **recensement** des habitants du 'township' (*census, count*)

recenser: plus de 200 offres d'emploi ont été **recensées** (*compile a register of*); aucune victime n'a été **recensée** (*report*)

recentrage (*m*): le **recentrage** de la gauche opéré par le Président (*occupation of centre ground; centrality*); il confirme le **recentrage** du groupe sur l'agro-alimentaire; le groupe achève son **recentrage** en vendant sa filiale suisse (*concentration*)

recentrer: une priorité absolue: **recentrer** la France (*move to the centre; occupy centre ground*); [se] la firme entend se **recentrer** de plus en plus sur la pharmacie (*concentrate*)

recette (*f*): les **recettes** pétrolières du Mexique (*income, revenue*); à la **recette des impôts** (*tax-collector's office*); les services de la **recette-perception** sont entrés dans leurs nouveaux locaux (*tax/revenue office*)

receveur (*m*): payable à M. le **Receveur des P et T** (*Administrator of the Post Office*)

rechange (*f*): l'Opposition est trop divisée pour offrir une **solution de rechange** crédible; il n'y a pas de **solution de rechange** à la coopération franco-allemande (*alternative*)

réchauffement (*m*): le **réchauffement** des relations entre Londres et Moscou (*improvement*)

récidive (*f*): le fort taux de **récidive** parmi les jeunes délinquants (*committing of a further offence; relapse*); le ministre avait averti qu'en cas de **récidive** les relations entre les deux pays en seraient affectées (*repetition, repeat*)

récidiver: il **récidive** à la première occasion (*commit a further offence; do again, repeat*)

récidiviste (*m/adj*): Yvelines: le violeur **récidiviste** inculpé (*repeated or habitual offender, recidivist*)

réciprocité (*f*): des **accords de réciprocité** négociés entre la France et ses partenaires (*reciprocal agreement*)

réciproquement: la France exporte et, **réciproquement**, les produits étrangers pénètrent en France (*conversely, in exchange*)

réclamer [se]: la moitié des habitants se **réclament** d'une autre nationalité;

sur l'essentiel, le Front national **se réclame** des mêmes valeurs que la majorité (*claim allegiance/kinship*)

reclassement (*m*): la CGT exige un **reclassement** des partants dans les PME locales (*redeployment*); des mesures pour faciliter la formation et le **reclassement** des salariés (*regrading*)

reclasser: les salariés de 45 à 55 ans **se reclassent** difficilement (*find new employment*)

réclusion (*f*): l'avocat général avait requis une peine de 15 ans de **réclusion criminelle** (*imprisonment*)

reconductible (*adj*): une grève **reconductible** de 24 heures a été déclenchée par la CGT (*renewable*)

reconduction (*f*): le P–DG a obtenu la **reconduction** de son mandat d'administrateur; **reconduction** exacte des déductions appliquées en 1990 (*renewal; continuation*)

reconduire: le cessez-le-feu a été **reconduit** indéfiniment (*extend, renew*); le ministre a été **reconduit** dans ses fonctions à la tête des Socialistes du Vaucluse (*re-elect*)

reconduisible (*adj*): une grève — vraisemblablement **reconduisible** (*extendable*)

reconversion (*f*): un programme d'aide à la **reconversion** des bassins miniers (*conversion to new industry*); les suppressions d'emplois se feront par départs en pré-retraite et **reconversions** (*retraining; redeployment*); toute la région a été décrétée **pôle de reconversion** (*special development area*)

reconvertir [se]: il va **se reconvertir** dans l'immobilier (*diversify; move into*)

recoupement (*m*): d'informations en **recoupements**, les policiers en sont venus à s'intéresser à cette société d'import-export (*cross-check*)

recourir: ils **recourent** à la violence en désespoir de cause (*have recourse to, take refuge in*)

recours (*m*): le PS toutefois décida de ne pas **déposer un recours** devant le Conseil constitutionnel (*register an appeal; appeal against*); l'ultime **recours en appel** s'est soldé par une fin de non-recevoir (*appeal*); le **recours en grâce** fut rejeté (*appeal for clemency*); ils **ont eu recours** à des moyens illégaux (*resort, have recourse to*)

recouvrement (*m*): la lutte pour le **recouvrement** des droits palestiniens inaliénables (*recovery, regaining*); le poste de percepteur a été supprimé, mais il est remplacé par un **agent de recouvrement** (*tax-collector*); des **sociétés de recouvrement** aux méthodes peu orthodoxes (*debt-collection agency*)

recouvrer: une amnistie leur a permis de **recouvrer** leurs droits civiques (*recover, regain*)

recrudescence (*f*): cette année a été marquée par une **recrudescence** de la

125

guérilla (*renewal of; renewed outbreak*)

recteur (*m*): on changea plus de la moitié des **recteurs** et 40 inspecteurs d'Académie (*regional director of education*)

rectificatif (*m*): *Le Monde* publia un **rectificatif** dans son numéro du 28 mars (*correction*)

rectoral <e> (*adj*): l'épiscopat attaque deux décisions **rectorales** supprimant le congé du mercredi (*of/by the* recteur)

rectorat (*m*): il réclame une large décentralisation au bénéfice des **rectorats** (*regional education department*)

recueillir: le PC **recueille** régulièrement 20% des voix exprimées (*obtain*)

recul (*m*): le **recul** du maire dans les sondages; on table sur un léger **recul** de la demande (*reduction; decline*); les libéraux sont **en recul** (*on the decline/retreat*)

reculade (*f*): on lui reproche cette nouvelle **reculade** (*about turn; retreat*)

reculer: le commerce mondial du pétrole a fortement **reculé** depuis 1973 (*decline, regress*)

récupération (*f*): ils dénoncent la **récupération** de leur mouvement par l'extrême-droite (*take-over*)

récuser: ils **récusent** l'analyse socialiste; il **récuse** totalement la démarche de son président (*refuse; reject*)

recyclage (*m*): le développement technique impose un **recyclage** périodique (*refresher course; retraining*)

recycler [se]: le directeur, ancien carrossier **recyclé** dans la fabrication d'engrais; il **s'est recyclé** dans le marketing (*retrain, convert*)

rédaction (*f*): la **rédaction** est composée d'une centaine de journalistes (*editorial staff*); la préparation et la **rédaction** du contrat d'assurance (*drawing up*)

reddition (*f*): ils tentent d'obtenir la **reddition** des rebelles (*surrender*)

redécoupage (*m*): le projet de **redécoupage cantonal** (*redrawing of electoral boundaries*)

redéploiement (*m*): devant la chute des commandes, la société envisageait un **redéploiement** industriel (*diversification; conversion*)

redéployer [se]: contraint de **se redéployer**, le Crédit National court après les PME (*diversify*)

redevance (*f*): la **redevance** TV augmenta de 10% en 1989 (*licence fee*); la société payera une **redevance** à IBM pour l'utilisation de ses brevets (*charge; fee*)

rédiger: un rapport confidentiel **rédigé** par son supérieur hiérarchique (*draft; write*)

redressement (*m*): démographie: le **redressement** se confirme (*recovery,* *improvement*); le **plan de redressement** fut arrêté en Conseil des ministres (*recovery plan*); la société a été placée en **redressement judiciaire** (≃ receivership); le fisc lui a imposé un **redressement fiscal** pour les deux exercices écoulés (*bill for payment of arrears of taxes*)

redresser: un nouveau P–DG sut vite **redresser l'affaire** (*turn a business round; make a business profitable*)

réduit <e> (*adj*): un nombre assez **réduit** d'articles sont soldés (*limited, small*)

rééchelonnement (*m*): la Pologne obtient un **rééchelonnement** de sa dette (*rescheduling*)

rééditer: l'industrie va sans doute **rééditer** sa performance de 1990 (*repeat*)

réévaluation (*f*): le ministre a annoncé une **réévaluation** des salaires des infirmières (*increase; rise*)

réfection (*f*): le conseil municipal a décidé la **réfection** du mur du cimetière (*repair*)

référé (*m*): la procédure du **référé** a pour objectif d'obtenir une décision rapide (*summary court action;* ≃ court injunction); ils ont saisi le **tribunal des référés** de Créteil (≃ court of summary jurisdiction)

réflexion (*f*): une **réflexion** en profondeur sur l'efficacité de l'ensemble de l'éducation (*debate; reflection*); la **commission de réflexion** étudiera notamment les problèmes soulevés par l'épargne-logement ('*think-tank*')

reflux (*m*): nouveau **reflux** du dollar, reprise des bourses des valeurs (*retreat; fall*)

refonte (*f*): l'opposition demande une **refonte** complète du texte; un projet de **refonte** du code de la nationalité (*recasting, redrawing*)

réforme (*f*): un rapport propose une **réforme** de l'impôt (*reform*)

réformer: engagé volontaire pour trois ans, il a été **réformé** et rendu à la vie civile (*declare unfit for military service*)

refoulement (*m*): le **refoulement** d'Algériens se rendant en France (*turning back*)

refouler: il a été **refoulé** à la frontière suisse (*send back*)

réfractaire (*adj*): plus des deux tiers de la population est **réfractaire** au changement (*hostile; resistant*)

refuge (*m*): les bijoux sont un placement **refuge** parfait par temps troublés (*safe*)

refuser [se]: bien qu'il **se refuse** à tout commentaire (*decline, refuse*)

regain (*m*): les négociations suscitent un **regain** d'espoir chez les blancs; l'Ulster connaît un brusque **regain** de tension (*renewal; revival*)

régie (*f*): il veut transformer le statut de la firme de celui de **régie** en celui de société anonyme (*partly State-owned company; guaranteed State group*)

régime (*m*): le **régime** en place est soutenu par l'étranger (*regime; government*); peut-on modifier un **régime** matrimonial après le mariage? (*regime*); l'équilibre financier des **régimes de retraite** (*retirement-pension scheme*)

règle (*f*): le ministre a vu son pays l'objet d'une accusation **en règle** de ses partenaires européens (*severe, formal*); on a intérêt à **être en règle** avec l'administration (*be straight with/in order*)

règlement (*m*): les **règlements** internationaux s'effectuent souvent à partir de lettres de change; un chèque en **règlement** d'achats est parfaitement légal (*payment, settlement*); pour parvenir à un **règlement** négocié du problème (*settlement*); cela tient surtout de **règlements de compte** personnels (*settling of scores*); la société est **en règlement judiciaire**, ne pouvant plus faire face à ses dettes (*compulsory liquidation*)

réglementation (*f*): la libération des prix exige une **réglementation** de la concurrence (*drawing up of rules*); la **réglementation** ici a tendance à être un peu protectionniste (*legislation, law*); aucun de ces pays n'a recouru à la **réglementation des prix** (*price control; retail price maintenance*)

réglementer: on a décidé de **réglementer** par voie législative; une proposition de loi visant à **réglementer** la publicité subliminale (*regulate, control*)

régler: pour **régler** le problème des sureffectifs (*solve, settle*)

régression (*f*): nette **régression** des valeurs minières à la Bourse (*decline, fall back*)

regroupement (*m*): partout, l'heure est aux **regroupements** (*coming together; fusion, merger*); des mesures prises pour faciliter les **regroupements familiaux** (*reuniting/bringing together of the family*)

regrouper: les Progressistes **regroupent** tous les mécontents du pays (*include, comprise*)

régularité (*f*): le Conseil constitutionnel est chargé de contrôler la **régularité** des élections (*fairness, legality*)

rehausser: ceci n'a fait que **rehausser** son prestige dans le pays (*enhance, increase*)

réinsérer [se]: une association qui aide les drogués à **se réinsérer** dans la société; les jeunes étrangers **se réinsèrent** plus difficilement que les Français (*reintegrate oneself; be rehabilitated*)

réinsertion (*f*): la **réinsertion** des anciens détenus dans la société (*readmission; rehabilitation*); les difficultés de la **réinsertion** des chômeurs de longue durée (*re-employment*)

réintégration (*f*): la demande de **réintégration** du Caire au sein de la Ligue arabe (*readmission; re-entry*); ceci n'entraîne pas la **réintégration** automatique du salarié (*reinstatement; rehabilitation*)

réintégrer: la France ne doit pas **réintégrer** l'OTAN (*rejoin*)

réinvestir: le taux de l'impôt sur les sociétés serait réduit de 42% à 39% lorsque les bénéfices sont **réinvestis** (*plough back; reinvest*)

réitérer: pour empêcher le maire de **réitérer** son exploit de 1988 (*repeat*)

rejet (*m*): un électorat qui manifeste son **rejet** de la classe politique (*rejection*)

rejoindre: les craintes de Londres **rejoignent** celles de Moscou (*resemble; be akin to*); [se] malgré leurs différences, les deux candidats **se rejoignent** sur l'essentiel (*be in accord/agreement; come together*)

relâche (*f*): lutter **sans relâche** contre le terrorisme (*without let-up, unceasingly*)

relâcher: ils sont interpellés, interrogés, puis **relâchés** (*free*)

relais (*m*): les Chinois vont **prendre le relais** des Japonais dans le secteur de l'informatique (*follow, take over from*)

relance (*f*): la **relance** de l'économie se fait toujours attendre (*reflation; expansion*)

relancer: il multiplie les voyages à l'Est pour y **relancer** le rôle politique de la France (*promote, boost*); la RFA refuse de **relancer**, mais accepte une réévaluation de sa monnaie (*stimulate the economy; expand*)

relativiser: la chute de Wall Street est importante, mais il faut **relativiser** les choses; ces chiffres doivent toutefois être **relativisés** (*put into proper perspective*)

relaxe (*f*): on annonce la **relaxe** des cinq mutins de la prison des Baumettes (*liberation, freeing*)

relaxer: le cinquième prévenu a été **relaxé**; les auteurs de la tuerie **relaxés** par le tribunal de Nouméa (*free, set free*)

relève (*f*): il faut une élite indigène pour **prendre la relève** au moment de l'indépendance (*take over*)

relèvement (*m*): on craint un **relèvement** de la cotisation vieillesse (*raising, increase*)

relever: le constructeur vient de **relever** ses tarifs (*raise, increase*); il a été **relevé de ses fonctions** (*sack, relieve of post*); la mise en route de la dissuasion nucléaire **relève** du Président seul (*be the preserve of*)

relief (*m*): ces graphiques **mettent en relief** l'importance du phénomène (*bring out, emphasize*)

remaniement (*m*): un **remaniement ministériel** est intervenu à Bonn (*cabinet reshuffle*)

remanier: Phnom Penh **remanie** profondément son gouvernement; la législation a été **remaniée** à plusieurs reprises (*reshape, change*)

remboursement (*m*): le **remboursement** moyen mensuel est de 350F; la part des revenus des particuliers consacrée au **remboursement de crédit** (*loan* *repayment*)

remédier: pour **remédier** au surpeuplement dans les prisons (*remedy, solve*)

remembrement (*m*): les efforts pour favoriser le **remembrement** des terres cultivables y ont échoué; grâce au **remembrement**, les exploitations seront d'une taille rentable (*reorganization into larger units of land; land restructuring*)

remercier: lorsque le gouvernement envisage de **remercier** le P-DG d'Elf-Aquitaine (*sack, remove from office*)

remise (*f*): ils consentent aux adhérents des **remises** importantes (*discount, reduction*); des formations de **remise à niveau des connaissances** (*refresher course*); la CGT refuse toute **remise en cause** du SMIC (*calling into question; abandonment*); une **remise en question** de la stratégie nucléaire (*reconsideration; calling into question*); le Président a décidé 25 **remises de peine** (*reduction of sentence; remission*)

remontée: (*f*): avec la **remontée** du chômage (*rise, increase*)

remonter: le chômage **remonte**, on assiste à une baisse des reprises d'emploi (*go up, rise*); la dernière augmentation **remonte** au 1ᵉʳ juillet (*date from, go back to*)

remous (*m*): l'affaire a provoqué des **remous** au sein du gouvernement (*controversy; stir; disquiet*)

remporter: l'opposition a **remporté** la majorité absolue (*gain, win*)

rémunérateur <-trice> (*adj*): on a préféré les cultures les plus hautement **rémunératrices** (*profitable; lucrative*)

rémunération (*f*): une hausse des **rémunérations** est survenue dans le secteur du bâtiment (*pay, earnings*)

rémunérer: Carrefour lance un compte **rémunéré** à 6% (*paying interest; interest-bearing*); un allègement des cotisations sociales pour les emplois **faiblement rémunérés** (*poorly paid*)

renchérir: on a vu le brut **renchérir** constamment (*get dearer, increase in price*); il a fait savoir qu'il **renchérirait** sur toute OPA lancée sur le fabricant de whisky (*outbid; raise the bid*); et le ministre de **renchérir**:-(*add; go further*)

renchérissement (*m*): le Japon, ébranlé par le **renchérissement** de l'énergie (*rise in price of*)

rendement (*m*): son **rendement** est passé de 20 milliards en 1975 à 50 en 1988 (*yield, capacity*); l'usine travaillait **à plein rendement** (*at full capacity*)

renflouement (*m*): le **renflouement** de la Sécurité sociale ne sera pas chose aisée (*refloating; bailing-out*)

renflouer: une société régulièrement **renflouée** par son actionnaire principal: l'État (*bail out; refloat*); en offrant ses services aux entreprises, la société **renfloue ses caisses** (*refill the coffers*)

130

renforcement (*m*): Washington s'inquiète du **renforcement** des troupes cubaines en Afrique australe (*strengthening, reinforcement*)

renforcer [se]: Lafarge **se renforce** en Amérique du Nord (*strengthen its trading position; expand*)

reniement (*m*): les **reniements** du maire sortant, et sa gestion incohérente (*broken promise*)

renouer: la France voudrait **renouer** avec Pretoria (*get back on good terms with*); le ministre **renoue le dialogue** avec les syndicats (*resume discussions*); les entreprises françaises **renouent** avec le profit (*re-experience, return to*)

renouveau (*m*): accusé d'être le saboteur du **renouveau** économique (*recovery; turn-round*)

renouveler: les élections permettront de **renouveler** le personnel (*renew, replace, change*)

renouvellement (*m*): le **renouvellement** partiel du comité central (*renewal, replacement*)

rénovateur (*m/adj*): les élus PC se sont constitués en groupe des élus **rénovateurs** (*reforming; modernizing*)

rénovation (*f*): la constitution d'une liste du centre et de **rénovation** (*reform; modernization*)

renseignement (*m*): la brigade criminelle de la police judiciaire, en liaison avec les **Renseignements généraux** [R.G.] (*secret police*)

rentabiliser: un éditeur **rentabilise** un ouvrage lorsqu'il en vend 2 000 exemplaires; il entend ainsi **rentabiliser** au mieux son investissement belge (*make a return on; make profitable*)

rentabilité (*f*): la **rentabilité** de l'investissement demeure faible (*profitability*); les obligations Écureuil vous assurent une bonne **rentabilité** (*financial return, profit*)

rente (*f*): il vit largement de ses **rentes** (*unearned income*); une **rente viagère** permet une réversion totale au conjoint (*life annuity*)

rentrée (*f*): la **rentrée** sociale promet d'être chaude (*return to work/school*); grâce à de bonnes **rentrées fiscales** (*tax revenue*)

renvoi (*m*): le **renvoi** devant une cour d'assises des six membres de la bande (*sending; referral*); le procès se termina par un **renvoi** pour complément d'instruction (*throwing out; sending back*); il a demandé le **renvoi** de la discussion au lendemain (*postponement*); 40% des sondés souhaitent le **renvoi** des travailleurs étrangers (*sending back; expulsion*)

renvoyer: pas question de **renvoyer** jusqu'après 1993 cette question cruciale (*put off; put back, postpone*); les inculpés sont **renvoyés** devant la cour d'assises (*send*)

répartir: elle a 280 filiales **réparties** dans 31 pays (*distribute, spread*)

répartition (*f*): la **répartition** des pouvoirs s'est faite sans difficulté (*division, distribution*)

répercussion (*f*): les **répercussions** des mouvements du dollar sur les prix (*effect, repercussion*)

répercuter: les entrepreneurs **répercutent** souvent ces augmentations sur leurs prix (*pass on the cost*); [se] ces incidents à l'autre bout du monde **se répercutent** sur la vie de chaque Français (*have an effect*)

répertorier: Amnesty International a **répertorié** la disparition de 272 personnes (*make a list of*)

répétition (*f*): s'ensuivent des mouvements de grève **à répétition** (*a continual series of; repeated*)

replâtrage (*m*): une hostilité telle que l'on imagine mal un **replâtrage** de leur alliance (*repairing; rebuilding*)

repli (*m*): cette position de **repli** est très précaire (*retreat, withdrawal*); la consommation des biens manufacturés a connu un **repli** sensible en mars (*reduction; decline*)

replier [se]: ils **se sont repliés** provisoirement (*withdraw, retreat*)

report (*m*): il a demandé le **report** de la conférence (*postponement*); un **report d'incorporation** pour cause d'études supérieures (*deferment of national service*); le candidat a bénéficié de très bons **reports de voix** des électorats communiste et radical (*transfer of vote*)

reporter: une partie des électeurs ont **reporté** leurs suffrages sur le candidat d'union (*transfer*); élection présidentielle **reportée** au Liban (*postpone, put off*)

repousser: ils ont **repoussé** à lundi leur décision (*put back*); la justice irlandaise a **repoussé** la démarche visant à interdire cette publicité (*reject*)

reprendre: ils voulaient **reprendre** l'entreprise en perdition; la filature de Guebwiller **reprise** par une firme allemande (*take over*)

repreneur (*m*): le nouveau **repreneur** n'est pas totalement étranger à cette activité (*proprietor*)

représailles (*f pl*): cette décision a été prise **en représailles** (*in reprisal*)

représentation (*f*): le Parlement, en France, assure la **représentation** du peuple (*representation*); les industriels français ont rouvert des **représentations** dans la capitale irakienne (*office; agency*)

répression (*f*): **répression** sanglante à la suite des émeutes de jeudi (*repression*)

réprimer: l'armée **réprime** brutalement des manifestations de rue (*quell; put down*)

repris de justice (*m*): l'homme, **repris de justice** notoire, est activement recherché par la police (*ex-convict*)

reprise (*f*): le vote sur la **reprise** du travail s'est soldé par la victoire des 'non' (*restart, resumption*); on espère une **reprise** modérée de la consommation (*revival, recovery*); après l'échec du projet de **reprise** de la firme allemande (*taking control; acquisition*)

requérant (*m*): le tribunal a débouté les **requérants** (*appellant*)

requérir: l'avocat-général a **requis** une peine de prison de dix ans (*call for, demand*)

requête (*f*): le Conseil constitutionnel rejeta la **requête** (*appeal*)

réquisition (*f*): contrairement aux **réquisitions** du procureur de la République, elle n'a pas été placée en détention provisoire (*request; demand*); la **réquisition** du parquet est accablante pour lui (*closing speech*)

réquisitoire (*m*): dans son **réquisitoire**, l'avocat général a insisté sur l'horreur du parricide (*indictment, charge*); il a prononcé un **réquisitoire en règle** contre la politique du gouvernement (*condemnation*)

réseau (*m*): un vaste **réseau** commercial dans les cinq continents (*network*); un **réseau d'espionnage** opérant au profit de l'URSS a été démantelé en RFA (*spy-ring*)

résidence (*f*): la mise en **résidence surveillée** du chef du parti de l'opposition (*house arrest*)

résiliation (*f*): demandez à votre propriétaire la **résiliation** de votre contrat de location (*termination, cancellation*)

résilier: il y a un temps de préavis à respecter pour **résilier** un contrat (*cancel*)

résolument: leurs convictions les placent **résolument** à gauche (*clearly*)

résorber: le déficit prévu de l'UNEDIC sera **résorbé** grâce à l'augmentation des cotisations (*absorb, reduce*); [se] le chômage **se résorbe** (*be brought down/reduced*)

responsabilité (*f*): en cas de blocage, il peut **engager ses responsabilités** en vertu de l'article 49/3 de la Constitution (*stake government survival on the acceptance without vote of a bill/ measure*)

responsable (*m*): un **responsable** américain a démenti cette affirmation (*representative; official*); il est fréquent que délégué du personnel et **responsable syndical** ne fassent qu'un (*trade-union representative*)

ressentiment (*m*): il n'y a pas de **ressentiment** ici contre les Américains (*antagonism*)

resserrement (*m*): le **resserrement** de la politique monétaire vise à mettre fin à la faiblesse du Mark (*tightening*)

resserrer: aux États-Unis, la réserve fédérale a préféré **resserrer** sa politique du crédit (*tighten*)

ressort (*m*): la défense est du **ressort** du chef de l'État (*province, responsibility*); utilisant tous les **ressorts** de la procédure parlementaire pour retarder l'adoption du texte (*resource; possibility*); c'est lui qui décide, **en dernier ressort** (*in the final analysis; finally*)

ressortir: c'est ce qui **ressort** du rapport établi par les enquêteurs (*emerge*); les traitements nets **font ressortir** une baisse du pouvoir d'achat (*indicate, point to*)

ressortissant (*m*): les **ressortissants** français dont les avoirs sont bloqués à Rabat (*national*)

ressource (*f*): Que font ceux qui n'ont pas de **ressource?** (*means, resources*); il leur reste toujours la **ressource** de quitter le pays (*possibility*)

restreindre: c'est le budget global qui **restreint** les dépenses hospitalières (*limit, keep down*)

restreint <e> (*adj*): cela s'adresse à un public assez **restreint** (*small; limited*); leurs discussions en **comité restreint** (*small committee; group*)

restructuration (*f*): 8% de la population active ont été touchés par les **restructurations** (*restructuring*)

restructurer [se]: Rhône-Poulenc Fibres **se restructure**: bilan, 400 personnes sans emploi (*be restructured*)

résultat (*m*): Michelet S.A. pesait 8,6 milliards de ventes, et 10 millions de **résultat** net (*profit*); la firme enregistra un **résultat d'exploitation** de 5,2 millions de francs (*operating profit*)

rétablir: il a l'intention de **rétablir** le scrutin proportionnel (*bring back*)

rétablissement (*m*): il demande le **rétablissement** de la peine de mort (*restoration*); il faut attendre 1995 pour que la firme achève son **rétablissement** (*turn-round; recovery*)

retenir: le tribunal n'a pas **retenu** la préméditation (*accept an argument*); le gouvernement a **retenu** une série de neuf mesures concrètes et immédiates (*decide upon, adopt*)

retenue (*f*): la **retenue** dont avaient fait preuve les autorités (*restraint*); les **retenues** pour la Sécurité sociale étaient de 6,5 % (*deduction, stoppage*); une **retenue à la source** par l'employeur sur tous les salaires (*deduction at source*)

réticence (*f*): le ministre s'est heurté aux **réticences** des députés socialistes (*doubt; opposition*)

réticent <e> (*adj*): ils sont **réticents** à s'engager plus avant (*reluctant*); certains ministres étaient **réticents** à l'idée, en raison de son coût (*hostile*)

retirer: les dossiers sont à **retirer** et déposer avant le 31 mai (*collect; pick up*)

retombée (*f*): cette mesure pourrait avoir des **retombées** politiques négatives (*consequence; result*); ils espèrent des **retombées** à la hauteur de leurs investissements (*spin-off, consequential benefit*)

rétorsion (*f*): ces mesures de **rétorsion** économique risquent d'être peu

134

efficaces (*retaliation*)

retournement (*m*): des entreprises en voie de **retournement** (*turn-round; recovery*); ce **retournement d'alliance** évoque une comédie de boulevard (*change of alliance; changing sides*)

retrait (*m*): la France réclame le **retrait** du corps expéditionnaire libyen; un **retrait de fonds** de votre compte peut s'effectuer à n'importe quel guichet (*withdrawal*); dans son discours, le Premier ministre a paru très **en retrait** par rapport au chef de l'État (*in retreat; not going as far as*)

retraite (*f*): des militaires **à la retraite** (*retired, in retirement*); leur **mise à la retraite anticipée** a été annoncée aux ouvriers (*early/premature retirement*)

rétrograder: 130 commissaires de la République sont **rétrogradés** (*downgrade; demote*)

retrouvailles (*f pl*): après les **retrouvailles** algéro-marocaines (*reunion; settling of differences*)

réunion (*f*): les ministres PR ont tenu une **réunion** (*meeting*)

réunir [se]: une table ronde nationale devrait **se réunir** à la mi-juin (*meet, get together*)

revalorisation (*f*): la **revalorisation** de l'enseignement du chinois en France (*promotion; up-grading*); ils demandent une **revalorisation** de leur statut (*regrading; improvement*); il confirme l'urgence de **revalorisations salariales** massives (*wage rise/increase*)

revaloriser: il faut **revaloriser** le rôle du Parlement (*give greater prominence/importance*); on exige que l'ensemble des rémunérations soit **revalorisé** de 1 500F au moins (*raise, increase*)

revendicatif < -ive > (*adj*): la CFDT est prête à s'associer à d'éventuels **mouvements revendicatifs** (*protest action*)

revendication (*f*): la **revendication** des syndicats pour une retraite à 60 ans (*demand*); la montée des **revendications salariales** (*salary/wage demand*)

revendiquer: l'attentat a été **revendiqué** par un groupe loyaliste; le mouvement **revendique** 20 000 adhérents (*claim*); territoire **revendiqué** à la fois par le Tchad et la Libye; les ouvriers **revendiquent** de nouvelles hausses de salaire (*claim, demand*)

revenir: le coût a chuté de 2 milliards de francs, **revenant** à 1,2 milliards en 1986 (*come down to*); la décision **revient** au Président, et à lui seul (*be the responsibility of*); une expérience qu'ils ont vécue et dont ils ne sont jamais **revenus** (*recover from*); le ministre a rappelé qu'il n'entendait pas **revenir** sur la liberté totale des prix (*abandon; retract*)

revenu (*m*): l'impôt sur le **revenu** des particuliers (*income*); les Britanniques paient un fort **impôt direct sur le revenu** (*income tax*)

revers (*m*): compte tenu des **revers** subis par la Gauche; c'est un **revers**

personnel pour le nouveau leader (*set-back; defeat*)

réversion (*f*): une **pension de réversion** est due au conjoint survivant non remarié âgé de 50 ans (*reversionary pension*)

revêtir: la grève des mineurs **revêtait** déjà une signification historique (*take on, assume*)

revirement (*m*): en annonçant un **revirement** de la politique énergétique (*reversal; turnabout*); ceci apparaît un **revirement total** (*U-turn*)

révocation (*f*): le ministre de la Justice a prononcé au moins 118 **révocations** (*dismissal; removal from office*)

revoir: il faut **revoir** un projet qui s'est révélé trop coûteux (*review*); l'OCDE **revoit en hausse** ses prévisions (*revise upwards*)

révoquer: le premier président d'industrie nationalisée à être **révoqué** (*remove from office, sack*)

revue (*f*): ils ont **passé en revue** l'état des négociations en cours (*review, survey*)

rigueur (*f*): Pays-Bas: manifestations contre la **rigueur** (*policy of austerity*); les effets du **plan de rigueur** se font déjà sentir (*austerity plan*); l'incident est clos: la Turquie semble ne pas **tenir rigueur** à Alger (*blame; feel resentment*)

riposte (*f*): la stratégie de la **riposte graduée** a beaucoup de partisans (*flexible response*)

ristourne (*f*): un dossier-clef: la '**ristourne**' accordée à la Grande-Bretagne (*rebate; refund*)

riverain (*m/adj*): on indemnisera les **riverains** les plus exposés; accès interdit sauf aux **riverains** (*resident; adjacent owner*)

rocade (*f*): l'ouverture de la **rocade** Nord-Est diminuera le flux des camions (*linking section between main roads/motorways*)

rogner: il **rogne** continuellement sur le budget militaire (*reduce bit by bit*)

rompre: le PS demande au RPR de **rompre** ses accords régionaux avec le Front national (*break off, cancel*)

rompu <e> (*adj*): il est **rompu** aux méthodes du Parti communiste (*experienced/knowledgeable in*)

rose (*adj*): l'Assemblée **rose** arrivée au Palais-Bourbon en 1981 (*Socialist*)

rotation (*f*): la **rotation du personnel** donne à penser que les cadences y étaient par trop élevées (*turnover of staff*)

rouage (*m*): ils connaissent les **rouages** de l'administration (*ins and outs, workings*)

rubis sur l'ongle: prix de la transaction: trois millions de dollars, **rubis sur l'ongle** (*paid in cash; cash on the nail*)

rubrique (*f*): il tenait longtemps la **rubrique** financière dans *Le Monde*

(*newspaper column; page*)

rude (*adj*): la concurrence est **rude** dans ce domaine-là entre tous (*tough*)

ruiner: des investissements qui les ont **ruinés**, les acculant à la faillite (*ruin*)

rumeur (*f*): la **rumeur publique** l'accuse, malgré le démenti de ses amis (*public opinion; rumour*)

rupture (*f*): une **rupture** de la coalition gouvernementale ne saurait tarder (*collapse, breakdown*); une **rupture** totale avec la politique suivie jusqu'alors (*break; change*); une **rupture diplomatique** entre Londres et Damas (*breaking-off of diplomatic relations*); il est désormais **en rupture** de contrat (*in breach of*); le magasin est **en rupture de stock** (*sold out*)

rythme (*m*): l'ampleur et surtout le **rythme** des réformes sont déconcertants (*speed; rate*); une nouvelle concertation sur la rénovation des **rythmes** scolaires (*tempo, pace*); une croissance de 3,7% **en rythme annuel** (*annual rate of growth*)

rythmer: la semaine a été **rythmée** par les évolutions du titre Compagnie du Midi (*mark; punctuate*)

S

sage (*m*): le rapport de la commission des **sages** sur le code de la nationalité (*experts*); les **neuf sages** vont plancher sur le projet de loi gouvernemental (*Constitutional Council*); (*adj*) les prix de gros progressent à un rythme plus **sage** (*reasonable; moderate*)

sagesse (*f*): une compression de la demande, et la **sagesse** de la consommation outre-Rhin (*moderation*)

saisie (*f*): les loyers montent: il y aura encore des **saisies** et des expulsions (*seizure of property*); il ordonna la **saisie** de l'hebdomadaire de gauche (*seizure; confiscation*); on estimait qu'une **saisie** de la commission des monopoles et des fusions s'imposait (*appeal to*); la compagnie a obtenu une **saisie-arrêt** sur les comptes bancaires de la société pour factures impayées (*distraint*)

saisine (*f*): il a demandé la **saisine** de la Chambre criminelle de la Cour de cassation (*submission of a case to the court*)

saisir: ses créanciers ont **saisi** tous ses biens (*seize, gain possession of*); la justice est **saisie**, il faut qu'elle mène l'enquête jusqu'à son terme; il a décidé de **saisir** de cette situation la Commission européenne des droits de l'homme (*appeal, refer to*); [se] le Sénat va **se saisir** à son tour de ce dossier (*take up, examine*)

salaire (*m*): l'ancien **salaire** minimum garanti [SMIG] est maintenant indexé sur l'évolution des prix [SMIC] (*wage, salary*)

salarial <e> (*adj*): il s'agit, comme toujours, de revendications **salariales** (*pertaining to salaries*); pour réduire leurs coûts, les entreprises essayent de réduire les **coûts salariaux** (*salary/wage costs*)

salariat (*m*): le **salariat** est aujourd'hui un privilège (*salaried status*)

salarié (*m/adj*): un **salarié** sur cinq n'a pas un emploi stable (*salaried person*)

sanction (*f*): la **sanction** des infractions aux règles de la navigation de la communauté (*punishment; penalty*); un DEUG — **sanction** de deux années d'études réussies (*ratification; reward*)

sanctionner: ses fautes doivent être **sanctionnées** (*punish*); le vote a **sanctionné** la politique française au Proche-Orient (*ratify, confirm*)

sans-: Soudan: plus d'un million de **sans-abri** à Khartoum (*homeless person*); au total, 16 millions de **sans-emplois** dans les pays de la CEE (*out-of-work/unemployed person*); les problèmes des sans-emploi et des **sans-toît** (*homeless person*); le taux des **sans-travail** doit avoisiner les 60% (*jobless, out-of-work person*)

Sarl (*f*): l'Assemblée générale de la **Sarl** *Le Monde*; il n'y a ni conseil d'administration ni P-DG dans les **SARL** [société à responsabilité limitée] (*limited liability company*)

satisfecit (*m*): il a décerné des **satisfecit** au Premier ministre (*commendation*)

saupoudrage (*m*): les pouvoirs publics voulaient résister à la tentation du **saupoudrage** des crédits (*sprinkling of small sums/grants*)

sauter: la voiture bourrée d'explosifs a **sauté** deux heures plus tard; on est venu **faire sauter** l'engin (*explode*)

sauvage (*adj*): pour assurer un contrôle de l'immigration **sauvage** ou clandestine; l'État n'encourage ni le monopole ni la concurrence **sauvage** (*uncontrolled; unrestricted*)

sauvegarde (*f*): il avait d'abord proposé la **sauvegarde** de 120 emplois (*saving; protection*)

sauvetage (*m*): ils ont mis au point un **plan de sauvetage** (*rescue plan*)

savoir-faire (*m*): les usines du tiers-monde offrent des débouchés aux exportateurs d'équipements et de **savoir-faire** (*know-how; ability; skill*)

scander: les manifestants **scandaient** des slogans (*shout, chant*)

scénario (*m*): trois **scénarios** peuvent être envisagés (*pattern of events, possibility*)

schéma (*m*): on est parvenu à retracer le **schéma** du trafic: faux certificats de destination finale (*pattern; diagram*); la Région a adopté un **schéma** régional d'aménagement des transports (*plan; scheme*)

schématiser: en **schématisant** un peu, on peut le présenter ainsi (*simplify*)

scission (*f*): cette décision entraînera une **scission** au sein du parti (*split*); les socialistes refusent l'union de la gauche et **font scission** (*split, secede*)

scrutin (*m*): on adoptera pour les prochaines élections le **scrutin** uninominal majoritaire (*vote, poll*)

séance (*f*): six mois de travaux marqués par 37 **séances** de travail (*session*)

sécheresse (*f*): il faut intervenir en faveur des victimes de la **sécheresse** (*drought*)

secouer: les militants ont été fortement **secoués** (*shake, shock*)

secourir: on chiffre à 2 500 les personnes officiellement **secourues** (*aid, help*)

sectarisme (*m*): à cause du **sectarisme** des socialistes locaux (*sectionalism; intolerance*)

secteur (*m*): les **secteurs** les plus touchés: la poste, l'enseignement (*area, sector*); dans le **secteur public** les augmentations ont été rares (*public sector*)

section (*f*): dans les **sections** et les fédérations du Parti socialiste (*local grouping*); patronat et **section syndicale [d'entreprise]** sont accusés de complicité dans la mauvaise gestion de l'entreprise (*trade-union representation within the work-place*)

sectoriel < -elle > (*adj*): les crises **sectorielles** sont de plus en plus aiguës (*sector-based; sectional*)

séculaire (*adj*): c'est une tradition **séculaire** dans ce pays (*time-honoured; centuries-old*)

sécuriser: la loi aura pour conséquence de **sécuriser** les immigrés (*make feel safe/secure*)

sécuritaire (*adj*): la question **sécuritaire** figure en bonne place dans les manifestes des partis (*pertaining to law and order/security*)

sécurité (*f*): l'Assemblée nationale a débattu les quatre projets de loi sur la **sécurité** (*security; law and order*); la **sécurité de l'emploi** sera un des principaux enjeux de l'élection (*job security*)

séduire: cette idée **séduit** les conservateurs; un atout important pour **séduire** la clientèle (*attract, win over*)

séduisant < e > (*adj*): perspective **séduisante** pour les petits investisseurs (*attractive*)

sein (*m*): relations tendues **au sein de** la majorité (*in, within the ranks of*)

sellette (*f*): déjà **sur la sellette** à propos de sombres histoires de pots-de-vin (*in trouble, in the 'hot seat'*); Corse: la révision des listes électorales **sur la sellette** (*under examination/scrutiny*)

semestre (*m*): la société de Dijon a enregistré de très bons résultats pour le premier **semestre** (*half-year, six-month period*)

semestriel < -elle > (*adj*): hausse de 20% du bénéfice **semestriel** (*half-yearly; semesterly*)

semonce (*f*): il a adressé une verte **semonce** à ceux qui perdaient l'espoir (*reprimand*); ces abstentions constituent un **coup de semonce** pour le gouvernement (*warning shot across the bows*)

sens (*m*): il vient d'envoyer une lettre **en ce sens** (*to this effect*); les autres pays ont fait savoir qu'ils **iraient dans le même sens** (*do likewise*); tout cela va **dans le sens de** l'apaisement (*in the direction of; towards*)

sensation (*f*): la **presse à sensation** s'est emparée de l'affaire (*popular press; gutter press*)

sensibilisation (*f*): c'est un problème de **sensibilisation** des jeunes (*making sensitive/aware*)

sensibiliser: il faut **sensibiliser** le grand public à l'intérêt de la chose (*make aware; bring home to*)

sensibilité (*f*): les **sensibilités** de gauche semblent y prédominer; le quotidien de Limoges, de **sensibilité** socialiste (*shade of opinion; tendency*)

sensible (*adj*): le PC conserve les portefeuilles **sensibles** de l'Intérieur et de la Défense (*sensitive*); le recul de leur candidat est encore plus **sensible** (*significant, appreciable*)

sensiblement: la retraite à 60 ans n'a pas **sensiblement** abaissé l'âge réel de cessation d'activité (*significantly*)

séparation (*f*): les époux mariés sous le **régime de la séparation des biens** (*husband and wife administering their possessions separately*)

septennat (*m*): la fin du **septennat** s'approche, les élections sont pour l'an prochain (*seven-year period of presidential office*)

septentrional <e> (*adj*): s'infiltrant à travers la frontière **septentrionale** du pays (*north, northerly*)

série (*f*): limogeages **en série**: 20 responsables mis à l'écart (*in large numbers; many*); la **construction en série** n'est pas prévue avant janvier (*mass production*)

serpent (*m*): le **serpent monétaire** [SME] doit réguler les monnaies européennes entre elles (*European currency 'snake'*)

serrer: une stratégie pour **serrer** les coûts de production (*squeeze; reduce*)

service (*m*): tout dépend du **service** dans lequel on travaille (*department; section*); (*pl*) les **services** en ont été les principaux bénéficiaires et non les industries manufacturières (*service sector*)

session (*f*): le projet de loi sera présenté au Parlement à la **session** de printemps (*session*)

seuil (*m*): des personnes dont les ressources sont inférieures au **seuil** de pauvreté; le **seuil** de tolérance a été largement dépassé (*limit, threshold*); le **seuil d'imposition** est très bas: 250 000F par personne (*tax threshold*)

sidérurgie (*f*): le charbon en Lorraine, la **sidérurgie** dans le Nord et dans l'Est (*iron and steel industry*)

siège (*m*): au **siège** du quartier-général des forces armées (*seat, headquarters, base*); il a perdu son **siège** de conseiller général aux élections cantonales (*seat*); en tant que **magistrat du siège**, il n'est tenu de rendre de compte à personne (*judge of the Bench*); les Ets Duforge ont désormais leur **siège social** à Lyon; on n'exclut pas cette éventualité, au **siège** de la banque, bd Haussmann (*head office; registered office*)

siéger: élu conseiller municipal, il **siège dans** l'opposition (*sit with*); le Parlement européen **siège** à Strasbourg (*sit*)

signalement (*m*): des affichettes portant les photos et **signalements** des deux malfaiteurs (*description*)

significatif <-ive> (*adj*): dans le bâtiment, on a constaté une amélioration **significative** (*significant*)

silence (*m*): ils ont **passé sous silence** la question la plus importante (*ignore*)

sinistre (*m*): un formulaire de déclaration de **sinistre** est joint à la police d'assurance (*accident*); le **sinistre** a été rapidement maîtrisé par le personnel de la prison (*fire*)

sinistrer: une tournée des régions **sinistrées** par la sécheresse (*disaster-stricken*); 17 communes du Vaucluse sont déclarées **zone sinistrée** (*disaster area*)

sis <e> (*adj*): l'institut, **sis** à Bruxelles (*located*)

situer [se]: la véritable alternative **se situe** sans doute ailleurs (*be found, reside*)

SMIC (*m*): le temps où il fallait se battre pour un **SMIC** à 2 000F paraît bien lointain (*legal minimum wage*)

smicard (*m*) (*fam.*): les **smicards** ont leur salaire indexé sur l'évolution des prix (*person in receipt of minimum legal wage*)

social <e> (*adj*): une semaine **sociale** agitée s'ouvre dans le monde enseignant (*social*); cette Europe **sociale** qu'appelle de ses vœux le Président (*of social justice*); 450 millions de francs dépensés pour 3 000 **logements sociaux** (*subsidized housing*); le groupe de Metz a réussi à prendre 62% du **capital social** de l'entreprise de Nancy (*share capital*); le **plan social** s'est traduit par 850 suppressions d'emploi (*recovery plan*)

société (*f*): Renault n'est pas absent du marché des **voitures de société** (*company car*); la sécurité est un problème global, un problème **de société** (*social; pertaining to society*); transformant la régie en **société anonyme** (≃ *limited company*); les rapports complexes entre les enseignants et la **société civile** (*society at large*)

sol (*m*): celui-ci veut supprimer le **droit du sol** en matière de nationalité (*right of nationality by birth within that country*)

solde (*m*): le **solde** doit être réglé un an plus tard (*balance; remainder; sum outstanding*); le **solde** industriel est **déficitaire** ce mois-ci; 20 000 postes seront supprimés et 7 000 créés, soit un **solde négatif** de 13 000 (*negative* *balance; deficit*): **solde** (*f*): il dénonça des meneurs professionnels **à la solde** de l'OLP (*in the pay of*)

solder [se]: l'affrontement **s'était soldé** par la mort de trois soldats; le scrutin **se solda** par un succès inattendu de la Gauche (*result in*)

solidaire (*adj*): les médecins d'hôpital sont **solidaires** des revendications des infirmières (*in support of*); ils tiennent à **rester solidaires** de leurs amis du PC (*stay united with*)

solidariser [se]: ils **se solidarisent** tous avec leurs collègues moins fortunés (*make common cause; sympathize with*)

solidarité (*f*): est-on prêt à renoncer, au nom de la **solidarité**, à certains avantages acquis? (*mutual support, solidarity*)

solliciter: la Grande-Bretagne, **sollicitée** d'y participer, réserve sa réponse (*ask, request*); il **sollicitera** aux élections de mars un troisième mandat (*seek; ask for*)

solutionner: c'est une question qui n'est pas près d'être **solutionnée** (*solve*)

solvable (*adj*): les banques prêtent de préférence à des débiteurs **solvables** (*solvent*)

sommation (*f*): la Ville lui a envoyé une **sommation** de quitter les lieux (*demand; injunction*)

sommeil (*m*): la **mise en sommeil** de la loi sur l'égalité professionnelle (*shelving; non-application*)

sondage (*m*): les instituts de **sondages d'opinion**, tel SOFRES (*opinion poll, survey*)

sondé (*m/adj*): 31% des **sondés** se déclarent prêts à abandonner leur droit de grève (*person questioned in opinion poll*)

sonder: pour en savoir plus, on a **sondé** toutes les catégories de personnel (*poll opinion*)

sortant <e> (*adj*): le maire **sortant** s'allie au Front national; l'équipe municipale **sortante** se représentera (*retiring, outgoing*)

sortie (*f*): pas de **sortie** de crise sans une croissance rapide de la consommation (*way out of; solution*); les licenciements représentent 21% des **sorties des entreprises** (*termination of employment*); avant même sa **sortie en librairie** (*publication*)

souche (*f*): nos compatriotes de **souche** nord-africaine; la moitié des pieds-noirs n'étaient pas de **souche** française (*origins; stock*)

souci (*m*): le **souci** du PCF de se présenter comme le défenseur du peuple (*desire, concern, intention*)

soucier: personne ne **se soucie** du fait qu'on viole constamment la Constitution (*care, worry, be concerned*)

soucieux <-euse> (*adj*): les États-Unis, **soucieux** de promouvoir la stabilité des taux de change (*desirous, concerned*); on est **soucieux** de ses possibles effets négatifs sur la démocratie (*aware, concerned*)

soudé <e> (*adj*): il veut une équipe très **soudée** (*solid*)

souffrance (*f*): même si beaucoup de problèmes restent **en souffrance**; conséquence de la grève des postes: activité ralentie, créances **en souffrance** (*delayed; held up*)

soulèvement (*m*): la tentative de **soulèvement** avortée de mercredi dernier (*uprising*)

soulever: en dépit de l'émotion que **soulève** cette affaire (*arouse; excite*); on a **soulevé** le problème du monopole (*raise, bring up*)

soumettre: on **soumet** le peuple à des pressions intolérables (*submit*); [se] le préfet est tenu de **se soumettre** à l'avis de la commission (*obey, submit*)

soumis <e> (*adj*): le régime, **soumis** depuis des années aux pressions venues de l'extérieur (*subject*); tous les contribuables **soumis** à l'ISF (*liable*); l'entreprise est **soumise** à l'obligation de publier un bilan social (*constrained; subject*)

soumissionner: documents à produire: déclaration d'intention de **soumissionner** (*tender for contract*)

souple (*adj*): avec des conditions très **souples** de durée et de taux; il a invité les deux pays à se montrer plus **souples** dans la négociation (*flexible*)

souscripteur (*m*): la liste des **souscripteurs** s'allonge (*contributor, subscriber*); 70 millions de titres ont été achetés par 270 000 **petits souscripteurs** (*small investor*)

souscrire: il était disposé à **souscrire** un contrat de vente (*sign*); il **souscrit une assurance** tous risques pour sa voiture neuve (*take out an insurance policy*); dans l'état actuel du plan, nous ne pouvons **y souscrire** (*agree; be in favour*)

sous-jacent <e> (*adj*): l'idée **sous-jacente**, c'est que les alliés de la France lui viendront en aide (*underlying; unspoken*)

sous-traiter: celle-ci a **sous-traité** plus de 70% des travaux à une firme anglaise (*subcontract*)

soutenir: il a, quant à lui, **soutenu** le contraire (*argue, maintain*); les dépenses consacrées à **soutenir** les prix agricoles dans la CEE (*support*)

soutenu <e> (*adj*): la demande reste **soutenue** (*buoyant; sustained*)

soutien (*m*): l'Occident, qui est le **soutien** d'Israël (*support, mainstay*); les dépenses communautaires affectées au **soutien** du lait (*price support*)

spécificité (*f*): conduits à affirmer chacun, violemment, sa **spécificité** (*separate identity; individuality*)

sponsorat (*m*): de plus en plus d'entreprises se convertissent au **sponsorat** (*sponsorship*)

spot (*m*): les **spots publicitaires** sont le dernier cri en matière de publicité médiatique (*advertising slot*)

stage (*m*): il faut accomplir un **stage professionnel** de six mois avant d'obtenir son titre (*work-experience/training scheme*); le développement des **stages d'insertion à la vie professionnelle** (*government-sponsored work-experience scheme*)

stagiaire (*m*): il obtint un poste de **stagiaire**, malgré le nombre élevé de demandeurs (*trainee; probationer*)

statuer: en dernier ressort, ce sera le tribunal qui **statuera** sur ce litige (*rule, give a ruling on*)

structure (*f*): le ministre a visité 15 **structures d'accueil** pour personnes âgées (*day centre/unit*)

structurel < -elle > (*adj*): évitons de confondre le conjoncturel et le **structurel** (*structural; underlying*)

stupéfiant (*m*): la législation sur les **stupéfiants** est draconienne (*drug, narcotic*); l'affaire a été confiée à la **brigade des stupéfiants** (*drug squad*)

subalterne (*adj*): il passa quelques années dans des emplois **subalternes** (*junior; minor*)

subornation (*f*): il a été inculpé pour **subornation** de témoins (*bribery*)

suborner: soupçonné d'avoir essayé de **suborner** le témoin principal (*bribe*)

subside (*m*): le ministre de la Recherche lui alloua les **subsides** nécessaires (*subsidy*); les travailleurs sans emploi ne bénéficient d'aucun **subside** (*grant, allowance*)

subsistance (*f*): les deux tiers de ces pays n'ont qu'une économie de **subsistance**; le droit à un revenu de **subsistance** ne devrait pas être lié à l'exercice d'un travail (*subsistence; bare survival*)

substitut (*m*): le **substitut**, spécialement détaché à la section anti-terroriste (*deputy public prosecutor*)

substitution (*f*): les prisons sont pleines, il faut trouver des **peines de substitution** (*alternative form of punishment; non-custodial sentence*)

subvention (*f*): on débattra à Bruxelles des **subventions** à l'agriculture (*grant, subsidy*)

subventionner: l'État **subventionne** le gros œuvre, la municipalité se charge du reste (*subsidize*)

succession (*f*): la mise en place d'un impôt progressif sur les **successions** (*inheritance*)

succursale (*f*): les banques vont-elle fermer leurs **succursales** dans les petites communes? (*branch*)

suffrage (*m*): le gouvernement devra en tenir compte s'il veut rallier les **suffrages** des centristes (*vote*); le chef de l'État est élu au **suffrage universel** (*universal suffrage*)

suite (*f*): le dossier sera-t-il **classé sans suite**? (*close a file/case*); le parquet décidera des **suites à donner** à l'affaire (*action to be taken*)

suivi (*m*): responsable de la mise en chantier et du **suivi** des travaux (*supervision; follow-up*)

suivre: la grève ne fut pas très **suivie** (*follow, obey*)

sujet <-ette> (*adj*): les nouvelles en provenance de Pékin sont **sujettes à caution** (*unconfirmed; unreliable*)

supercherie (*f*): les prétendus documents authentiques étaient en fait des **supercheries** (*fabrication*)

suppléant (*m*): le député, décédé le 15 septembre, sera remplacé par son **suppléant**; il s'agit du **suppléant** à l'Assemblée du secrétaire d'État à la Jeunesse et aux Sports (*stand-in, deputy*)

supplétif (*m*): il s'agit de l'unité de **supplétifs** de l'armée tchadienne (*reservist*)

suppression (*f*): la **suppression** des subventions gouvernementales (*abolition*); 1 290 nouvelles **suppressions d'emplois** (*redundancy*)

supprimer: 600 emplois bientôt **supprimés** chez Brandt (*abolish, suppress; axe*)

surcapacité (*f*): il faut essayer de réduire une **surcapacité** de 20% et des prix trop élevés de 25% (*excess productive capacity*)

surchauffe (*f*): une reprise de l'inflation, dûe à une **surchauffe** de l'économie (*overheating*)

surcoût (*m*): le **surcoût** sera très important pour les petites entreprises (*increased cost; overspend*)

sureffectif (*m*): les militants sont conscients du problème des **sureffectifs**; la chasse aux **sureffectifs** a entraîné la fermeture de l'usine du Mans (*overmanning; surplus labour*)

surenchère (*f*): il prépare une **surenchère** à l'offre de l'industriel australien; la CGT, vite dépassée par la **surenchère** de la base (*higher bid; over-bid*); sa **surenchère** réactionnaire va hypothéquer les chances de son parti (*excess, exaggeration*)

surenchérir: il est forcé de **surenchérir** ou de renoncer à son OPA (*raise the bid/offer*)

sûreté (*f*): les policiers de la **sûreté** urbaine de Strasbourg (*criminal investigation department*)

surimposition (*f*): ayant payé une **surimposition**, il aura droit à un abattement sur la prochaine imposition (*excess tax*)

surimposer: le fisc l'ayant **surimposé** deux années de suite; la nécessité de ne pas **surimposer** les artisans et les commerçants de la commune (*overtax*)

surnombre (*m*): comment résorber le problème du **surnombre** auquel fait face l'administration pénitentiaire?; le problème des 1 500 salariés **en surnombre** (*excess, surplus*)

surpeuplement (*m*): les gardiens sont les premières victimes du **surpeuplement**

carcéral (*overcrowding*)

sursaut (*m*): le brusque et rapide **sursaut** du dollar (*sharp rise*)

surseoir: c'est au Président de recommander que l'on **sursoie** à l'exécution des deux condamnés à mort (*defer, postpone; suspend*)

sursis (*m*): deux ans de prison **avec sursis** ont été requis contre l'accusé (*suspended sentence*); les jeunes Français peuvent bénéficier d'un **sursis d'incorporation** (*deferment of military service*); **sursis à exécution** pour deux cliniques nantaises (*temporary reprieve*)

sursitaire (*m/adj*): en tant que **sursitaire,** il fera son service militaire plus tard (*deferred conscript*)

surveillance (*f*): le tout sous la **surveillance** étroite du ministère de la Santé (*supervision*)

survie (*f*): ils se battent pour la **survie** de leur langue; la **survie** du gouvernement, de plus en plus problématique (*survival*)

susceptible (*adj*): les électeurs **susceptibles** de voter pour le candidat centriste (*likely*)

susciter: un discours qui a **suscité** bien des controverses (*cause, give rise to*)

sympathisant (*m*): au cours d'affrontements entre manifestants de l'opposition et **sympathisants** du gouvernement (*supporter*)

syndic (*m*): pour la reprise de la société en faillite, les **syndics** se sont prononcés pour le groupe belge (*official government receiver*); une assurance de copropriété est souscrite par le **syndic d'immeuble** (*tenants' managing agent*)

syndicalisation (*f*): avec le taux de **syndicalisation** le plus faible d'Europe (*union membership; unionization*)

syndicat (*m*): la question sera soumise à un **syndicat** interdépartemental (*association*); de moins en moins de Français appartiennent à un **syndicat ouvrier** (*trade union*)

syndiqué (*m/adj*): en 1979, les **syndiqués** y étaient encore au nombre de 12 millions (*member of a trade union*)

syndiquer [se]: les femmes de 30 à 40 ans **se syndiquent** plus fréquemment que leurs aînées (*join a trade union*)

T

table (*f*): on ne saurait **faire table rase** de la législation sociale du gouvernement sortant (*change completely*); les quatre **tables rondes** chargées d'examiner les problèmes sociaux (*round table committee/ conference*)

tabler: les experts **tablent** sur une baisse des prix des céréales de l'ordre de 15% (*expect; count upon*)

taille (*f*): la seule société française de **taille** européenne (*dimension*); dans les discussions à Bonn, l'enjeu sera **de taille** (*considerable, redoubtable*)

tailler: il faudrait **tailler** dans les programmes sociaux et augmenter les impôts (*make large cuts in*); [se] il **s'est taillé** une réputation d'incorruptible (*secure/gain for oneself*); lors des élections le RPR **s'est taillé la part du lion** (*gain the lion's share*)

talonner: la France arrive cinquième, **talonnant** la Grande-Bretagne (*be just behind/on the heels of*)

tampon (*m*): une **zone tampon** servant de cordon sanitaire aux localités frontalières (*buffer zone*)

tarder: si le gouvernement **tarde** à négocier avec les mineurs (*be slow to; delay*); il faut aller de l'avant **sans tarder** (*without delay*)

tarif (*m*): les compagnies baissent leurs **tarifs** (*scale of charges; fare*)

tarifer: le ministre a autorisé les banquiers à **tarifer** les chèques (*make a charge for*)

tarification (*f*): on relance le débat sur la **tarification** des comptes bancaires (*charging for; putting a charge on*)

tas (*m*): un animateur social formé **sur le tas**; il a tout appris **sur le tas** (*on the job*)

tassement (*m*): hausse des exportations, **tassement** des importations (*slow-down; stagnation*)

tasser: on a beau **tasser** les prix (*squeeze, reduce, compress*); [se] les ventes vers les États-Unis **se sont tassées** en 1990 (*fall, slump*)

taux (*m*): la chute du **taux des naissances** (*birth-rate*); les banques relèvent leur **taux de base** (*base lending rate*); la Banque du Japon avait abaissé son **taux d'escompte**, taux auquel elle prête aux établissements financiers (*discount rate; bank rate*)

taxation (*f*): il s'est prononcé contre la **taxation** plus forte des plus-values des entreprises (*taxation*)

taxer: elle se voit **taxée** de protectionnisme par les États-Unis (*accuse*)

tel quel: le texte fut adopté **tel quel**, sans débat (*as it stands; without modification*)

témoignage (*m*): de nouveaux **témoignages** sur les circonstances de la mort des otages (*piece of evidence; version of events*)

témoigner: ceci **témoigne** de l'importance que la France attache à ses rapports avec le Maroc (*show, indicate*)

témoin (*m*): l'absence de ce **témoin** crucial pour la défense (*witness*); il y avait deux **témoins à charge** (*witness for the prosecution*)

tenant (*m*): les **tenants** de la ligne dure voulaient proclamer la loi martiale (*advocate, supporter*)

tendance (*f*): la **tendance** était, en effet, à une augmentation annuelle du nombre de chômeurs (*tendency, trend*)

tendre: le dépôt d'un amendement **tendant** à porter le taux de l'impôt sur les sociétés à 50% (*the effect/aim of which*); [se] les cours **se sont tendus**, enregistrant une progression de 100% en un an (*rise*)

tendu <e> (*adj*): c'est dans un climat très **tendu** que les discussions ont commencé (*tense*)

tenir [se]: la réunion **s'y tiendra** du 21 au 24 août (*be held*); pour **s'en tenir** à la période 1958–1962 (*limit/restrict oneself to*)

ténor (*m*): les principaux **ténors** du PS ont pris la parole (*leading personality*)

tentative (*f*): reconnu coupable d'une **tentative de** hold-up; une **tentative de** coup d'État échoua (*attempted*)

tenue (*f*): avant la **tenue** d'élections (*holding; taking place*); la relative **bonne tenue** du Franc suisse (*healthy state; firmness*)

tergiversation (*f*): de longues **tergiversations** ont précédé l'adoption du projet (*prevarication; shilly-shallying*)

tergiverser: Téhéran, après avoir **tergiversé** pour ne pas répondre à l'appel lancé par le Conseil de sécurité (*delay; play for time*)

terme (*m*): on espère ainsi **mettre un terme** à 40 ans de socialisme (*bring to an end*); **à terme**, tous les intérêts sont menacés (*in the end; eventually*); **aux termes de** la loi, l'employeur n'est pas obligé de le faire (*according to*)

terrain (*m*): une politique qui soit proche des réalités du **terrain** (*field; actual situation, reality*); c'est **sur le terrain** des droits de l'homme que cette mesure est critiquable (*in the field of, area of*); l'étude **sur le terrain** révèle l'ampleur du problème (*on site; in the field*); nul ne peut exclure qu'un **terrain d'entente** soit trouvé (*area of/basis for agreement*)

tertiaire (*adj*): c'est aujourd'hui l'industrie qui décline, au profit du [secteur] **tertiaire** (*service industries; tertiary sector*)

tête (*f*): il espère être **tête de liste** pour les élections municipales (*top of voting list*); les industriels étrangers trouvent ainsi une **tête de pont** en France (*bridgehead; foothold*); ils en veulent aux centristes, **têtes-de-turc** traditionnels (*whipping-boy; Aunt Sally*)

texte (*m*): la Chambre des représentants vient de voter un **texte** visant à réduire les pouvoirs du Président (*piece of legislation; bill*)

thèse (*f*): il se disait favorable aux **thèses** des séparatistes (*idea, argument*)

ticket (*m*): ce **ticket modérateur** peut être partiellement remboursé par les mutuelles (*patient's contribution to cost of medical treatment*)

tiers (*m*): l'assurance dite **aux tiers** garantit la réparation des préjudices causés à d'autres personnes (*third-party insurance*); les pays du **tiers-**

monde ont réagi de façon positive (*Third World; non-aligned countries*); le **tiers provisionnel**, un acompte sur l'impôt sur le revenu (*interim tax payment*); (*adj*) des accords de pêche avec des pays **tiers** (*third; other*)

tirage (*m*): aucun journal français n'avait un **tirage** supérieur à 50 000 exemplaires (*circulation; print run*)

tirer: les exportations **tirent** la croissance dans la plupart des secteurs de l'industrie (*promote, give momentum to; lead*); Le Monde **tire** à 400 000 exemplaires par jour (*have a print run/circulation*)

titre (*m*): ce jour-là, 70 000 **titres** changèrent de main à la Bourse de Londres (*stock; share*); employés **au titre** de la co-opération; les immigrés entrés depuis 1975 **au titre** du regroupement familial (*under a scheme for*)

titrer: Le Figaro **titrait**: 'A bas la Droite' (*run a headline*)

titulaire (*m/adj*): tous les postes ont été pourvus de nouveaux **titulaires**; un quart sont **titulaires** de revenus fonciers; **titulaire** de la double nationalité française et algérienne (*person holding/in possession of*)

titularisation (*f*): le statut des enseignants qui n'optent pas pour la **titularisation** (*tenure; granting of tenure*)

titulariser: instituteur, il a été **titularisé** en 1987 (*confirm in a post; establish*)

tollé (*m*): ce fut un **tollé** de la part des syndicats; une décision qui a provoqué un **tollé** général dans les milieux laïques (*outcry, protest*)

tort (*m*): la Cour européenne **donne tort** à la France (*blame; find against*)

totalité (*f*): en cas de retard, la **totalité** des droits peut être exigée immédiatement (*all, the whole of*)

toucher: il aurait **touché** d'importantes sommes d'argent (*receive*); les secteurs les plus **touchés** par la grève (*affect, hit*); un pétrolier a été **touché** par un missile dans les eaux koweitiennes (*hit*)

tournant (*m*): ce **tournant** historique s'est fait dans le calme (*turning point; crucial moment*); il a voulu donner un nouveau **tournant** aux relations franco-allemandes (*direction; impetus*); l'opposition fait des gorges chaudes de ce **tournant** du PC (*volte-face; turn-round; change of policy*)

tourner: l'usine doit commencer à **tourner** en octobre prochain (*begin production; operate*); les firmes d'armement **tournent** l'embargo vers le golfe Persique (*get round; find a loophole in*); le vrai taux annuel **tourne autour** de 3% (*be in the region of/approximately*)

tournure (*f*): la **tournure** prise par les discussions laisse présager une cessation des hostilités (*turn*)

tract (*m*): il édita les **tracts** et affiches électoraux (*tract, pamphlet*)

tractation (*f*): après six mois de **tractations**, les deux partis sont arrivés à un accord (*laborious negotiations*)

traduire: 13 personnes ont été **traduites en justice** (*bring before the courts*)

trafic (*m*): deux officiers de police mêlés à un **trafic** de voitures volées (*trade, dealings in*); inculpé de corruption et de **trafic d'influence** (*trading of* *favours*)

train (*m*): l'entrée en vigueur d'un **train de mesures** d'austérité économique (*batch/package of measures*); la réduction du **train de vie** américain apparaît comme la seule issue (*standard of living*)

traîne (*f*): **à la traîne** au début des années 80 (*lagging behind*)

trait (*m*): deux rapports, **ayant trait** aux droits des détenus (*concerning, relating to*)

traite (*f*): il n'avait plus de quoi payer les **traites**; une maison dont les **traites** mangent la moitié de leur revenu (*bill, draft; hire-purchase/ mortgage repayment*)

traitement (*m*): les **traitements** dans le secteur du bâtiment restent stables (*wage*); les élections s'approchent, et le **traitement social** du chômage [stages, TUC] bat son plein (*government action on social/employment questions*)

traiter: il **traita** l'auteur du livre d'affabulateur et de menteur (*call*); [se] une tonne d'aluminium **se traite** aujourd'hui à 23 000 dollars (*be sold/ bought*)

tranche (*f*): dès 1992, la première **tranche** du projet sera achevée, assure le promoteur (*section, stage*); dans la **tranche d'âge** 15–44 ans (*age bracket*); toutes les **tranches d'imposition** sont relevées (*tax band*)

trancher: le tribunal s'est donné jusqu'au 28 mai pour **trancher**; les élections du 16 mars **trancheront** (*decide, settle an issue*); le ministre soviétique **tranche** avec son successeur (*be very different from*)

transalpin <e> (*adj*): les services secrets **transalpins** y furent pour quelque chose (*transalpine; Italian*)

transfuge (*m*): **transfuge** du RPR, qu'il avait quitté en 1989 (*renegade; deserter*)

transiger: dans cette affaire, les États-Unis refusent de **transiger** avec les principes (*compromise*)

transiter: ces opérations frauduleuses avaient **transité** par un compte bancaire (*be put/go through*)

transitoire (*adj*): la mise en place de mesures **transitoires** (*transitional*); ils auront un mandat de cinq ans **à titre transitoire** (*as a transitional measure*)

transparence (*f*): le débat sur la **transparence** du patrimoine des élus (*openness; publicizing*)

travail (*m*): les **grands travaux** ont l'avantage de créer des milliers d'emplois (*major building /constructional developments*)

tremper: ils semblent avoir largement **trempé** dans l'affaire de ventes de drogues (*have a hand in; be involved in*)

trésor (*m*): le **Trésor public** finance, en fin de compte, ces activités (*Treasury; public purse*)

trésorerie (*f*): une baisse de sa **trésorerie** lui a fait perdre la confiance de ses banquiers (*funds, cash*); en proie à des **difficultés de trésorerie** (*cash-flow problems*); une **gestion de trésorerie** personnalisée et sans risque (*money management*)

trêve (*f*): une fragile **trêve** s'est instaurée entre Palestiniens et miliciens chiites (*truce*)

tri (*m*): il faudrait opérer un **tri** pour n'en garder que les meilleurs (*selection; sorting out*)

triangulaire (*adj*): il l'avait emporté en 1982 dans une [élection] **triangulaire** au deuxième tour (*three-way electoral contest*)

tribunal (*m*): le gouvernement décida de **porter l'affaire devant les tribunaux** (*bring before the courts; take to court*); le **tribunal de police** juge les contraventions (*police court*)

tribune (*f*): on a organisé une **tribune** sur les questions sociales (*discussion, forum*)

tributaire (*adj*): l'économie algérienne est largement **tributaire** des hydrocarbures; la progression des transports maritimes est **tributaire** de l'évolution de la conjoncture (*dependent*)

tricolore (*m/adj*): la plupart des grandes marques **tricolores** étaient représentées (*French*)

trimestre (*m*): dès le premier **trimestre** de 1990 (*term; quarter, three-month period*)

trinquer (*fam.*): les actionnaires sont contents, mais les salariés '**trinquent**' (*suffer; pay*)

tripotage (*m*): une sombre histoire de **tripotage** électoral (*malpractice*)

troc (*m*): dans le cadre d'un accord de **troc** conclu récemment (*barter/ exchange*)

troisième âge (*m*): les promesses du candidat aux personnes du **troisième âge** (*senior citizens; age of retirement*)

trou (*m*): le **trou** du régime général de la Sécurité sociale dépasse quatre milliards pour l'année (*deficit*)

trouble (*m*): des **troubles** sanglants à la suite d'une manifestation antinucléaire à Rome (*disturbance*)

truchement (*m*): l'État exerçait sa tutelle sur les départements par le **truchement** du Préfet (*intermediary*)

truster: ils **trustent** toutes les premières places; ses supporters ont **trusté** les places au Congrès (*monopolize; win a majority of*)

Tuc (*m*): 495 000 personnes en stages, dont 193 000 en **TUC** [travaux d'utilité collective] (*government job-creation scheme*)

tuciste (*m*) (*fam.*): ces chômeurs, tous deux '**tucistes**' désabusés (*person employed on government job-creation scheme*) tutelle (*f*): la **tutelle** humiliante de l'Amérique; les départements sont soumis à la **tutelle** de Paris (*supervision; overseeing*); en intervenant auprès de leur ministre **de tutelle**, rue de Rivoli (*with administrative authority*)

U

ulcéré <e> (*adj*): il se déclara **ulcéré** par ce refus de transiger (*sickened, angered*)

ultérieur <e> (*adj*): les versements **ultérieurs** sont de 3 600F (*subsequent; later*)

unanimité (*f*): on regrette que l'**unanimité** ne se soit pas faite à ce sujet (*unanimous agreement*); il a été réélu **à l'unanimité** (*unanimously*)

une (*f*): le grand quotidien lui consacrait la **une** de son supplément dominical (*front page*); la visite **faisait la une** des journaux (*make the front page/headlines*)

uninominal <e> (*adj*): le scrutin **uninominal** majoritaire revient en faveur (*single-member voting*)

union (*f*): le secrétaire de l'**union** locale CGT (*interprofessional trade-union grouping*)

unité (*f*): la société construira une nouvelle **unité** de 30 salaries près du Havre (*production unit; factory*)

urbanisme (*m*): un plan d'**urbanisme** et de résorption des bidonvilles (*town planning/development*); la **commission d'urbanisme** a émis un avis défavorable (*planning committee*)

urgence (*f*): l'**urgence** de rétablir un équilibre conventionnel en Europe (*urgent need*); l'**état d'urgence** a été levé (*state of emergency*); un **plan d'urgence** a été lancé pour créer 200 000 emplois (*emergency plan*)

urne (*f*): dimanche prochain les Français **se rendent aux urnes** (*go to the ballot box; vote*); le gouvernement **sorti des urnes** en mars 1986 (*return, vote in*); les électeurs hier ont **boudé les urnes** (*abstain; fail to vote*)

us et coutumes (*m pl*): ceux qui ne sont pas familiers avec les **us et coutumes** du pays (*habit, custom*)

usage (*m*): avec toutes les garanties **d'usage**; les policiers ont procédé aux constatations **d'usage** (*usual*); les policiers ont **fait usage** de leurs armes (*use, employ*)

usager (*m*): grèves: les **usagers** mis à rude épreuve; l'**usager** subira une forte augmentation (*member of the public; user of a public service*)

usufruit (*m*): il en a l'**usufruit**, le terrain passant à son fils après sa mort (*use; usufruct*)

usure (*f*): la **guerre d'usure** entre gouvernement et opposition (*war of attrition*)

utile (*adj*): l'édifice du Musée d'Orsay présente 47 000 m² **utiles** (*usable space*)

utilisation (*f*): les **frais d'utilisation** d'une voiture (*running costs*)

V

vacance (*f*): le président du Sénat assura l'intérim pendant la **vacance** du pouvoir en 1969; il y a toujours **vacance** du pouvoir au sommet de l'État (*vacancy, falling vacant; vacuum*)

vacataire (*adj*): le personnel **vacataire** ne bénéficiait pas de couverture sociale (*temporary*)

valeur (*f*): une hausse record des **valeurs** françaises (*securities; stocks and shares*); une baisse du niveau des investissements **en valeur absolue** (*in real terms*); le secteur public représente 30% de la **valeur ajoutée** industrielle (*added value*); un bel appartement, **valeur locative** 8 500F par mois (*rental value*); la **valeur locative cadastrale** d'une propriété est fixée par le service des Impôts (*rateable value*)

valoir: opération manquée qui lui **a valu** une peine de prison de quatre ans (*earn*); les adversaires du projet **font valoir** qu'il sera très coûteux (*argue, point out*)

valorisation (*f*): il assure la promotion et la **valorisation** de l'image de marque Schneider (*prestige; promotion*)

valoriser: il faut **valoriser** le bilan, l'œuvre accompli déjà par le gouvernement (*put emphasis on*); un rôle essentiel des avantages en nature est de **valoriser** le salarié qui en touche (*give a sense of achievement/importance to*); en **valorisant** voiture et logement de fonction, on arrive à 20 000F nets mensuels (*calculate/estimate value of*)

valse (*f*): après les élections, ce fut, comme d'habitude, la **valse des préfets** (*wholesale replacement of* Préfets); la mesure a provoqué une **valse** immédiate **des étiquettes** (*price increases*)

valser: les garagistes, les hôteliers **faisaient valser les étiquettes** (*raise prices sharply*)

vedette (*f*): sa mort a ravi la **vedette** dans la presse outre-Rhin (*news headline*); les **valeurs vedettes** étaient les plus demandées hier en bourse (≃ *'blue-chip' shares*)

véhiculer: il **véhicule** ouvertement les obsessions racistes de l'extrême-droite

(*advocate; be a vehicle for*)

velléitaire (*adj*): le gouvernement est très **velléitaire** sur ce chapitre (*indecisive, lacking in resolution*)

velléité (*f*): dès que se manifeste la moindre **velléité** de contestation; il y a eu en 1981 des **velléités** de révolution culturelle (*hint, sign of; desire for*)

vente (*f*): après la fixation du **prix de vente** (*selling price*); la **vente au privé** de Saint-Gobain défraye la chronique boursière (*privatization*)

ventilation (*f*): une **ventilation** géographique du déficit commercial américain (*analysis, breakdown, distribution*)

ventiler: les enquêteurs du *Figaro* ont **ventilé** les divers contrats de ces sociétés (*analyse, break down*)

verbaliser: l'agent **verbalisait** pour stationnement non-autorisé (*book, report*)

vergogne (*f*): il exploita le thème raciste **sans vergogne** (*shamelessly*)

vérifier [se]: si les prévisions de fréquentation **se vérifient** (*turn out to be true; be confirmed*)

vérité (*f*): le mot d'ordre sera: **vérité des prix** (*fair/realistic prices*)

verrou (*m*): un citoyen belge **mis sous les verrous** en France (*put behind bars; imprison*)

verrouiller: un autre groupe tenté, lui aussi, de **verrouiller** le marché informatique (*gain a dominant position*); les Socialistes **verrouillent** les postes clefs en région parisienne (*dominate; monopolize*); dans un système aussi **verrouillé** et bloqué que celui de l'URSS (*tightly controlled*)

versement (*m*): payable en 12 **versements** annuels (*payment*); les **versements** s'échelonnent sur 2 ans (*instalment*)

vert <e> (*adj*): le problème récurrent des **politiques vertes** (*agricultural policy*); la '**banque verte**' n'a pas été nationalisée mais mutualisée (Crédit Agricole *bank*); le **parti Vert** a recueilli 14% des suffrages (*ecological/Green party*)

véto (*m*): l'OLP a **mis son véto** à un tel projet; le Président va pouvoir **opposer son véto** à la loi sur le commerce (*veto*)

viabiliser: 75 000 m² de terrains, **viabilisés** tous réseaux (*equip with services*)

viabilité (*f*): ainsi la **viabilité** de l'entreprise serait compromise (*viability*)

viable (*adj*): des entreprises pourtant économiquement **viables** (*viable, healthy*)

viager <-ère> (*adj*): il perçut une **rente viagère** en vertu d'une clause de réversion (*life annuity*); il **vendit** la ferme **en viager** moyennant une rente qu'il toucherait jusqu'à sa mort (*mortgage a property in return for a life annuity*)

154

vice (*m*): la demande fut rejetée **pour vice de forme** (*on a technicality*); le jugement fut cassé **pour vice de procédure** (*on a legal irregularity*)

vignette (*f*): il y aura une nouvelle **vignette** automobile pour les voitures de 15 et 16 chevaux (*road-fund licence*)

vigueur (*f*): les taux de cotisation **en vigueur** au 1ᵉʳ novembre 1990 (*in force/ operation*); l'**entrée en vigueur** du cessez-le-feu (*coming into effect/ force*); la nouvelle Constitution **entre en vigueur** le 4 décembre (*come into force*)

vindicte (*f*): les députés ne devraient pas être livrés à la **vindicte** publique (*condemnation; vilification*)

viol (*m*): pour **viol** des règlements nationaux et internationaux (*violation*)

virage (*m*): le **virage** de 1983 explique la défaite de 1986; le **virage** économique et commercial a été amorcé (*change of direction/policy*)

virement (*m*): le transfert de fonds s'est effectué par **virement** bancaire (*transfer*); les pressions se multiplient pour un complet **virement de bord** (*change of direction/policy*)

virer: la somme a été **virée** à son compte (*transfer*); (*fam.*) le chef d'état-major brésilien **viré** pour avoir trop parlé (*fire, sack*)

visée (*f*): les **visées** gouvernementales n'échappent à personne; il déplora les **visées** expansionnistes d'Israël (*design; intention*)

viser: notre démarche **vise** la catégorie des 18 ans (*target/be directed at*); il faut faire **viser** le formulaire à la mairie du domicile (*vet; visa, stamp*); le texte **vise** à garantir les droits des petits épargnants (*aim*)

vivre: les accords du Louvre **ont-ils** définitivement **vécu**? (*be at an end; no longer exist*)

vocation (*f*): il a rappelé que le revenu minimum d'insertion avait une double **vocation** (*purpose*)

vœu (*m*): au FN, on en est ravi, car on **appelait de ses vœux** une telle solution (*hope for*)

voie (*f*): les pays **en voie** de développement (*on the way to, in the course of being*); la réforme a été réalisée **par voie** de référendum (*by means of*); d'où ils sont expédiés **par voie terrestre** (*overland; by land*); une procédure judiciaire pour outrage et **voies de fait** (*assault; violence against the person*)

voirie (*f*): grâce aux efforts de la **voirie** municipale, les routes ont été dégagées (*highways department*); des plans de **voirie** qui ignorent les quartiers traversés (*road systems*)

voisin (*m/adj*): c'est un pourcentage **voisin** de celui qui fut observé en 1981 (*similar; in the neighbourhood of*)

voix (*f*): le candidat centriste a reçu 12 000 **voix**; la répartition des **voix** et des sièges (*vote*)

vol (*m*): son inculpation pour **vol à l'étalage** (*shop-lifting*); deux cambrioleurs inculpés de **vol avec effraction** (*breaking and entering*)

volet (*m*): le train de mesures comporte trois grands **volets**; deux **volets** inséparables de la politique du gouvernement (*aspect*)

volontaire (*adj*): inculpé de coups et blessures **volontaires** sur un enfant âgé de moins de 15 ans (*deliberate*); lorsque sera dressé le bilan définitif des **départs volontaires** (*voluntary redundancy*)

volontairement: cette convention se résume en 21 articles **volontairement** vagues (*deliberately*); le Japon limite **volontairement** ses ventes aux États-Unis (*voluntarily*)

volontariat (*m*): la CGT conteste que les départs aient lieu sur la base du **volontariat** (*volunteer scheme*); une journée de travail **en volontariat** (*unpaid*)

volonté (*f*): l'absence de **volonté** de démocratisation du pays; il a affirmé sa **volonté** de voir la Turquie entrer dans la CEE (*will, wish, desire*)

volontiers: il se reconnaissait **volontiers** une parenté avec le FN (*willingly, readily*); une Turquie mieux armée et **volontiers** offensive (*given to being, tending to be*)

volte-face (*f*): cette **volte-face** se traduit par une grave crise de confiance pour le gouvernement conservateur (*about-turn; U-turn*)

vote (*m*): avant même le décompte des **votes**, il était donné gagnant (*vote*); le **vote** du budget interviendra la semaine prochaine (*voting; vote on*); grâce à la procédure du **vote bloqué**, le gouvernement s'assura la victoire (*package vote; single vote on whole bill*)

voter: le groupe centriste n'a pas **voté** la motion de censure (*vote; vote in favour of*)

X

X: l'ouverture d'une information judiciaire contre **X** (*person/persons unknown*)

Z

ZAC (*f*): les **ZAC** [Zones d'aménagement concerté] visent souvent à la transformation d'un quartier ancien par rénovation ou réhabilitation (*integrated development zone*)

ZAD (*f*): les **Zones d'aménagement différé** permettent à la collectivité de s'assurer des réserves de terrains pour logements ou équipements collectifs (*area reserved for development*)

zélateur (*m*): les **zélateurs** de la 'perestroïka' veulent aller vite en besogne (*supporter, advocate*)

zénith (*m*): il est **au zénith** de sa popularité (*at the top/highest point*)

zizanie (*f*): un diviseur qui crée la **zizanie** au sein du PS marseillais (*discord, strife*)

zone (*f*): un enfant d'immigrés, né dans la **zone** (*slum belt*); ils réclament un **abattement de zone** pour compenser la cherté de la vie en Corse (*reduction/allowance granted on a regional basis*)

ZUP (*f*): les **Zones à urbaniser en priorité** [ZUP] sont une forme aujourd'hui périmée d'urbanisme concerté; au fin fond de la **ZUP** nord de Nîmes (*industrial zone*)

ACRONYMS AND ABBREVIATIONS

Besides the most useful acronyms and abbreviations, this list contains a selection of frequently used addresses of ministries, headquarters of political parties, trade unions etc. These are widely used as convenient shorthand for the bodies, offices and organizations to which they refer.

ACP	Afrique, Caraïbes, Pacifique
AEF	Afrique équatoriale française
AELE	Association européenne de libre échange [Eng: EFTA]
AF	Action Française
AFNOR	Association française de normalisation
AFP	Agence France-Presse
AFR	Allocation formation-reclassement
AGEO	Assemblée générale extraordinaire
AGIRC	Association générale des institutions de retraite des cadres
AGO	Assemblée générale ordinaire
ALPE	Association laïque des parents d'élèves
ANPE	Agence nationale pour l'emploi
AOF	Afrique occidentale française
APEL	Association de parents d'élèves de l'école libre
APL	Aide personnalisée au logement
Ardt	Arrondissement
ARRCO	Association des régimes de retraite complémentaire
ASSEDIC	Association pour l'emploi dans l'industrie et le commerce
Beauvau	<place> Ministère de l'Intérieur
BEP	Brevet d'études professionnelles
Bercy	<rue de> Ministère de l'Économie et des Finances
BIT	Bureau international du travail
BNCI	Banque nationale pour le commerce et l'industrie
BNP	Banque Nationale de Paris
BO	Bulletin officiel
BOURBON	<Palais-> Assemblée nationale
BPF	Bon pour francs
Brienne	<Hôtel de> Ministère de la Défense
Brongniart	<Palais> Bourse de Paris
BRP	Brigade pour la répression du banditisme
BSP	Brigade des stupéfiants et du proxénétisme
BT	Brevet de technicien
BTS	Brevet de technicien supérieur
CA	Conseil d'administration
CAC	Compagnie des agents de change
CAC 40	Paris Stock Exchange 40 Share Index
CAF	Coût, Assurance, Fret;
	Caisse d'allocations familiales
CAP	Certificat d'aptitude professionnelle

CAPES	Certificat d'aptitude au professorat de l'enseignement du second degré
CC	Corps consulaire
CCI	Chambre de commerce et d'industrie
CCP	Compte chèque postal
CCR	Coefficient de capitalisation des résultats [Eng: PER]
CD	Corps diplomatique
CDD	Contrat à durée déterminée
CDF	Charbonnages de France
CDS	Centre des démocrates sociaux
CEA	Commissariat à l'énergie atomique
CECA	Commission européenne du charbon et de l'acier
CEE	Communauté économique européenne
CEG	Collège d'enseignement général
CER	Comité d'expansion régionale
CERES	Centre d'études, de recherches et d'éducation sociales
CERN	Centre européen de recherches nucléaires
CES	Conseil économique et social; Collège d'enseignement secondaire
CET	Collège d'enseignement technique
CF	Communauté française
CFA	Communauté financière africaine; Centre de formation d'apprentis
CFDT	Confédération française et démocratique du travail
CFE/CGC	Confédération générale de l'encadrement Confédération générale des cadres
CFTC	Confédération française des travailleurs chrétiens
CGC	Confédération générale des cadres
CGT	Confédération générale du travail
CGT-FO	Force ouvrière
CHU	Centre hospitalier universitaire
Cie	Compagnie
CNCL	Conseil national de la communication et des libertés
CNI[P]	Comité national des indépendants [et des paysans]
CNPF	Conseil national du patronat français
CNR	Conseil national de la Résistance
CNRS	Centre national de la recherche scientifique
COB	Commission des opérations en Bourse
CODER	Commission de développement économique régional
CODEVI	Compte d'épargne pour le développement industriel
COGEFI	Conseil en organisation de gestion économique et financière d'entreprises
CPA	Classe préparatoire à l'apprentissage
CPAM	Caisse primaire d'assurance-maladie
CREDOC	Centre de recherches, d'études et de documentation sur la consommation
CRS	Compagnies républicaines de sécurité
CSA	Conseil supérieur de l'audiovisuel
CSM	Conseil supérieur de la magistrature
CU	Communauté urbaine

Acronyms and abbreviations

DATAR	Délégation à l'aménagement du territoire et à l'action régionale
DDASS	Direction départementale à l'action sanitaire et sociale
DES	Diplôme d'études supérieures
DEUG	Diplôme d'études universitaires générales
DGSE	Direction générale à la sécurité extérieure
DGSN	Direction générale de la sûreté nationale
DOM	Département d'outre-mer
DST	Direction de la surveillance du territoire
DTS	Droits de tirage spéciaux
DUEL	Diplôme universitaire d'études littéraires
DUES	Diplôme universitaire d'études scientifiques
DUT	Diplôme universitaire de technologie
ECP	École Centrale de Paris
EDF	Électricité de France
EGF-GDF	Électricité/Gaz de France
Élysée	<Palais de l'> Présidence de la République
EMP	École des Mines de Paris
ENA	École nationale d'administration
ENC	École nationale des chartes
ENPC	École nationale des Ponts et Chaussées
ENS	École normale supérieure
ENSAD	École nationale supérieure des arts décoratifs
ENSJF	École normale supérieure de jeunes filles [Sèvres]
EPIC	Établissement public industriel ou commercial
ESC	École supérieure de commerce
ESSEC	École supérieure des sciences économiques et sociales
ETAM	Employé, technicien, agent de maîtrise
E-U	États-Unis
Fabien	<place du colonel> siège de la CGT
FDES	Fonds de développement économique et social
FEN	Fédération de l'Éducation nationale
FFA	Forces françaises en Allemagne
FLN	Front de libération nationale
FMI	Fonds monétaire international [Eng. IMF]
FN	Front national
FNE	Fonds national de l'emploi
FNS	Fonds national de solidarité
FNSA	Fédération nationale des syndicats agricoles
FNSEA	Fédération nationale des syndicats d'exploitants agricoles
FO	Force ouvrière
GDF	Gaz de France
Grenelle	<rue de> Ministère des Affaires sociales; Ministère de l'Industrie
HEC	École des hautes études commerciales
HLM	Habitation à loyer modéré
Iéna	<Palais d'> Conseil économique et social
IEP	Institut de sciences politiques [Sciences-Po]
IFOP	Institut français d'opinion publique
IGAME	Inspecteur général de l'administration en mission

	extraordinaire
IGF	Impôt sur les grandes fortunes
IGR	Impôt général sur le revenu
ILM	Immeuble à loyer modéré
INED	Institut national des études démographiques
INSEAD	Institut européen d'administration des affaires
INSEE	Institut national des statistiques et des études économiques
INSERM	Institut national de la santé et de la recherche médicale
IRPP	Impôt sur le revenu des personnes physiques
ISF	Impôt sur la fortune [ex-IGF]
IUT	Institut universitaire de Technologie
IVD	Indemnité viagère de départ
JCR	Jeunesse communiste révolutionnaire
JEC	Jeunesse étudiante chrétienne
JO	Jeunesse ouvrière;
	Journal officiel
Lassay	< Hôtel de > Président de l'Assemblée nationale
LCR	Ligue communiste révolutionnaire
LEP	Livret d'épargne populaire;
	Lycée d'enseignement professionnel
Lille	< rue de > RPR
LO	Lutte ouvrière
Luxembourg	< Palais du > Sénat
MATIF	Marché à terme d'instruments financiers;
	Marché à terme international de France
Matignon	< Hôtel > Premier ministre
MEP	Mouvement d'écologie politique
MGEN	Mutuelle générale de l'Éducation nationale
MJC	Maison des jeunes et de la culture
MOCI	Moniteur officiel du commerce et de l'industrie
MRG	Mouvement des Radicaux de gauche
NDLR	Note de la Rédaction [Eng: Editor's note]
OAS	Organisation de l'armée secrète
OCDE	Organisation de coopération et de développement économique [Eng: OECD]
OECE	Organisation européenne de coopération économique
OLP	Organisation pour la libération de la Palestine [Eng: PLO]
OMS	Organisation mondiale de la santé [Eng: WHO]
ONG	Organisation non-gouvernementale [Eng: ≈ QUANGO]
ONU	Organisation des Nations unies [Eng: UNO]
OP	Ouvrier professionnel
OPA	Offre publique d'achat
OPE	Offre publique d'échange
OPAEP	Organisation des pays arabes producteurs de pétrole
OPCVM	Organisation de placements collectifs en valeurs mobilières
OPEP	Organisation des pays producteurs de pétrole
OQ	Ouvrier qualifié
Orfèvres	< quai des > Police judiciaire
Orsay	< quai d' > Ministère des Affaires étrangères
ORSEC	< plan > [plan d'] Organisation des secours

Acronyms and abbreviations

ORTF	Office de la radio et de la télévision française
OS	Ouvrier spécialisé
OTAN	Organisation du traité de l'Atlantique nord [Eng: NATO]
PAC	Politique agricole commune [Eng: CAP]
PAF	Paysage audiovisuel français;
	Police des airs et des frontières
Palais-Royal	< rue du > Conseil d'État
	< place du > Conseil constitutionnel
PAP	Prêt à l'aide à l'accession à la propriété
PC	Prêt conventionné
PCC	Pour copie conforme
PC/PCF	Parti communiste français
P-DG	Président-Directeur Général
P et C	Ponts et Chaussées
PEL	Plan d'épargne-logement
PIB	Produit intérieur brut
PIL	Programme d'insertion local
PJ	Police judiciaire
PLM	Paris-Lyon-Marseille
PME	Petites et moyennes entreprises
PMI	Petites et moyennes industries
PNB	Produit national brut
PR	Parti républicain
PS	Parti socialiste
PSD	Parti social-démocrate
PSU	Parti socialiste unifié
P et T	Postes et Télécommunications
PTT	Postes, Télégraphes, et Téléphones
PUD	Plan d'urbanisme directeur;
	Plan d'urbanisme en détail
PV	Procès-verbal
QG	Quartier-général
RATP	Régie autonome des transports parisiens
RC	Registre du commerce
RCS	Registre du commerce et des sociétés
R et D	Recherche et développement
RDA	République démocratique allemande [Eng: GDR]
RER	Réseau express régional
RES	Reprise d'une entreprise par les salariés
RF	République française
RFA	République fédérale allemande [Eng: FRG]
RG	Renseignements généraux
Rivoli	< rue de > Ministère de l'Économie et des Finances
RMI	Revenu minimum d'insertion
RN	Route nationale
RPR	Rassemblement pour la République [1976]
RTF	Radio-Télévision française
SA	Société anonyme
SAFER	Société d'aménagement foncier et d'établissement rural
SARL	Société à responsabilité limitée

SAU	Surface agricole utile
SDAU	Schéma directeur d'aménagement et d'urbanisme
SDECE	Service de documentation extérieure et de contre-espionnage
SDF	[personne] sans domicile fixe
SDN	Société des nations [1919–45]
SEITA	Société nationale d'exploitation industrielle des tabacs et allumettes
SFIO	Section française de l'Internationale ouvrière
SGDG	Sans garantie du gouvernement
SICAV	Société d'investissement à capital variable
SICOB	Salon des industries du commerce et de l'organisation du bureau
SIDA	Syndrome immunodéficitaire acquis [Eng: AIDS]
SIRET	numéro d'immatriculation de l'entreprise
SIVOM	Syndicat intercommunal à vocation multiple
SIVOS	Syndicat intercommunal à vocation spécialisée
SIVP	Stage d'initiation à la vie professionnelle
SIVU	Syndicat intercommunal à vocation unique
SME	Système monétaire européen [Eng: EMS]
SMIC	Salaire minimum interprofessionnel de croissance (*1970–*)
SMIG	Salaire minimum interprofessionnel garanti (*1950–70*)
SNCF	Société nationale des chemins de fer français
SOFRES	Société française d'enquêtes par sondage
Solférino	< rue de > Parti socialiste
SR	Service des renseignements
SRPJ	Services régionaux de la police judiciaire
SS	Sécurité sociale
SUD	Solidaires, Unitaires, Démocratiques
TAAF	Terres australes et antarctiques françaises
TGI	Tribunal de grande instance
TGV	Train à grande vitesse
TIG	Travail d'intérêt général
TIL	Travail d'intérêt local
TOM	Territoire d'outre-mer
TTC	Toutes taxes comprises
TUC	Travail d'utilité collective
TVA	Taxe à la valeur ajoutée [Eng: VAT]
UDC	Union du centre
UDF	Union pour la démocratie française
UDR	Union pour la défense de la République [1968]; Union des démocrates pour la République [1971]
UDV^{c}R	Union des démocrates pour la Ve République [1967]
UER	Unité d'enseignement et de recherche
UFR	Unité de formation et de recherche
UNAPEL	Union nationale des associations de parents d'élèves de l'école libre
UNEDIC	Union nationale pour l'emploi dans l'industrie et le commerce
UNR	Union pour la Nouvelle République [1958–1962]
URSSAF	Union pour le recouvrement des cotisations de la Sécurité

	sociale et des allocations familiales
Valois	< place de > Parti radical-socialiste
Varenne	< rue de > Hôtel Matignon
Vendôme	< place > Ministère de la Justice
Vivienne	< rue > Bourse de Paris
VRP	Voyageurs de commerce, représentants, placiers
ZAC	Zone d'aménagement concerté
ZAD	Zone d'aménagement différé
ZEP	Zone d'environnement protégé;
	Zone d'éducation prioritaire
ZIF	Zone d'intervention foncière
ZPIU	Zone de peuplement industriel ou urbain
ZUP	Zone à urbaniser en priorité